Mesh Collaboration

Creating New Business Value in the Network of Everything

Andy Mulholland and Nick Earle

Evolved
Technologist
Press
New York, NY

Mesh Collaboration
Creating New Business Value in the Network of Everything

Andy Mulholland and Nick Earle

Published by Evolved Technologist Press, an imprint of Evolved Media Network, 242 West 30th Street, Suite 801, New York, New York 10001

This book may be purchased for educational, business, or sales promotional use. For more information contact:

Evolved Technologist Press
(646) 827-2196
info@EvolvedTechnologist.com
www.EvolvedTechnologist.com

Editor/Analyst: Dan Woods
Writers: Dan Woods, James Buchanan, Kermit Pattison, and Dan Safarik
Production Editor: Deb Gabriel
Cover and Interior Design: 1106 Design
Illustrator: Tory Moore
First Edition: March 2008

ISBN: 978-0-9789218-5-9; 0-9789218-5-2

Contents

Foreword

Until virtual reality becomes commonplace, we will rarely have the chance to experience and plan for change while it's happening. *Mesh Collaboration* and its predecessor *Mashup Corporations* provide, through the eyes of the executives of the fictional Vorpal Inc., a view of the changes facing corporations in what is being touted as the era of collaboration. Reading their story accelerates our ability to respond strategically; it lets us in effect look back at the future.

Historically, revolutionary advances usually start with innovators and early practitioners thriving outside the policies and procedures of those chartered with the role of managing technology. Remember how the PC, LAN, file server, web server, blog, and wiki entered the corporate environment?

In one of my first technology jobs, I was the kid, working in computer operations, who dared venture out past the locked door to the mainframes. Why? People were calling for help with the PCs they'd bought without approval. This did not make me very popular in the IT department, but on the other side of the door, I was a hero, the glue between the institution of computing and those attempting to improve their own environments through technology. Since then, I've been actively engaged in the ongoing technology revolution.

In essence, technology has been adopted in layers, causing us to constantly refocus on the newest layers. What is often missing is an explanation of how the newest layers, added to the older layers, create new value. Without this explanation, the layers appear to be an ever-increasing pile of complexity. Fortunes have been and are being made by those harnessing innovation and organizing complexity into value—think of the beginnings of IBM, HP, Microsoft, Intel, Cisco, Dell, Netscape, Saleforce.com, Google, Skype, Facebook, YouTube...

Today, many IT departments don't even have mainframes and internationally the term IT is evolving to Information and Communications Technologies (ICT). But, true to form, we ICT types are still trying to protect our users from the dangers that lurk beyond our control. Try substituting the locked door to the mainframes with corporate firewalls, community-generated content, open source code, or even just people outside the company.

I applaud the authors for addressing topics that usually go untouched in a book targeted at corporate leaders. Andy and Nick showcase how success in one area can lead to inefficiency in another. The reality of any change is that it places new stresses on an organization. Refreshingly, the story goes on to address the issues, pointing out that the way to streamline and improve processes stressed by change is often found by using the very tools associated with the change.

Perhaps the book's most uncomfortable concept for traditional IT types is that of Mesh Collaboration, what the authors call strong collaboration as opposed to previous forms of collaboration in which relationships were limited and carefully defined. It's based on the premise that the knowledge needed to solve most problems is most likely located outside your company and that using new behaviors and tools (often associated with Web 2.0) can accelerate your ability to benefit from the collective knowledge of the global whole.

Here is where some discomfort begins. The emerging technology-aware labor force is probably using more advanced technology in their personal collaboration than most corporations have deployed or allow today. In Mesh Collaboration, you don't know who the critical participants in your knowledge community are. Engaging the right people often requires blog postings, messages on mailing lists, comments on other content, videos on YouTube, and articles wherever they appear. This complex mass of content and connections is the network (mesh) of everything. It is no longer carefully designed web pages; it's content that's easy to create (such as blogs, wikis, and videos) and that is instantly indexed by search engines. It's real-time collaboration through instant messaging, telepresence, VOIP, or web conferencing. It's making, recording, and maintaining social networking connections. Your ideas start flowing through this digital nervous system, finding their way to people who help you as much as you help them. Until you've made a few such collaborative journeys, you won't believe how productive they can be.

Using the Long Tail business model as an apt example, *Mesh Collaboration* shows how this stronger form of collaboration can be systematically applied in the corporate world. In an era of extreme coding, Rapid Application Development (RAD), Software as a Service (SaaS), and Cloud Computing, the book accentuates the impact of network-powered collaboration by showing how smart services can deepen and expand the relationship between customers and vendors.

Using a creative format, the authors also address the difficult area of changing sales and business models. They examine how the global community can benefit from technology and how new models are emerging to ensure that people obtain true value from products. This book provides an illustrative roadmap that shows how the transformation of the world economy will take place over the next 20 years, ending with an examination of the role that ecosystems play in enabling and expanding such transformations.

While its style makes *Mesh Collaboration* easy to read, it is the kind of book that inspires further thinking each time you read it. More importantly, as you finish reading, it spurs you to consider the part you're playing in this rapidly changing landscape.

Chris S. Thomas
Chief Strategist, World Ahead
Intel Corporation
Coauthor: *Mashup Corporations*

Acknowledgments

I would like to thank Ron Tolido for acting as my sounding board and advisor throughout the development and writing of this book, Peter Evans-Greenwood who provided most of the content for at least one chapter, and Pierre Hessler who has been a constant inspiration for many years by challenging me, mentoring me, and generally making me look at things in new ways. I also want to thank my colleagues. Without your contributions to the great debate on how technology is developing and impacting business, it wouldn't have been possible to write this book. Finally and most importantly, I want to extend my greatest thanks to my wife Gwen for her patience when I took time to work on this book at Christmas and on holiday.

— Andy Mulholland

From Cisco Systems, I'd like to acknowledge Rebecca Bell and Gretchen Ushakova for their invaluable help adding content and their careful proofreading. Smart Services content was derived from conversations with many people but particularly Glen Allmendinger, of Harbor Research, as well as Pascal Severins and Jim McDonnell. Mike Pilbeam gave valuable technical input on Virtual Systems Engineering and Jorgen Ericsson was a key driver of the thought leadership on collaboration and network-based business processes. Additional input came from Bill Ruh, Dave Lyon, Ian Symes, Anja Jacquin Langer, and Jesus Galindo. On a personal note, I'd like to thank my wife Debbie for her love and support, our children Laura and Sophie for putting up with me during the long hours of typing, and our dog Jasper for not eating any of the paperwork.

— Nick Earle

Prologue

In order to set the stage for the story we are going to tell we first will join Jane Moneymaker, CEO of Vorpal, near its middle...

"Hi Josh, it's me Jane," says Moneymaker into her cell phone as she rides in a taxi through the streets of Amsterdam to the Schiphol Airport. She is on her way home to Boston after a very intense meeting with her boss, Charles Dodgson. He is the CEO of Jabberwocky, which is Vorpal's parent company.

"Yeah, hi Jane how did it go?" asks Lovecraft, Vorpal's CIO.

"It went well," says Moneymaker. "Apparently Charles did some checking on his own, after I told him what I had found out about Power Plus, and it seems that the company really is in quite a bit of trouble."

"Well, I think the information that essentially landed in our lap pointed in that direction," says Lovecraft.

"This is true, and knowing Power Plus' CEO I'm not surprised that he hasn't been able to develop a vision for how to get his company out of trouble," says Moneymaker. "The issue now, though, is that Charles has looked past our financials to gain a glimpse into what we are really doing at Vorpal and he wants us to prepare a presentation for the other CEOs."

"Really," says Lovecraft, somewhat surprised. "I always sort of figured he was more concerned with the results as opposed to how we actually get to those results."

"No, you don't get to be CEO of a group such as Jabberwocky without having a desire to look past results for details," says Moneymaker matter-of-factly. "I think, too, that his assistant, Jenny Thompson, had something to do with it as well. She is a young up-and-comer and I think she appreciates the efforts we have made around collaborative working and business model transformation. She has probably been working behind the scenes to connect some of the dots for Charles."

"What do you mean?" asks Lovecraft.

Moneymaker normally would not talk so openly with a colleague, but she views Lovecraft as more of a peer and a confidant whom she can discuss these kinds of internal politics with.

"Well, Charles didn't say anything explicitly, but I have the feeling that he may look to what we are doing, and maybe even to us, to try and make some rather serious changes at Power Plus," says Moneymaker. "Think about how far we have come in a very short amount of time at Vorpal. We introduced using the Web as a means to develop and sell customizable products to online communities fairly quickly, without really considering how that would affect our internal back office support systems and processes. For a time it seemed as if these sales were going to fragment the company along a number of fault lines, with some fairly serious consequences.

"However, in a few months we have been able to use the Web, some innovative thinking, and a handful of new technologies to turn the situation around to where we are making good profits on these sales. I can't help but think that Charles has been quietly watching and I also can't help but think that Jenny has helped him gain a better grasp of some of the strategies and concepts we have been using, though he doesn't seem to fully understand it yet."

"And now he thinks we can use these same things to completely turn Power Plus around?" asks Lovecraft.

"I think that's where he is going," says Moneymaker. "Our situation wasn't that much different. Our sales were flat, the markets were growing modestly if at all, cost-cutting and efficiency initiatives weren't enough to grow our margins significantly, and we were being hit by low-cost competitors. We found a way out of that and managed to transform our business model and reinvent our internal systems and processes to better serve the new model very quickly. I think he is very interested to hear how we managed to do that."

"No, I know, but Power Plus' generator and motor market is quite a bit different from our kitchen and home wares business," says Lovecraft. "We faced some very big issues in order to turn the situation around here at Vorpal, but are those things going to translate to other businesses and other industries?"

"It seems to me that some will, but I take your point and really don't have an answer to that yet," says Moneymaker. "I do know, though, that we can at least put together a report and present what we have done to the other CEOs as we have been asked to do. I also know that Charles hasn't asked me to do anything beyond that yet."

"True," acknowledges Lovecraft. "I'll start pulling together what we will need at this end for you and I suppose we'll just go from there."

"Thanks Josh," says Moneymaker glad for the help. "If nothing else this should be a good exercise to help us get a better understanding of all we have managed to do with Vorpal."

With that Moneymaker says goodbye to Lovecraft as she arrives at the airport. She has a long flight ahead of her, but she can use it to reflect on the challenges she has already faced with Vorpal and those that may lay ahead with Power Plus.

Part 1

The Growing Pains of Vorpal's Long Tail

Chapter 1

We Have a Problem: Revenues and Margins are Up, but Profits are Flat

In *Mashup Corporations: The End of Business as Usual*, the first book in this series, we explained how Jane Moneymaker, the CEO of the fictitious company Vorpal, has been very successfully moving the company into a number of niche markets using the Long Tail principle. This principle asserts that specialized niche markets in aggregate create a much bigger market than traditional mass markets, and lead to increased revenues for the company.

Enabling this transformation has been a new generation of Web 2.0 technologies, which, in total, have provided a platform for a number of web-based communities and hosted services. Further, Web 2.0 is not wrapped around one core product or technology. If anything, the core product or technology is people, particularly web-literate users with the ability to find innovative ways to use technology to pursue a wide variety of interests—everything from professional pursuits to engaging with fans of favored sports teams. These technologies have provided novel and rather powerful opportunities for people with common interests to build connections around those interests and create web-based services that reflect those interests. This is what has made the Long Tail effect possible.

At the beginning of our story, Hugo Wunderkind, former marketing manager at Vorpal, but now the company's director in charge of online marketing efforts, came up with a novel idea while at home watching a New York Jets football game. The idea was that it would be fun to have a popcorn popper with his team's emblem on it. He also thought that other people might be interested in such a product, and wondered why not sell Vorpal's brand of popcorn popper, the Pop-Matic, in a way that would allow any fan to place an image of their favorite sports team on the side of the popper?

Wunderkind garnered the help of a friend to build a web application that would allow users to select a team emblem or image and render that image onto the side of a popcorn popper. He then placed this application on his personal blog for people to access. In this way, by creating a web application that combined his blog entries on the Jets, and football in general, with a service that would allow visitors to his blog to customize their Pop-Matics as well, he created a prototype mashup.

This "toy" of Wunderkind's sparked something of a craze, and soon he had people trying to place orders with payments for their team's emblem on his blog. As the marketing aspects of his creation became apparent, he went to Moneymaker.

Seeing the reaction Wunderkind received from merely posting his toy on his blog, she realized that providing a web-based service, leveraging online communities to sell customized poppers, could prove helpful for improving the company's stagnant sales and marketing share in a flat and unchanging market.

Josh Lovecraft, Vorpal's CIO, was concerned about the negative effects of allowing anyone that much control over even this one aspect of Vorpal's IT environment. After first overcoming this concern, Moneymaker very quickly moved forward on the initiative. Soon Vorpal was transformed from mass-marketing one brand of popcorn popper into marketing customized poppers in many niche markets.

Success with this one product line was met with similar success using the same method with Vorpal's other products. Soon Moneymaker and Wunderkind had sparked something of a revolution at Vorpal. The basis was selling customized products via web-based services and connecting with various sales channels—communities of people with common interests—via Web 2.0 technologies. In all, Vorpal was succeeding at creating a unique and personal experience for its customers around its products.

However, as the story moves forward there are storm clouds on the horizon and Moneymaker is wondering if she has unleashed something that she may not be able to control. Yes, her efforts have met with success, but not without some issues that are now beginning to worry her and her CFO, Frank Cashtender.

As we pick up our story it's Monday evening, and Moneymaker is at home waiting for delivery of yet another dinner of take-out. She is talking on the phone with her long-time friend and business school roommate Hannah Grant...

Something's Wrong

"Sometimes I wish I had taken a slightly easier path than the corporate world. I mean, perhaps I should have followed your example and opened a flower shop," Moneymaker says, leaning back into her rather plush couch. She has her shoes off and is relaxing for the first time that day. A glass of wine sits idly on an end table and her husband has yet to arrive home.

"Yeah, well flowers do sometimes die," says Grant.

A sharp nervous laugh blows past Moneymaker's lips. "I suppose, too, that I wouldn't have been happy with just one shop. I would have had to have been the Starbucks of flowers, one on every corner."

"This is true," says Grant with an impish lilt to her voice, "you always were something of an overachiever in school, which stands in stark contrast to me. I'm more than happy with my modest little flower shop."

"Modest? Little?" says Moneymaker softly mocking her friend's false humility.

"Please, you must allow me my petite idiosyncrasies," says Grant jokingly. "But yes, I suppose business is doing well and it doesn't matter in my humble industry whether I am the Starbucks of florists or not—people are still pulling a few dollars from their purses for a nosegay."

A laugh bursts from Moneymaker and she remembers how much fun it can be to just chat with a close friend. "It's nice to know that in some places brand doesn't matter so much, you know, that people can trust and recognize the unique qualities of your busy little shop. I suppose it relates to what some of our professors in school used to say about trust models and…"

"Oh please don't bring *that* up," says Grant laughing, "I'm having a glass of wine and the store is closed for goodness sake."

"I know, I know, but I just have to say that I may have found out why Starbucks so rigidly rejects customizing its stores and products," presses Moneymaker.

"So now I know why you've called. What's going on?"

"Was I that obvious?" asks Moneymaker taking a small sip of her wine. "I'm worried; I certainly wouldn't say panicked, but worried that I may have unleashed something at the company that I may not be able to control."

"A Pandora's box kind of thing?"

"Yes, well, perhaps. You see, there is this fellow at work, Hugo Wunderkind…"

"I remember reading about him in a newspaper article about you and the things you had done at Vorpal."

"Of course, then you'll know that he came up with this way for people who went to his blog on his football team—I think they're the Jets that he likes so much—anyway, he created this way for people to customize popcorn poppers, specifically the Pop-Matics that we make. This created something of a stir even though the application he built was only on his blog. It seems that other Jets fans, and then fans of other football teams, have something of a communal experience watching the games and tend to eat a lot of popcorn."

"Yes, people do find joy in some rather amazing ways," interjects Grant.

"And I'm glad they do," says Moneymaker. "Anyway, up until that point people just bought a popper and that was that. We decided that if people are going to have this communal experience, why not place our product at the center of it. The way to do that is to allow them to customize the popper to their favorite team, and we expanded this to include sports other than football. So we built our own application, which we call PopMe! and placed it on our web site. We then had to work out deals with decal makers, which was easy enough to do…"

"I remember you talking about how excited you were as it was happening," says Grant, "and it went very well, too, as I remember."

"Yes, it did. It went so well in fact that we used these same concepts on about two dozen other products."

"Yep, I have one of them. You can customize the design of the clock and it has a USB port so it can be plugged into a computer. When you log onto its website there are a bunch of services around that clock, such as setting it to the exact day and time, downloading music, displays, and even various alarm voices and sounds. I love mine. Every morning I wake up to George Clooney cooing 'Breakfast time hon.' My husband hates it," says Grant laughing.

"Yes, exactly, that and quite a few others…"

"And if I remember correctly from that one newspaper story—and there were a bunch of others, it seems like you and Vorpal were in just about every business magazine around, which is how I got my idea to add a customized flower pot web service to my web site—but anyway, I remember you managed to post a double-digit increase to your revenues," says Grant.

"We did, *and* we could also charge a premium for the customization because Hugo was connecting us with all of these niche market channels. Then we opened up our technology by offering a toolkit with a common API, to essentially amateur developers in various niches, so that they could innovate on what we are already doing and add additional sales channels and volume to those that we could create on our own. This has been downloaded more than 200,000 times, which means that 80% of our custom appliance orders are made online, and of those only a small fraction come from Vorpal's web site. This came with some risks, as my CIO Josh Lovecraft told me over and over, but we worked out his security and operational concerns by using our various web services as something of a top layer above our internal IT architecture. The web services are our interface with these communities of people, but our internal information systems are protected. Now our customers, and even suppliers and partners, are telling us how to better serve them. We're letting them serve themselves better, and, in the end, they're better serving us, too.

"So in all, we've been selling not only more popcorn poppers than ever, but more of everything; the clocks, kitchen appliances, bathroom appliances, and on and on, and all of them are customized around a community with a shared interest. It has been breathtaking to see all of this activity and all of this revenue and sales growth."

"Yeah, and? We all should have such problems," says Grant.

"Well, then we took it a step farther. Josh realized that the kind of work that Hugo was doing on his own is probably being replicated by tech-savvy employees throughout the company. He even came up with a great term for it, which is 'Shadow IT.' Most of these people are our younger new employees and Josh discovered they were using technology in all sorts of interesting and useful ways right under our noses. So, being the savvy CEO that I am…"

"As always," chimed in Grant.

"We set policies that would nurture these uses and harness them to the overall business, but would also manage risks. So we sent out a memo saying that the company and I would provide the technology and support their efforts, these 'labors of love,' if you will. What this did was add to what was already taking place, which was the slow transformation of our enterprise from back-office-centric IT toward using technology to change our way of doing business in the front office."

"I'm still failing to see how any of this is a problem," says Grant.

"Well, what if I told you that while revenues are up and our margins on each item sold are higher than before—both are way up actually—we aren't generating the profits to match?"

"What do you mean? You are selling more stuff at a higher margin. How could you not be making more money?" says Grant.

"I'm not really sure on the specifics yet, though I have a few ideas, but basically our overall costs across the business are up, way up, which is holding profits relatively flat. And if this continues as it is, this situation will slowly choke the gains the new model should be making."

"And here you are way out on a limb, with everybody in the world watching what you are doing thanks to all of the media attention," says Grant.

"Exactly, and worse, the head office in Amsterdam is watching, too. They haven't really noticed yet that profits are flat because they have been so focused on growing sales revenues. We still have the rest of the quarter to at least come up with a way to deal with the spike in costs, but we, I mean I, am running out of time and may be headed for a very big fall if I can't turn it around."

"So you've let this genie out of the bottle and it's out there doing all sorts of things, things you wanted it to do, but things you didn't expect it would do, and now you have to shove it back in the bottle," says Grant.

"Well, no, I want to better control those things it is doing that I don't like. I want to keep it out of the bottle because I think it can work, but I want it to listen to me better and I want to better understand why, and see when and where it may be doing things I don't like. Besides, I don't think I could force it back into the bottle anyway."

The doorbell rings.

"Hannah, thanks for listening. I'm getting my team together tomorrow to work on this, but right now I'm tired and my dinner has finally arrived."

"No problem, my dear. Best to you."

Searching for a Diagnosis

It's early the next day—Tuesday—and Moneymaker has called a meeting of her core team. They are gathering in her executive conference room, which she jokingly refers to as her "home-field advantage." Josh Lovecraft, Vorpal's CIO; Frank Cashtender, the company's CFO; David Firehammer, the CTO; Wendy Chiselpenny, VP of operations; David Wannamaker, VP of sales and marketing; and Sarah Brown, VP of customer service, are already there. Hugo Wunderkind is lagging as usual, but walks through the door with a cup of coffee in one hand, his laptop under one arm, and his BlackBerry in his other hand just as Moneymaker is closing the door.

"Hugo, you made it in the nick of time," says Moneymaker with a faux look of sternness on her face.

"Well, I was just finishing up a few things at my desk, but I know you like to bolt the door at the precise hour so nobody can sneak in late," says Wunderkind impishly. "By the way, the system seems a bit sluggish this morning, has anybody else noticed?"

"No, not really," says Chiselpenny, leaning forward and opening her laptop.

"My computer was practically swimming," says Cashtender, leaning back into his chair and crossing his legs.

"Hugo, it's probably because our system isn't designed for you and your friends' workstations doing about 10 to 15 things at the same time," says Lovecraft, sharing a chuckle with Firehammer. "I swear, with the way I've seen you work you're carrying on about 5 instant message conversations with one hand, sending 3 or 4 emails with the other, and bouncing around Facebook, MySpace, and lord knows what other web sites with…well I'm not sure what's left."

"Alright then," says Moneymaker cutting in with the slightest suggestion of a smile at Lovecraft's remark, "Well, it's good that all of you were free this morning on such short notice."

"Yes, I only got the meeting notice yesterday, which was lucky that I got it at all, as I was in a phone conference with the head office in Amsterdam about some changes to some of the reporting templates we're using," says Cashtender, brushing an imaginary bit of lint from his shirt sleeve.

"Sorry about that, Frank, but I wanted us to meet before our regular Thursday get-together to sum up a few things with regard to the changes we have been through, and to talk about what we need to do next.

"As you all are very aware of, we've been through a lot of changes over the past year and by most accounts it seems as if we've been doing very well. Starting with the PopMe! web application, and then extending on to nearly every line of products we have, we're allowing our customers to customize our products to their tastes, thereby supporting their interests. This has included a variety of product details, different finishes, and the participation of a wide array of designers, so that our kitchen and home appliances are creating new experiences beyond the ones that people originally got them for.

"In fact, I was just talking with a friend last night and she loves our customizable line of clocks, to her husband's distress," she says with a smile.

"Have we heard anything from corporate about all of our efforts?" asks Wannamaker.

"You've been unusually quiet, David. I was wondering if you had your Bluetooth tucked behind your ear trying to make a sale…" says Moneymaker.

"Well, you know, always have to be closing," he responds, to a few quiet chuckles.

"No, I know, keep up the good work. But to answer your question, the head office is, I think as you have been told, very pleased with the way our sales revenue and market share is rising," says Moneymaker. "If this carries on, I imagine the board will start wondering if the same approach could be used across the whole group, even though I'm sure they aren't exactly sure what that approach is. They seem to be mostly focused on results at this point, as opposed to learning the details of how we are doing it, but that likely will change. So, don't be surprised if you and Hugo start getting calls from your counterparts in the UK and Europe.

"Anyway, where was I?" says Moneymaker leafing through a couple of papers in front of her. "Oh yes, alright, just as we found with the initial idea for the PopMe!—various communities came to us via Hugo's blog—we're finding that the Web is a tremendous marketing channel for us. And we have a variety of web sites up that are introducing our products to new communities, finding new audiences for us. As a result, we're selling a lot more products than we ever have before.

"I want to emphasize here, though, that the great news is that this Long Tail, niche-type business is growing much faster than our traditional mass-market efforts were, and the margins, well they make me smile. So I imagine, Frank, that you're pleased as well."

"Actually Jane…" says Cashtender, leaning forward with a rather earnest expression on his face.

However, Moneymaker cuts him off saying, "Frank, I'm aware of your concerns, which is the primary reason I called this meeting, but if you could just hold off for a moment.

"Hugo, could you give everyone a brief explanation as to how we're finding these new markets and revenue streams?"

"Yep, well, as most of you may already know, every week we're able to identify new groups—essentially people with whom we could build a relationship, who may have some form of constituency that would be interested in one or more of our products, or who may help us find ways for our products to connect with them. Then we have something of a back and forth where we show them a product or products; we show them other sites that we're working on; and then we brainstorm with them about how we can bring it all together to develop that relationship.

"We're also starting to actually put together new niches that involve not just our products and the person who understands the niche, but also other products as well. For example, we're talking with representatives from a famous chef-slash-personality. I'm not able to say who yet because it's still in development, but this person has a line of what are essentially designer bread recipes using organic whole grains and that sort of thing. So, we're working with the chef's company and the owners of a chain of organic markets so that we can link the recipes to the organic markets' ingredients and our bread-makers, via an online distribution system.

"When we put it all together, the customer will be able to go online, or make orders at the various market locations, or via this person's web site—she will also promote these products on her show—and purchase the recipe and ingredients *and* one of our bread-makers, customized to the person's tastes, such as how it makes the bread as well as certain design elements and finishes."

The room looks slightly stunned after hearing all of this.

"Who's the personality?" asks Brown, somewhat eagerly.

"Can't say yet as we're still developing the deal," says Wunderkind.

"Thanks, Hugo," says Moneymaker, again with the slightest hint of a smile.

"Okay, now, not to diminish anyone's spirits, but there is some bad news to report and this is where we really need to focus our efforts, to resolve these issues," says Moneymaker, quickly shifting into a rather serious and stern demeanor. "As well as we're doing, there are some clouds on the horizon and they may be rather big ones. We have some problems we need to deal with that have to do with the way in which we keep score in this company, which is through making money for our investors. If *they* are happy then *we* can be happy.

"We're owned by Jabberwocky. They are who we report to, ultimately, and let me tell you, I am going to have some rather bad news about some of our numbers at the end of this quarter. I can't believe it, given our growth in revenues and sales margins on the products, and I don't completely understand it yet, but it looks like our revenues will rise by about 25% while it doesn't look like we're going to do much more than 2% of profit.

"I don't know why this is so, but I asked Frank to take at least a cursory look at it. Again, Frank, sorry for the short lead time, but as you know, we need to attend to this situation with all due haste."

"Well," said Frank, "what I have here is a rather informal report, as I was rushed, but, as Jane said and I began to say earlier, the revenue situation looks very good, but the costs of operating our business are rising in an unusual way. For example, all of our central services that support sales, manufacturing, and so forth, are all going over budget. It seems that the indirect support costs for each line are higher than we allowed for and are eating into the profits on these products. Basically, the extra margins we thought we would see were based only on the direct costs we expected to incur for labor and materials, which is why I blanched a bit when Hugo described his latest effort. It's great and I don't want to diminish his efforts, but we obviously need to figure out how to make these new types of deals work better for us, and we need to do it quickly.

"There are also a number of new suppliers of many different items and their relative costs are higher than we estimated, based on those we already achieve under a more traditional business model based on our longstanding volumes.

"The call center is doing far more in direct support because people are accessing our products' sales online, and, because we are selling more products, we're also seeing more in returns and other related services. I have a feeling some of this may be due to higher expectations among customers in these new niche markets.

"Then, because we sell so many customized products and a very wide variety of products to match all of the markets Hugo is finding, our inventory is much larger than it has ever been before, which is driving up warehouse costs. Based on this knowledge, I can already anticipate that a host of similar incidental costs that we didn't predict, or expect, are going to be up as well.

"Also, because everything has an IT function attached to it, our IT costs are growing too. I suspect it may be symptomatic of what is happening elsewhere in our business, or maybe it's even the direct cause with these new ideas of Hugo's."

"Could you explain that a bit more for me please, Frank?" asks Moneymaker.

"Well, as you mentioned a moment ago, Jane, we have all of these web sites," says Cashtender, "but we have to design them and host them and manage the various functions and applications they support. Content has to be populated onto the pages and updated. They have to be managed in case, say, one goes down or gets hacked. So, our IT costs are quite a bit more. But, once again, it's showing up in the unallocated indirect costs, while the allocated direct costs for each product suggest that we should be earning very good margins."

"Thanks, Frank, that was better than I thought you could do on short notice," says Moneymaker. "Look, so what's different? When we did the PopMe! by itself, we did very well. Now that we are doing it in 20 different niches we're having these serious and, really, fundamental issues. Any ideas on what could be causing the problem?"

"Well for one thing," says Brown somewhat sheepishly, "We're interacting with a lot more customers in a lot more ways, and we have to be able to respond to them in ways that are aligned with the particular niche they fill. After all, the people who watch football and buy the Pop-Matic and our Wing-Dipper chicken cooker are not the same as the people we'll see with the bread-maker and the organic recipes."

"If I may," says Chiselpenny, VP of operations, "the number of suppliers has gone up, which has also placed a much larger emphasis on the mechanisms we use to manage our supply chain. Every niche we go into is its own small market that, so far, has required a new supplier of some sort, or a new relationship with a current supplier."

Wannamaker, VP of marketing, raises his hand and Moneymaker gives him a nod. "Margins may be much higher, but the volumes are lower with a much briefer product cycle. There are only so many Jets fans interested in a customized popcorn maker, so perhaps there is something we're doing there that could shed a little light."

"On its surface," says Cashtender, "what you're describing means that the business has to run faster and faster to keep up with markets, but our people, and perhaps even our systems, simply can't keep up."

Lovecraft chimes in, "Is anything really tuned into all of this? Have we really thought through how different everything is that we do now as compared to a year ago?"

"I think I'm starting to see the big picture here, at least," says Moneymaker breaking in. "We have been so busy running after this new way of doing things that we haven't really looked at how it would affect the company from a more holistic perspective. We have just been chasing the money, and I have been the one telling you to do that, and we are getting it. But then it's going out the door, through a number of drafty doors and windows. I think we need to take a bit of time to consider what is going on here within our respective areas.

"I want everybody to go back and analyze your departments with what we have discussed in mind. Don't make a lot of noise, but do as thorough a job as you can to find out how and why things are different in this new world we seem to be inhabiting. Then let's meet again in two weeks on that topic. We'll still have our Thursday meeting, but we have some other agenda items we can talk about while you people go out and gather this information.

"Thanks everybody, this has been great. I think we are going to get hold of this genie before it escapes us."

"What?" asks Cashtender.

"Oh, nothing, it's just something a friend said to me the other day."

Questions for Further Analysis

Later in this book we have included a section of questions and answers that cover the specific issues raised in each of these chapters. The questions are intended to spur further consideration and explanation of the points raised so that the reader may take these ideas and find innovative ways of their own to apply them to their business.

The questions for this chapter are:

1) An Overview of Mashups and Mesh

2) Who Owns What as You Transform the Role of Technology in Your Business?

3) How is the Long Tail Different from Other Business Models?

4) What are the Challenges of Pursuing a Long Tail Strategy?

5) Where is the Long Tail Growing?

Chapter 2

Mass-Market Infrastructure— Meet the Long Tail

Over the past two weeks Jane Moneymaker's team has been looking at what they're doing now that is different from before. They're seeking a clearer understanding of the underlying cause for why the company is bleeding profitability even as revenues and margins are up. Why are they so inefficient and unable to allocate costs as they traditionally have?

Though the original idea for all of this frenetic activity to discover and exploit the various niche markets came from Hugo Wunderkind, director of online marketing, Moneymaker knows that she has taken ownership of the initiative—and a lot of very important people are watching.

As Moneymaker's team has been out looking at their respective roles and how they have been altered, Moneymaker has focused her attention on the big picture. She knows that there is something very different about what the company is doing. But the big question for her is whether the costs and inefficiencies are systemic, requiring a significant change in how the company manages its operations from the front office to the back office, or something much simpler, such as that the operational areas have grown slack and are now under new pressures to perform at capacity as revenues rise.

Moneymaker understands that they have made a truly innovative change in what and how they are selling, so she must come to the realization that the company's unchanged back office and business administration model can't handle what they are doing. The challenge Moneymaker then faces is how to redesign the back-end processes so that they are able to efficiently support a diversified mass-personalized sales model delivered by one company. Further, is it possible to redesign these processes so that they're able to support the Long Tail as efficiently as traditional mass-market sales? Or will they need to accept that there are some limits, and make a compromise as to how innovative and diversified the company can be? Perhaps though, the question that is nagging at Moneymaker the most is whether this beast can even be tamed—has she unleashed an unmanageable tiger?

Also, as Moneymaker has gone on her daily walks through the various public areas in the company's headquarters she can sense two competing emotions. Around the sales and marketing offices the activity is frenetic but upbeat, as this one team is responding to the fact that they have increased revenues and each product sale is made at a higher margin than it would have brought a year ago.

However, in the areas where these sales are supported—in the traditional departments handling accounting, purchasing, and other transactional support operations—she senses a general unease, a frustration that sales are moving full steam ahead without much consideration of the costs and the efficiency of the processes associated with supporting those sales.

In addition, Moneymaker knows that problems are begetting more problems, and she also understands—from her pulse-taking walks and discussions with Cashtender, the CFO, and the company's CIO, Lovecraft—that the environment created by this new way of doing business cannot solve these new challenges and problems quickly enough.

Moneymaker takes some measure of relief by the fact that though the business press initially reported Vorpal's success, it has not yet followed along to report on the very serious issues facing the company. Adding to her unease is the knowledge that the many new channels being explored and exploited by Hugo have introduced a new level of connectivity with the outside world—the world beyond the company's firewall.

How Open Can We Be?

The team is beginning to gather in her conference room when Moneymaker pulls Josh Lovecraft, Vorpal's CIO, aside as he is entering the room.

"How are things going, Josh?" asks Moneymaker, attempting a confident smile as she shifts a small stack of papers from one arm to the other.

"Well, Jane, why do you ask?"

"What I mean is that it seems rather obvious that there is…well, there is a high degree of stress among many of the employees," says Moneymaker, "especially those in the operational areas of the company, the people that are tasked with supporting all of these new sales. Of course the folks in sales and marketing are running full steam ahead. What seems to be happening is that we have essentially transformed our go-to-market, the way in which we sell products, but not our processes to support those sales, and the people in those departments are taking the brunt of this load. We're close to having the system come undone—and the people with it."

"I know, it's something that I've thought about, too. On the one side they know all too well that things are not going well, while on the other they're chasing after the money, and succeeding at it, so they are pushing hard on these sales. But I think, too, that the sales side knows that inefficiency and costs could sink things for them as well."

"They do?" asks Moneymaker with some concern.

"Yes, the other day Hugo came to me and mentioned his concern about some negative comments being posted on a few sites with respect to the quality of our service," says Lovecraft. "If we don't deliver, we won't be forgiven. I can't help but think of some early tech inventors who never saw a penny from what they created because someone else came along and found a better way to use it."

"That's true. I'm wondering, though, if the stress some of our own people are feeling may find a similar outlet on a web site someplace, and we certainly don't want the business media or analysts sniffing around here right now," says Moneymaker, almost blushing at the realization of how self-conscious her words have just made her look. She knows that, as a CEO, betraying any self-doubt is akin to a mortal sin.

Josh smiles a little because he knows that in her own way Moneymaker has taken him into her confidence.

"No, I think that if things were getting a little leaky around here we'd know about it," says Lovecraft.

"That's what I thought, too. Shall we…" Moneymaker says, allowing Lovecraft to enter the room before her.

The Initial Analysis

Once in the room Moneymaker sees that the members of the team are in their usual seats and Wunderkind is fiddling with the buttons on his phone and his laptop is in front of him. Cashtender is sharing a few words with Lovecraft as he takes his seat, and the others are quiet. It's not the usual chatty scene she would have walked into a few months ago. The mood in the room is one more piece of anecdotal evidence that Vorpal is in serious peril, which only increases her unease and frustration.

Another sign of the turmoil within her company is a note in the papers she is carrying from the head of HR, telling her that staff turnover has climbed steeply in the past two months. She coolly places the papers down on the conference room desk.

"Alright, thanks for being here on time," she says. "I'm going to get to the point: We have some very serious problems here and if we don't begin to resolve them life is going to get difficult for all of us.

"Before coming to this meeting I was thinking of my father. He is no longer alive, but he spent the bulk of his career as the CEO of a much larger company, and I remember two things he told me over and over while I was earning my masters in business administration. The first is that senior management is in the business of being dissatisfied. To say that I am dissatisfied would be an extraordinary understatement.

"The second thing he told me is, if you need to get people's attention—fire somebody."

Moneymaker pauses for a moment to look around the room. Wunderkind is no longer fidgeting with his cell phone and everyone is focused on her.

"I don't believe I need to separate anyone from the company in order to get your attention. It isn't my style and I don't really think that at this point there is any one person that is responsible for our troubles. But we need to rein in costs and find out why this company has become so inefficient.

"It is my opinion that we are close to getting this right. Our revenues are up, even though a significant challenge remains in regaining control of our operating costs. If we don't get this side—the cost side—right, too, and do it quickly…well, there may be some accountability moments around here."

Moneymaker looks to Cashtender, who looks more perturbed than anything else, even as the rest of his peers seem to be slightly shocked by Moneymaker's pronouncement.

"Frank, I know it has only been a short while since our last meeting, but could you give us an update on the financials please?" asks Moneymaker.

"It has only been two weeks, but I have spent that time trying to get a better hold of where we stand," says Cashtender. "The fact of the matter is that I can't make any kind of reliable prediction at this moment as to what the quarter will look like because—and this is something we need to discuss—sales are outstripping our ability to assess and control the costs to support them. I can barely tell you what happened yesterday and what is happening today, but there is no way to get any accurate fix on what is going to happen tomorrow or a week from now or a month. The one trend I can report is that, if we go along as we are now, we may just break even at the end of the quarter—maybe."

"In our last meeting you said we may pull some profit," says Moneymaker.

"We may, but, like I said, I can't give you any guarantee it will be more than 1 or 3%, which are pretty tight margins even for us," says Cashtender.

"Alright, well, what I would like to do is look at what we know we have changed, and perhaps we can start generating some ideas," says Moneymaker. "Since technology has been the primary driver of the changes we've been through, I want to look at this more closely. We obviously are supporting far more pages through the APIs than we have been creating, so… Hugo, is your laptop connected to the overhead projector?"

"Um, yes it is. Let me just get this going…" says Wunderkind, drifting off as an image of his computer's desktop is projected onto a screen at the far end of the table from Moneymaker.

"Okay," continues Wunderkind, "here's one of the first web sites, it's a blog site for fans of the New England Patriots football team, with our PopMe! software embedded in it."

"Alright, could you take us to another site with PopMe! embedded in it?" asks Moneymaker.

"Um, yes, here's a fan site, sort of a discussion board, for Jets fans," says Wunderkind.

"So, as I look at this, there really isn't that much of a difference between this one page and the other, except that there are different logos and graphics, but the fields and information that are presented to help someone customize and then purchase a popcorn popper are essentially the same," says Moneymaker.

"Well, one of the rules that we established with PopMe! is that there is some uniformity within the construction of the page and the fields contained in it," says Lovecraft, jumping in. "With each web site, whether it's sport related or not, there's a certain ubiquity as to how the fields are presented and information on the product is accessed."

Moneymaker pauses for a moment. The room clearly tenses.

"Alright then," says Moneymaker. "Why are we spending so much money on contractors? I may not have the details right, but it seems that they all bill us for rewriting the same stuff time and time again.

"I talked with Frank the other day and he happened to mention to me that we are paying these invoices, and not for small amounts either, to four or more different contractors, to develop each one of these new services. How many do we have now Josh?"

"I'm not sure," says Lovecraft, "Hugo keeps needing new things all the time; it's hard to keep up."

"David," says Moneymaker sharply to Firehammer, Vorpal's CTO, "could you tell me, beyond having to pay all of these contractors, what effect carrying all of these new and different services is having on us?"

"Well, off the top of my head…"

"I don't want off-the-top-of-your-head, I need more specifics than that," interrupts Moneymaker.

"Well, I don't have clear visibility to say what we are doing in house and what specifically is being outsourced to contractors, which is something that Josh or Frank should have been on by now…"

"Look, our information systems are functioning properly," says Lovecraft defensively, "but the fact of the matter is that these markets, the speed at which sales are made and expenses are incurred to support those sales, means there's something of a disconnect between what I would call the front office operations—Hugo's brave new world, which is essentially sales in the different niches—and our well structures and managed back office IT operations."

Moneymaker eyes Lovecraft coolly, "But really too, Josh, you should have some idea of where your resources are going in supporting the business."

"Frankly, I'm not all that sure who is calling the shots in this," responds Lovecraft, his voice tinged with frustration. "Currently it's a case of the sales guys doing what they claim they need as they need it, and if I try and stop them I get accused of trying to get in the way of sales."

"Alright, I see what you're saying," says Moneymaker turning her gaze from Lovecraft to Firehammer. "David, you've had some time to think about all of this; what can you tell me?"

"Alright," says Firehammer shooting a brief look at Lovecraft. "Maintaining a number of services to do what are essentially similar tasks is obviously a lot more difficult to maintain than if we only had one, but it's actually worse than you think as every other extra one we add has the additional effect of increasing the number of variables that are in use at any one time. This makes it harder to keep track of everything, which I am embarrassed to have to admit to, but there you have it."

"David, we're looking at problems in this meeting and, as I said, there is no single place to put any blame," says Moneymaker. "Is there more?"

"Yes, it takes more programmers because we not only have to build each new service, but we support them and keep them online, and if they get buggy, then they tend to become even more buggy amongst themselves.

"We have some other fundamental problems, too. I've noticed that each contractor favors a different way of doing things and, as we push them for speed and cost, this becomes increasingly apparent. Right now, we have Java script for some, PHP for another, and so on. So that is just one inefficiency I can clearly define…"

"What about markup language and the tags for inserting our stuff into a site?" interrupts Lovecraft. "Is that ubiquitous or does it…"

Cashtender suddenly leans forward, clearly frustrated by the direction of the discussion so far. "I'm sorry, but all that we've been discussing is trivial compared to the very real issues we have right now, which is, with all of these different elements—the new sales, markets, contractor agreements, and on and on—we simply don't have a firm policy or procedure that allows me, rather, us," says Cashtender, looking at Jane, "to tell the auditors that we know what is going on in the commercial booking and billing of orders."

"Okay, Frank," says Moneymaker sternly, "calm down. I understand what you are saying, but we need to go through this methodically, by looking at what *has* changed, so we can get a grasp of what we need *to* change."

"Actually," says David Wannamaker, VP of sales and marketing, "what Frank is describing also means that if we cannot provide a smooth and satisfying experience for customers we are at risk in the marketplace of upsetting them and losing business. I saw a study the other day on a marketing blog—yes, Hugo, you're not the only one who now reads blogs—that talks about if a customer on a web site receives one of those annoying 404 error pages, which shuts down the interaction, they're likely to just give up on the interaction rather than try again. Or if they really want the product they will try and make the transaction manually by phoning the call center."

"That would explain some of the calls we have been receiving," says Sarah Brown, VP of customer service.

"What do you mean?" asks Moneymaker.

Brown looks down at a sheaf of papers stacked in front of her. The top page reads, "Customer Service: External Issues Affecting Customer Service Operations."

"Well, in the past, the calls that we would receive primarily revolved around the products—returns, questions about rebate issues or mechanical problems, those sorts of things—but now our call volume is way up and the content of those customer contacts is over a much broader range of issues," says Brown, looking around the room.

"Which would explain why you have allowed your costs to go up so significantly," says Cashtender quickly. "We are spending more on the call center than we ever have before."

"Well, Frank, that isn't really my fault, now is it?" shoots back Brown. "We can't exactly hang up on everyone who calls after we've reached our call budget, can we?"

Cashtender begins to open his mouth, but Brown beats him to it.

"Think about this: we still handle the same amount of calls for our traditional mass-market brands, they haven't disappeared, while at the same time we are receiving calls on all the new products, and, as we know, there are a lot of them. We get everything from 'Why doesn't this programming function the same way on this product as the other one?' to 'Why haven't I received a confirmation that my payment information has been accepted?' to 'Do you think the Jets are going to trade their quarterback?'

"We're also getting more in returns and more in service calls, and more in every kind of call you can think of. We had one woman tell us our mixer that is supposed to be ecru is actually khaki. I think we hadn't realized that the people who go to the trouble of buying unique customized products online will have higher expectations than the ones who buy standard models off the shelf in a store."

"What about the increased cost in our 1-800 service?" says Cashtender, clearly stretching to make some sort of retort.

"Yes, we are spending more on our 1-800 service and we have increased the number of phones lines," responds Brown. "And to cut you off on your next question, Frank, personnel costs are up as a result, because I have had to bring in more temp workers, and both our current service reps and the temps need additional training to be able to handle all of these calls. Put simply, we have still got the call center for our traditional business and now we have had to bolt on a new one for the new niche business model."

"Could we outsource the call center to India?" asks Cashtender.

"Look," interrupts Moneymaker, "I'm all for cutting our costs, this is what this exercise is all about, but I don't want to get into establishing an overseas infrastructure just yet."

Moneymaker looks to Lovecraft, "Josh, you've been quiet. I can't imagine any of what Sarah is saying is news to you."

"No, Jane, it isn't," responds Lovecraft. "I knew that we were spending more on the call center, but Sarah hasn't exactly been forthcoming on the more granular details of why she is spending so much more money."

"Jane," growls Cashtender, "we're drifting from the real point; costs are up and need to go down. We need to get this business back to where it was, using the tried and trusted procedures, and put an end to all of this adventuring. Can we please look at how to get back to where things feel a bit more like normal around here?"

Moneymaker gives Cashtender a cool look. He has been bending her ear about what he perceives to be the heart of the issue for the past month, which Moneymaker largely agrees with. But she has told him she needs to get a better view of how the niche markets are affecting these many internal support systems and processes.

"Do we have a communication problem?" asks Moneymaker, looking to Brown.

"No...well, yes," stammers Brown. "No, I haven't explicitly met with Josh to discuss these issues in detail, but neither have I met with you. I thought that's why we're here now."

"That's true," responds Moneymaker.

Moneymaker looks up at the overhead screen where the PopMe! web page is still up, and looks at it for a moment.

"You know, one of the solutions is right here in front of us," she says. "When I look at this page, our customer service number is all over the place."

"That's because we clearly want customers to be able to easily reach us without having to go through the web site owner's or webmaster's contact information," says Wunderkind, clearly trying to regain some ground with Moneymaker. "So one of the rules we have wrapped around the use of our content is that our contact information should be clearly visible."

Benefiting and Learning from Experimentation

"Didn't one of your clever contractors think that perhaps we should also include links to a FAQ page on one of our web sites or some other form of online help center?" asks Moneymaker. "You know, if we are going to be using all of this collaborative technology we might as well get the most utility from it."

"No, they didn't, but I don't see why this is exclusively my fault," says Wunderkind. "David, as our CTO, should have been more involved in developing these services and…"

"Actually a lot more people should have been involved," interrupts Moneymaker, "because then we likely would have only a single set of services on which these business niches could have been built, and we would have saved a lot of money."

"Look, we were able to go in parallel and get these services done once so that we could move on these niches very quickly," says Wunderkind. "I shouldn't have to tell you that as we were moving forward you wanted us, well, me, to move very quickly, and that the services should be responsive. Now you are changing the rules and saying that I should have been thinking internally about our own IT systems first."

"Actually, Jane," interrupts Lovecraft, "I don't think what you said is entirely true."

"What do you mean?" asks Moneymaker.

"Well the fact of the matter is that all of this is very new to us and we did want to move quickly," says Lovecraft, "I remember conversations that you and I had where you were concerned we weren't executing quickly enough…"

Moneymaker's jaw juts out slightly and she purses her lips, remembering that she and Lovecraft did have a back and forth on how fast she wanted the company to move on the original niche marketing idea.

"…so it would have been impossible for us to have known in advance where we were going to end up, and therefore what our requirements for a single set of services would have been," continues Lovecraft.

"That's true," says Firehammer. "Without knowing what our requirements were ahead of time, we would have been operating on assumptions, which means we would have likely created something that really wouldn't have functioned properly for us."

Adapting Internally to External Change

"At last an admission that they didn't even think about our crucial systems," mutters Cashtender to himself.

"Frank, is there something you wanted to say?" says Moneymaker sternly.

"Yes, which is what I have been saying for a while now, which is that as we raced ahead on this initiative, we never took the time to stop and reflect on how all of these changes to the front of the business would affect the back of the business," says Cashtender. "While I would definitely agree that we gain value in the front; critical to making that value equate to profits and accountable procedures, and all of the things we learned in the first year of business school, are the back-end systems *and* processes. We never considered and dealt with the impact that changing one would have on the other."

"You're right, Frank," says Lovecraft, leaning toward Cashtender, "but you have to remember that what Hugo, and really all of us have been doing, was a lot of experimentation to figure out what our requirements are and what the effect on the business would be. Now that we know these things, for example, there is no reason why we couldn't take what are essentially the best features from all of our currently diverse services and turn them into one cohesive services set that we could support internally for all of the products and niches."

"There are going to be issues for sure, as we consolidate, but you are right, we need to do it," says Firehammer. "We should be able to manage integrating existing services over to whatever it is we come up with."

"Alright, that's good. This is what I wanted this meeting to be about; talking through what is going on and looking for the real causes and solutions, not just blaming each other for the symptoms," says Moneymaker, scanning the room.

"Wendy," continues Moneymaker, "we haven't heard much from you, and when I look at our financials, our vendor costs are awful, which is your world."

"Well, I'll tell you what," says Wendy Chiselpenny, VP of operations, "you're right, the vendor costs don't look good, but so, too, does the process I'm working under to supply all of these new sales. Yeah, Hugo and the marketing guys can move very quickly to find new markets and new ways to sell left-handed spoons or whatever they come up with, but it's as if they don't realize that not all of us can operate in the same world. Most of our vendors can't be as flexible as Hugo wants them to be, and when they try to be flexible it comes at a much higher cost to us."

"Agreed," says Moneymaker, "but we do take responsibility for those things that *are* in our world, and for you that is making sure we're not losing hard won margins through poorly defined vendor relationships."

"Like I said, I'm working to support new processes, and the tools that I currently have are not working," says Chiselpenny. "Think about it this way, Hugo, or some other person in marketing, comes up with a new service to customize a product and then that service gets embedded in one web page, and then another, and soon I have to deal with sometimes hundreds and thousands of orders for customized products. And get this, there is no substantial volume to any of it, nor is there a manufacturing schedule to work to. Think about the relationship we have with Cogswell Motor Corp., where we get a discount on small motor assemblies because we buy in bulk with our sibling company Power Plus. I simply haven't been able to put together, in any cohesive manner, what our needs are for small motors across the customized products, so we could attach those orders to our bulk traditional mass-market products.

"Also, the product orders almost seem as if they are coming out of the blue. Where is Frank on this stuff? Where is Josh? Hugo is off in cyberspace and none of these people are managing what is coming in and rationalizing with me what I'm going to have come up with in order to support those sales from a materials point of view."

"Wendy, you know that the rest of us are racing around trying to make sense of what is happening on any given day, but our systems and processes aren't giving us the visibility we need yet," says Lovecraft.

"I know that," responds Chiselpenny, "but what all of this means is that I have to essentially establish a vendor relationship for each sales channel and set of products, because I don't have the time or ability to take a more rational look at what we need. In our mass-market products I have the time and ability to look across the landscape and see what I'm going to need for the next six months or year, and I can go out and establish relationships with vendors based on bulk purchases. But I haven't been able to do that because there is never any time to do anything now; every day is a new set of changes and we are not set up to deal with this."

"So if you knew this was an issue, why haven't you been able to do anything about it?" interrupts Moneymaker.

"For the same reason that Hugo moved in the way he did and pulled in contractors. We moved so quickly, and the volumes coming from a number of small sales channels are all so new to us, so it made it impossible to anticipate and plan based on some degree of stability. Worse, it has meant that I never can find the time to establish what I was going to need to develop as a better system to connect to our existing processes. We've been flying by the seat of our pants, and it's a simple Business 101 issue to understand that smaller volumes from an individual vendor mean higher prices for us and bigger margins for the vendor.

"But you know, as I said, Frank and Josh are supposed to help support operations by providing better management so we don't have these kinds of issues."

"You know, Wendy," says Cashtender, glancing at Moneymaker and wondering if she will finally allow him in the conversation, "None of us has the visibility we need right now. New markets are being found and products created to match, but our transactional systems aren't aligned in a manner that allows me the detailed visibility I need to see it all before it has happened and is a foregone conclusion on the balance sheet, by then it's too late for me to see trends and manage the financial picture.

"The risks I'm seeing right now are more than just financial, but are compliance related as well. We're bleeding away our profitability right now, as well as tearing this company apart just trying to stay afloat in the face of this thing you have unleashed. Hear me well on this point, because of Sarbanes-Oxley, if our processes are not sound and everything we know isn't reported, we are at risk of noncompliance for signing off on financial statements we really don't understand."

"Frank, you are overreacting a little bit," says Moneymaker cautiously. "I mean, nobody has gone to jail because their costs have risen."

"No, that's true," says Cashtender, "but my concern is not so much what we do see as what we aren't seeing, and that we need to be confident in what we are reporting. For example, and I'm speaking hypothetically, but this could be an issue: does this new business model mean we should be taking a more aggressive stance on accruing for potential bad debt? If we are selling more products to people who can't actually pay for them, because perhaps these online transactions aren't as well vetted as they are in a brick and mortar retail store, we need to be able to recognize it, establish a means to mitigate it, and accurately report it. If we know this is a problem, then we have to mention this on our SOX return. If this situation is true and we fail to report it, we could be in trouble."

"Not to mention the PR disaster a SOX issue would create," adds Wannamaker, considering the true impact these back-end inefficiencies could have on sales.

"PR disaster?" says Cashtender. "By that point I don't think I'm going to be spending my time worrying about how all of this looks for the company. Right now, and let me make this perfectly clear to you, Jane, we have to sign these financial reports for SOX compliance each quarter, that means four times per year..."

"I know what that means, Frank," interrupts Moneymaker.

"...and we're essentially doing this on faith because, not only are my systems *and* processes not linking well with the front office, but also, they aren't linking very well with what the other back office systems and processes are really doing right now to cope with what's going on. If we look at the tangible results in terms of understanding our business, we're not in control."

"I understand that, Frank," says Lovecraft, breaking in to the conversation. "And I'm seeing the same thing, or rather, I'm not seeing the same thing. We have a gaping wound between the front office and all of our back office operations designed to support sales and market creation—this includes informational, operational, and transactional systems, the things we rely on to help us manage the financials, or Wendy do a better job with the supply chain, and even Sarah's call center. These processes and the supporting applications—ERO, CRM, SCM, and so on—are not designed for this new hybrid sales model we're working under. "

"Excuse me, but I'm still in charge of this meeting," says Moneymaker strongly. "You know, I'm beginning to wonder if all of this Web 2.0 stuff is something similar to the dotcom boom, which is that it's more hype than substance. I'm also wondering if these underlying business models and processes are unchangeable.

"That said, so far we have only been focusing on the things that we can see, the visible symptoms, but not on what I think is the root cause of these issues, which is a business facing a new set of challenges; moving from the mass-market sales model that everyone understands and nearly everyone else is also doing, to one that is dynamic, fast, and driven by creating opportunities and niches that are in a constant state of change and enables us to be innovative in order to gain market share."

Looking to the Outside for Answers

"Jane, may I?" asks Wunderkind.

"Go ahead Hugo."

"Over the past week or so I've noticed most of what everyone here has been talking about; it's been hard not to with the level of frustration people seem to have," says Wunderkind, "so I talked over some of these issues with a few friends in my social network."

Moneymaker looks at Wunderkind coolly.

"What issues?" she says.

"Well, issues around our cost and efficiency," says Wunderkind, inching forward a bit in his chair. "I wanted to see if there are others going through what we are experiencing, or even those that have already been through it that could provide some much needed information or ideas of even where to go looking for possible solutions."

"Hugo!" yells Moneymaker. Wunderkind immediately withdraws into his chair. "I have been losing sleep wondering when I'm going to wake up to a headline in the business press or an analyst's report saying our growth is flat, that leadership has lost control of the internal processes of the company, that the company is on the brink of failure, and you have picked up a bullhorn and broadcast what is going on here to the entire world!"

"Did you at least use a screen name while you were having these conversations?" says Lovecraft quickly.

"Josh, it doesn't matter..." says Moneymaker.

"Yes, but not for all of them because I'm able to define who my 'friends' are and establish trust models and...," says Wunderkind, cringing under the attack.

"For goodness sake, Hugo," breaks in Cashtender, "I was just issuing what I thought was a rather blunt assessment of our compliance capabilities right now, in particular the risk of failing to comply with SOX, and here you have thrown the door wide open to landing our asses in some serious trouble. Do you even know what is material for compliance?"

"Look," says Wunderkind trying to fight back a bit, "this is how I've been finding and developing all of these markets; it's how the PopMe! came into being..."

"This is a lot more serious than talking with a few football fans," says Moneymaker. "Who are the people on these blogs? Is it our competitors? The SEC? Is it some stock analyst that is going to rake us over the coals in his next report and make us look like a bunch of idiots?

"What if I get a call from the group CEO, about all of this before we have established a plan of action? Do you know what information is okay to disclose and what isn't? Are we going to end up with fines or worse because you're standing up in a room full of strangers and telling them everything that is happening behind our closed doors?"

"You're right, Jane, I don't know everything, I don't know what is material for compliance or who all of the people I'm talking to are," says Wunderkind. "But I do know that the only way to get the information we need to solve these problems, and as you said these are very big problems, is to find information from outside of the company. What are people saying and doing who have been through this? After all that we've done I thought we had learned by now that there are no closed doors in this new world we're working in so we all have to modify our behavior in the new world."

"Well, you have just added to our problems, Hugo," responds Moneymaker. "You've done a lot for this company, but this may be it for you."

"Josh, can we get a log of his instant messaging and email trail?" asks Cashtender. "If we do, at least we could see what he was telling people and start to react to what may be out in the public domain by now."

"No, we don't record instant messages right now," says Lovecraft.

"Josh, what do you mean?" asks Moneymaker. "With all of the hardware and software we keep around here for our compliance and risk initiatives I thought we would have that capability."

"We do, but," Lovecraft pauses for a moment, "we felt that our firewall capabilities and manual governance surrounding use of instant messaging and email was enough, but Hugo, and really everyone in marketing, is an exception because he needs to be able to communicate freely and via a number of mediums outside of the company."

"Jane, this is just the sort of material example of what I'm talking about," says Cashtender. "We have given Hugo too long a leash and there is no way to connect his activities with one of my key support tasks, which is compliance. This is obviously a massive failure of our business' operational process."

"Josh, after this meeting, and I mean right after this meeting I want those log rules updated and I want you to find whatever you can, with Hugo's help, of his communications," says Moneymaker. "You will need to work with Frank to understand exactly what we should be tracking and controlling for compliance and our own safety. Hugo, this is too much and I'm..."

"Jane, a lot of people have been talking so at least let me tell you what I found out," interrupts Hugo. He continues without waiting for an okay from Moneymaker. "I did find some people and they gave me some very good information and ideas. By reaching out to these communities, which I have to say seems like a far more efficient way to go about it than this meeting has been, I had a handful of very good conversations with people who are going through many of the same issues as us. We aren't the only company going through this kind of change."

"Such as?" says Moneymaker. "I want examples."

"Off the top of my head there have been some pretty big names such as eBay, Amazon, Netflix," answers Wunderkind, "but it's the smaller and more specialized companies that have been the ones that have been online sharing their experiences. I've even talked fairly extensively with one guy who does print-on-demand classic books with custom covers and other details. He started out thinking he could make money on specialized products at higher margins because these books are hard to find, but then he found he wasn't making the kind of money he expected to. It seems he was using a package set of applications for the publishing industry and..."

"Alright," says Moneymaker interrupting him, "what have you learned from these people?"

Wunderkind leafs through a few papers in front of him to find the page he's looking for.

"In a general sense, that the sales environment moves very quickly, which stresses the support systems causing—and this is a quote from nearly everyone at any company that has done something similar to us—causing fragmentation not only between the underlying support systems and the sales environment above those systems, but fragmentation within the support systems themselves."

Reconnecting the Front Office with the Back Office

"What Hugo is saying," says Lovecraft, "actually does make a lot of sense. We have literally transformed our business model in the front office around just about every dimension: what we sell, to whom, and how we sell it, and so on, without any real thought as to what this means to our existing systems and business model in the back office operations. And guess what? It shouldn't be any big surprise that it can't cope."

"That's what I'm seeing too," says Moneymaker.

"Think of it this way," continues Lovecraft, "We have a mass-market sales model and now this newer niche model, both of these overlay our traditional and very static back office support systems. These systems are trying to do two things at once—one thing they are designed to do and the other they aren't. As they try and keep up with the faster moving and shorter lifecycle niche markets, they can't keep up, we lack what I hear referred to often as 'adaptability,' though in truth I think it's more than that. It's not the speed to change our existing systems that matters, it's our ability to behave completely different. In the terms of another of the new technologies, Service Oriented Architecture, we lack orchestration—the ability of the back office to respond to business needs as they are generated by remaking on the fly any necessary processes from existing elements or subprocesses that we already have."

"So I think you're saying that there is a fundamental disconnect and fragmentation between the niche sales model and the as yet unaligned back office processes," says Cashtender, "which will in turn cause further disconnects and fragmentation between all of our other existing processes as we try and accommodate both the new niche and the traditional sales models."

"Yes, right," says Lovecraft standing and walking to the whiteboard and beginning to draw. "Think of it this way. If the back office is something that needs to be standardized, such as electrical voltage, and the front office is something that is not standard such as waffle makers, upright lamps, computers, and so on, then there needs to be a common plug and socket so the differentiated sales channels can plug into standardized support systems."

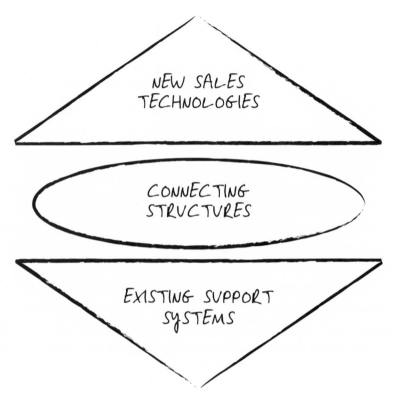

Figure 2-1. Diamond Model Drawing

"What we're doing now is trying to run adaptable markets with both AC and DC voltages," adds Wunderkind. "Jane, please trust me when I tell you I have not been running my mouth off in just any forum, I have been looking at and interacting with resources established by highly credible and trusted business schools and blogs. Some of the professors I talked to have hinted at wanting to talk with us, perhaps to offer some direct help. Many of them have been following the discussions around the potential of using the Long Tail to gain market share and revenue and have been gaining some understanding of the organizational side of dealing with the impact. They even have a special phrase for this whole issue, it's called 'Innovating your Business Model.'"

"Yeah, what they are really thinking though is that we're a company that is classically screwed up and would make a great case study on what not to do," says Moneymaker.

"No, I don't think so…" stammers Wunderkind.

The Emergence of Shadow IT

"Jane, another point I would add," says Lovecraft, "is that because our systems have been under such stress and are fragmenting at numerous weak points, our employees have been feeling this stress too and we likely are forcing them to develop their own Shadow IT approaches to survive. This may be solving the issue in the short term on a tactical level, but in the long-term it will contribute to creating even more issues. We should remember what happened when individuals and departments introduced PCs—short-term benefits then long-term and expensive issues to fix."

Firehammer, who has so far remained on the sidelines, breaks into the dialogue, "I heard this great point at a recent Business Intelligence event that I went to. It seems that 20 years ago 80% of the knowledge a person required to do their job was kept in their head, but now it's only 20%. Nobody has gotten dumber; in fact it's the reverse. The new reality is that there's so much happening and it's happening so quickly around us that 80% of what we need to know to make the right decisions is now located beyond our own minds.

"When you think of it that way it goes a long way to explaining the pressures on everyone, why we all turn to Shadow IT in self-defense, and why we need to find more people to help us; even those outside of our own company."

"I think, in defense of Hugo," says Wannamaker, "what Hugo did is a serious issue and he should have provided notice of his intentions rather than just launching out on his own. On the other hand, what he did reflects the new reality. All he was doing is what David just said, using a customized Shadow IT approach to find information held outside of this company to help us."

"Hugo, I'm going to want to speak with you after this meeting," says Moneymaker. "We have rules around here and we need to follow them.

"Josh, if we need to be able to reach outside of these walls from time to time I want a clear set of policies in place and appropriate IT controls so we can minimize risk and make sure we are always in compliance. Signing a quarterly report should be more than an act of faith."

The Beginning of Business Model Innovation

"We should now share a common understanding that we need to transform our business model," continues Moneymaker. "Using the new term from the business schools we need to 'Innovate our Business Model.' It seems that we have done half the job in respect to the external sales and markets, so now we need to rapidly act to transform internally in order to support both the existing and the new sales models. And believe me, we will need to be innovative in how we do that so I want everyone focused on one set of goals and not on private turf wars around their existing P&Ls and departmental responsibilities.

"I'm not sure how we should go about this. A possible starting point is that we should use the same technology that we used to transform the front office to redesign the back office. However, I'm cringing at the thought—and, Frank, you likely will agree—but I don't want to even have to think about changing our existing ERP systems.

"Josh, it seems that since technology is what got us into this situation and will likely get us out that I assign you the task of getting the redesign process started. I want you to start mapping out a series of focus meetings on how we can build a different approach to supporting these new market channels and services while at the same time linking to our key existing IT systems that we need for compliance. We also need to start thinking about the *controlled* use of outside resources for information discovery as we move forward on innovating our business model.

"In general, it seems that we need to address a few different areas. The first is that we have a problem with our people; they are dissatisfied with working here now and some are leaving the company. The second is that we still will need to be able to differentiate our products in the market, but do it in a controlled way so that we are efficient, costs are controlled, and so on. The third is to identify processes that will be able to support this tight balancing act we need to perform. We'll also need to understand better how this new sales model affects our compliance requirements. After all, we want Frank to be able to sleep nights so he's less cranky," says Moneymaker with a bit of a smile.

"That's it for now people, but mind you, I want to see action on these things begin to take shape very quickly. There's a lot on the line, but at least now, unlike at the beginning of this meeting I think I can see where we need to be working on the solution. Perhaps we'll be the case study for getting this right instead."

Questions for Further Analysis

1) Has Business Model Innovation Become the Key to Sustainable Competitive Advantage?

2) Why do Traditional Models for IT Fail to Support Continuous Business Model Innovation?

3) How is Do-It-Yourself Shadow IT Enabling Users to Fill the Gap Between What IT is Providing and What They Need to Compete in the New Marketplace?

4) What are the Characteristics of Innovative Companies?

Chapter 3

Flowing Toward Synergy

It's now just one hectic month of hard work for the team since Jane Moneymaker expressed her deep dissatisfaction with the failure of the company to contend with rising costs and inefficiencies related to Vorpal's Long Tail initiative. Though there is still much work to be done, the team has managed to overcome its immediate challenge of finding a way to control costs through increased operational efficiency.

Initially the team had failed to recognize the difference between the new generation of technology that provides "interactions" based on services across the Web in the front office enabling the ability to create new markets and revenues from the traditional applications in the back office, which are used to automate the capture of a "transaction" as a cost-saving capability. This crucial difference had resulted in a fracturing of not only their internal IT systems, but also their whole business model.

Further, with the speed of change being a crucial success factor in capturing new markets in the front office, it was difficult to impossible for the more static and difficult-to-change back office systems to keep up.

This lack of synchronicity caused what had once been efficient end-to-end systems to break up and become inefficient and disconnected subprocesses, leading to increased costs and replication of activities with little visibility.

However, Moneymaker and her team have realized that at the heart of their problems is the need to transform Vorpal's business model. The company needed to find a way to express both its new business and its older IT systems in a common manner that could both support the existing relatively static mass-market sales processes and accommodate the new, very dynamic and fast-paced market niches to be found in the Long Tail without fragmenting.

This realization and the resulting transformation that it will lead to means that Vorpal will be better able to find and execute in a number of differentiated markets and products. The company will understand where differentiation creates value, as well as be able to identify where shared and synergistic systems supporting those markets should be common and thereby understand where differentiation increases costs. Put simply, they have found the way to connect what is common—back office operations—with what is differentiated—front office operations.[1]

In reality it will not be that simple as there are degrees of commonality and differentiation in all they do, so they must learn how to break down their activities into granular tasks that can readily be reorganized, extended, edited, or reused as and when needed. To do this, the concept of a business task must become synonymous with a technology service.

However, the increased efficiency created by addressing the most obvious issues has reduced the level of stress that employees had formerly felt. In particular, Moneymaker is able to breathe a little easier.

Her improved mood is evident as she opens a meeting with the team to discuss the company's ongoing efforts…

---

[1] See also the discussion on Diamond Model in previous chapter

Feeling Like a New Company

"Hello everyone," says Moneymaker, surveying the room. "As I said a few months ago, my father was a CEO and one of the things he often told me as I began my education and career is that upper management is in the business of being dissatisfied. Well, he was right, though I must say that I am a bit *less* dissatisfied today than I have been in the recent past. But I believe we still have our work cut out for us in order to continue the changes we have begun, but it feels to me, and there is strong evidence to support this, we know that we are a new business now; we've identified that we need to be doing things differently—that we're in the process of a real business transformation. One based on technology changing the game for us and our markets.

"For example, maybe as Hugo pushes our online marketing efforts he no longer has to be so concerned that the markets and products he was trying to develop could be supported…"

"Jane?"

"Yes, Hugo," responds Moneymaker.

"Well, to clarify, I have to be mindful that what I'm doing is being noticed by the back office operations, and yes, you are right I'm much freer to focus on those activities that have the most effect on generating sales. But it still is not exactly easy to do new things out front without it being a significant strain back in the operation."

"Right, but I still want to make the larger point I was driving at, which is that we can feel that we are moving toward becoming a much different company," says Moneymaker. "Wouldn't you agree?"

"Yes I would," says Wunderkind, anxious to show his agreement. "For example, a little more than a year ago a lot of my time was consumed by mass solicitations such as direct mail—something which we were lucky to get a return of less than 1% on—but now I am interacting with various web communities who help me, through collaborative efforts, to find new opportunities. The other day I was reading through a couple of blog entries by a chef in New York when he mentioned it would be great to have utensils—spatulas and spoons, the things he has in his hands all day—be more ergonomic and convenient. I took that idea and went on Facebook and then MySpace, where there are numerous networks for professional and amateur chefs and found there is a great deal of interest for a web-based service where cooks could customize these tools of the trade. The potential sales from those few interactions would far surpass what I could have accomplished with a mass-marketing appeal…"

Seeking Synergy

"Okay," interrupts Moneymaker, "and the problem in the past is that we were essentially building a separate structure to support such an initiative in terms of business processes as well as inefficiently allocating IT resources to support those individual efforts."

"That's right," says Lovecraft. "Because things were moving so fast we were missing synergistic opportunities. We were experimenting, which was good, but processes and information weren't flowing evenly or efficiently throughout the model—from the markets and product sales down to the support mechanisms and across those mechanisms—and that meant we weren't able to recognize the inefficiencies and determine the synergies.

"We are much better at this for a number of reasons, but one thing we have done is established, and this meeting could be considered really as part of this effort, but we have established regular rationalization cycles to take all of this new learning and apply it to existing and new markets and products so that we can capture more standardization and synergistic opportunities within the underlying business processes. Really, what we're doing is offering a set of support services to Hugo and the marketing department that are standardized, which allows them to go out and follow whatever ideas may come to them."

"If I may," interjects David Firehammer, Vorpal's CTO. "One result of this change is that we realized that rather than offer multiple APIs, and services to help others embed our products into their web sites, we have created one API that is easily adaptable and capable of aligning with any initiative. As Hugo moves forward on his utensils idea, each network that he finds on Facebook or MySpace or wherever can use that API, which is essentially the same as those for the Mix-Décor and every other web service we offer, to create a web page where people can customize their spatulas and spoons.

"Not only has this eliminated the need to use contractors to continually write new APIs for us, but our underlying IT environment is better aligned to support the services that are grafted onto our network via the API."

"Right, I certainly didn't mean to undersell the role of IT in all of this," says Lovecraft. "We have realized that our new business model is in fact a technology model and it's not about the conventional alignment of IT to what business needs, it's about the total convergence of business and technology into a common business model.

"So to add a little bit to that, where we have existing IT and business processes, which you might say are aligned as in the old business model, we can also link them to the new. As an example, we already offer a line of utensils within our mass-market side of the business, so as we may move forward on Hugo's idea, processes and IT support services are in place to allow us to determine what the material needs for the products will be and find where they are common with those that we already receive from vendors, which is easily automated and scalable."

Changing Supplier Relationships

"Okay, good. I wanted this meeting to be about reinforcing that we are operating under a very new business model," says Moneymaker, looking toward Wendy Chiselpenny, VP of operations. "Haven't we also been receiving enhanced services from our suppliers as well?"

"Well, yes actually we are," says Chiselpenny. "As I have worked with suppliers to find ways to better service the markets we sort of came to the same realization that what we were really doing is looking for ways for suppliers to help customize our products for other people. In terms of the web-aware products, you know, like the clocks with USB ports and so on, we have found deals on placing those devices in the products.

"With Hugo's latest idea, I would probably go to an existing supplier and say, 'Look, we're going to be selling a lot of these customized kitchen utensils and since you already supply the utensils for our mass-market brands, how can we set this up so that you receive orders directly and can produce what we need; how can we help each other out with this?' They have been responsive because while we need smaller batches of customized items, overall we're buying a much larger volume and they want to be our vendor of choice. I'm also beginning to wonder if they are not subconsciously adopting the same changes to their business model as we are."

"I had noticed this," says Moneymaker, "and I like the cascading effect our efforts are having. As we need to solve supply issues for these sales channels our vendors are expanding to offer solutions to us."

"And we're getting better deals with our distribution partners too," adds Chiselpenny. "Rather than establishing separate distribution networks for each product, we're combining channels for products where it makes logical sense to do so."

"Right," interrupts David Wannamaker, VP of marketing, "yes, I love this one because when we were meeting with Wendy initially to look at our processes and see where we could find commonality, we realized that if a Jets fan wants a popcorn popper with the team logo, they're likely going to want a grill and a deep fryer to make food on game day. So to leverage off these unified distribution channels we have offered what we call the 'Game Day Package,' which includes a grill, fryer, and popper customized to their team. And the distribution partners are helping with unique packaging for these products. We're able to take product differentiation one step further while maintaining our costs and therefore retaining the extra margins customers are prepared to pay for their customized product."

"Actually, I had noticed that sales of our 'Tailgater's Grill' have gone up with the 'Game Day Frialater' and the popper," says Cashtender. "Though, I want to mention that not everything has been cookies and cream…"

Balancing Security with Opportunity

"No, you're right," says Moneymaker. "Josh, could you update us on the security aspect?"

"Yes, it has not been easy, as our security was based on either the authentication to our internal applications or denial of access by the firewall. We have a whole new game here based on services and networks and that means new methods," says Lovecraft. "We did actually get caught out early on by releasing a service that did not have appropriate authentication mechanisms embedded within it. It wasn't properly vetted, which is an issue we have addressed. It allowed external access so that somebody could see their own purchase order with us, but it turned out that they could easily see all of the purchase orders on hand with the company. This in turn allowed one of our competitors to peek in and essentially make offers to underbid us to customers where we had yet to deliver the goods. But in the end things didn't turn out badly for us..."

"Well except for forcing us to react to this from a compliance point of view..." says Cashtender crossly.

"Yes, it wasn't a good thing, it was a security breach, but it was noticed, it taught us a lot, and we did close it quickly," says Lovecraft. "However, when we saw what this one competitor was trying to do and how they were able to use the information we had inadvertently allowed them access to, it sparked the realization that by allowing suppliers, and I stress, in a secure and controlled way, to see more of what we're doing across the product lines and markets, that they could take that information and use it as a dynamic feed to their own forecasting systems, thus speeding up their abilities to accommodate our requirements.

"This made us rethink our approach to the whole topic, and we realized that the real question was not access to applications, which is where we were starting from, but access to any form of content and that includes email and a hastily compiled PowerPoint slide as much as the data in our corporate applications. In fact, the more we thought about it the more we realized that actually this was the very 'data,' if we still would use that word, that we were at most risk over. The back office enterprise applications transacting our commercial systems are broadly not as involved in this new world as the people-to-people new technology capabilities.

"Once we realized all of this, it got much easier to find the solution."

"Which is?" asks Moneymaker, displaying CEO impatience at having to draw out the details.

"Digital Rights Management, DRM," says Lovecraft.

"Okay," sighs Moneymaker, not trying to hide her exasperation at being introduced to yet another familiar, but unknown technology buzzword.

"It's the ability for the creator or owner of any document to be able to control who uses the contents and how they can use it," says Lovecraft. "As an example, I can send you an email that you can read, but not forward to anyone, or a document that you and you alone can edit, and so on. It's the perfect answer to being able to share, but in a controlled way. And we're working on a proposal to set up a DRM solution internally right now."

Capturing Profits

"Okay, that sounds like something we probably should have been thinking about quite a while ago," says Moneymaker, turning to Cashtender. "So, Frank, with all of these changes, what has the effect been on our books?"

"They are starting to look much better," says Cashtender slowly. We've started to regain control over some of the bigger cost issues and with that we've regained some of our lost efficiency.

"Meanwhile, we're still growing revenues as new markets come online and the predicted margins on each sale are very good. In all, if we continue to surmount our issues in the same way, then we should capture more of that predicted margin into our profits.

"I should also add that my visibility about what is really happening across the business has greatly improved. For example, as the utensil market that Hugo talked about moves forward, I'm going to better be able to notice those transactions and see how we're managing related costs. I'm also able to better document the processes from the time Hugo finds a market, resources are brought to bear to execute on the market, and sales are made, which means compliance and audit functions are starting to come up to where they need to be, though, of course, there is still a lot to do as we haven't done more really than pick the low hanging fruit."

Moneymaker looks to Firehammer, "Did you want to add something?"

Converging and Aligning Technology with Business

"Yes, I do. I want to pick up on Josh's point about the role of IT going through a change as well," says Firehammer. "As Hugo noted earlier, he is able to essentially go out and seek new markets using a variety of collaborative technologies such as wikis, blogs, Facebook, MySpace and so on, though with a new set of governance policies and monitoring of those activities.

"But now we're also right there with him interacting in the same way at the same speed. In short, we have moved from being a catch-up delivery source working sometime later to deliver our projects, to becoming real-time partners with Hugo; doing things together in real time. So while there is great differentiation between the products, markets, and the technologies being used by the front office, so to speak, we are also able to supply the connections and use of underlying IT-supported back office business applications at the same time.

"As we continue, we're moving toward working together in, well, like one huge interconnected mesh of people, systems, and activities rather than just a handful of predetermined connections set up by the IT department for the business. We could probably think of this as something of an evolution from Matrix Working, which is what we called the change in how people worked when the PC networks first started to appear."

"Did you say 'Mesh,' M-E-S-H?'" asks Moneymaker, jotting a note on the corner of a piece of paper.

"Yes I did, this change we are moving toward looks something like a mesh rather than a matrix," says Firehammer, wondering if Moneymaker even heard him as she is still intently making a note to herself.

Service Oriented Architecture as Enabler of Transformation

"You know," Firehammer says slowly as if to wait for Moneymaker to catch up, "this has taught me something else, too. For the first time I think I really understand what Service Oriented Architecture, you know, SOA is all about, and it is not just for technology integration that we had limited our thinking to. It does that, but its use is more than that; it's to define, or maybe I should say redefine business processes into specific tasks and elements. Now that we've approached SOA that way it's been possible to solve the aspect of joining the two halves of our business together."

"You know," says Lovecraft, "this has been a big learning curve and we've been looking at a lot of these new technologies as something to use in our existing IT systems. What we now know is that they add a whole new layer of different capabilities, and that we have to approach how we do things very differently. It's not any longer about business and IT alignment, what we're doing now is creating business in new markets made possible by new technologies. If you get it right, it's really a total convergence now.

"This is true," says Moneymaker, putting her pen down. "I suppose if you consider the big picture, the business model we seem to have evolved into, if you really think about it, is a visual model. I mean, the markets and all of those distinct interactions are unique points—there really isn't much commonality between Jets fans and their popcorn poppers and those who may follow the recipes of a celebrity chef and their higher-end kitchen utensils, but underneath is a layer where the underlying resources, such as the kitchen and the electricity, *are* shared in common.

"It sort of makes me think of a crown where the points on the top of the crown are all of these differentiated front office processes and the band that connects them are the support systems, the things they share in common…"

Questions for Further Analysis

1) How Does the Design of Business Processes Change to Meet the Needs of Long Tail Business Models?

2) How Does the Structure of IT Change to Support the Crown Model?

3) How can SOA Be Used as a Tool for Business Transformation?

Part 2

Leveraging the Mesh— Exploiting the Power of Strong Collaboration

Chapter 4

Moneymaker, Facebook, and Mesh Working

Jane Moneymaker and her team are deeply involved in what they now realize is a business model transformation based on the concept of "Business Model Innovation." Basically, they are looking at how they should rethink existing or extend new processes as a series of granular business tasks captured as SOA-type services.

The result has been that they no longer see their business as a set of separate departments based around applications, but as a totally connected network of people, processes, and resources that can be deployed in any combination to create value or to respond to events.

However, as Jane Moneymaker has continued to ponder the concept of a mesh and what it could mean to the company she recognizes that Vorpal is so far missing a crucial element in its efforts to transform its business model. In particular, she is considering the role that Vorpal's people could play in driving synergy and innovation as opposed to simply seeking cost-cutting initiatives.

The changes so far have helped the staff work better with each other and within their roles, but they are still largely working in much the same way as they did prior to the PopMe! moment of change.

As Moneymaker takes time to consider this issue she has worked to break down what she can see happening around her. What is readily apparent is that a segment of employees, which is generally composed of an older generation of employees, is largely working in a fairly traditional manner—spreadsheets, email, internal proprietary applications, and so forth.

Meanwhile, another segment, largely composed of younger workers, is using a different set of technologies and using them to work in a different way. They have grown up in an online world and view technology and its use as something they can define and apply in a personalized manner. This is the generation of Web 2.0, the instinctive collaborators sharing and creating content in many different forms. As such, they have new skills that can be tapped into.

Moneymaker is coming to the realization that in order to fully take advantage of all that Web 2.0 has to offer, the company needs to do more than just use it to develop new sales leads. They need to learn how to use these technologies as a proactive problem-solving capability to respond to events and develop solutions by finding the right combination of people, resources, content and so on. This is a concept that has come to be known as "Strong Collaboration."

Web 2.0–type technologies reinforce this capability in two ways. The first is to remove the technology limitations imposed by traditional applications and their deployment inside the enterprise's firewall. The second is that by being standardized and people focused, collaborations can be set up and changed and dismantled as dictated by circumstances in order to connect and support internal and external people.

By contrast, existing or "Weak Collaboration" means staff only have access to a preassigned and defined structure of people and content with no capability to align this rapidly into actions.

By making this change Vorpal will be adopting an Enterprise 2.0 model. The definition of such an enterprise is given in full later, but for now think of it as a business that has succeeded in connecting people, processes, and events together in a dynamic way to optimize any situation.

However, prior to taking action Moneymaker needs a sounding board to develop her thoughts. She is discussing these ideas and what she has learned with her friend Hannah Grant.

It is Saturday and Moneymaker and Grant have met for a morning cup of coffee and a day wandering around town doing some shopping in preparation for the upcoming holidays. The café the two women are in is trendy, noisy, and hectic as other shoppers wander in for a warm coffee or espresso to steel themselves for dealing with more crowded stores.

Moneymaker and Grant have settled into a table in a relatively quiet corner of calm…

Work Smarter not Harder

"I hate the holidays," says Grant.

"No? Really? Come on doesn't everybody love Christmas? The crowds, the expense, the never-ending evening engagements…" says Moneymaker as a young father carries his crying child out the door of the café yelling behind him to his wife that she should make it a triple shot of espresso.

"Yeah, right. Actually, my life is even more hectic, which I hold you at least partially responsible for," says Grant.

"Me?"

"Yes you, with your, 'Use the Internet to increase your sales at the flower shop,' and all that jazz," says Grant.

"Well, you didn't *have* to listen to me, did you?"

"No, but this time of year is busy enough for a florist without having all of the orders flying in from the web business you helped me establish. You know, teaming up with potters and other like-minded people who also have web sites so that people can select personalized arrangements from these web sites or they can purchase specific items from a page on my web site from these so-called partners," says Grant.

"Well, maybe you need to change the way you work," responds Moneymaker.

"What, get up earlier and work later? That's what I'm doing now. I only barely was able to find the time to be with you today," says Grant.

"I'm not sure exactly what I mean, or rather, how it would work for you, but, you know, the other day, Friday, I was looking at some of our sales figures and our online business is continuing to grow steadily and at the heart of it is the work of Hugo, he's in charge of our online marketing efforts, but in other ways he's acting as something of an inspiration for everyone else to understand new technology," says Moneymaker.

"Didn't you nearly fire him?" asks Grant. "Something about him being indiscreet?"

"Yes, I was mad at him," says Moneymaker. "It was right at the time of the crisis meetings so it was sort of a heat of the moment thing because he had been seeking advice with regard to a major issue with the company from people on his blog and a couple of other sites," says Moneymaker.

"Kind of like having a husband who likes to spread the family's dirty laundry to his buddies at the bar?"

"That's why I got so annoyed with him initially," says Moneymaker. "I mean, he was talking to people without any idea of who they were. We're working on establishing governance around that so he can be free to continue his marketing efforts, but do it in a controlled way…"

"Right, but what does this have to do with me?"

"Okay, I was thinking that he's using all of this technology to develop relationships with people and to learn from them and develop strong sales leads. So why couldn't some of that help with the processes that are internal to the company. We are trying to change, really transform our business model, to be more innovative in how we find ways to make things work better and in a more logical manner, and at the heart of that is communication."

"Still not seeing how that relates to me," says Grant, glancing up to see a young couple enter the café.

"Let me explain this and I think you will get it, okay?" says Moneymaker without pausing.

"You're slipping into CEO mode again, dear," says Grant flashing a bit of a grin.

Mesh Working

"Sorry, but as I was thinking about communication and the things that Hugo is doing, I came to see that really at the heart of it is a new and stronger form of collaboration. So if you think of collaboration as facilitating innovation I realized we needed to do a better job with our internal operations of collaborating not only with each other, but with the outside world as well."

"But isn't that what you nearly fired Hugo for?" asks Grant.

"Yes, but as I said, we're working on governance to better define how that kind of communication or collaboration can be done," says Moneymaker, "and when I think about it, we can do the same throughout the company—with our CFO, CIO, me, and on down the line."

"You know, don't forget that we went to business school together and though things have likely changed since then," says Grant, glancing at a young man passing by their table, "our professors would have been rather upset over stuff like this—saying you must control information to ensure that you know more than others. You need more supervision to make sure people are working in the right way on the right things. Also, how do you know someone isn't going to spend all day 'collaborating' with their latest boyfriend or girlfriend?"

"You're right," Moneymaker says smiling, "but the times, people, and business have all changed and there has been a change in the discussion to include ways to create value in a business by augmenting the ability of people to collaborate. And there are new IT tools that we can use to monitor interactions and governance policies. One of these tools is Digital Rights Management to control some of the risks inherent in sharing too much with the wrong people. It seems we can actually embed policies as to not only who sees what documents, but also what they are allowed to do with the document, including preventing them from copying or forwarding it. Basically, there are controls we can use, though there are some risks.

"But you know, a lot has changed and that includes what the new generation of business professors has to say on this subject. People are used to behaving differently now. It's less about keeping to office hours than it is about working at any time and any place to suit the circumstances. Think about this, surely there is a bigger risk in doing nothing. Look at you, you're as busy as ever and I'm sure that you would like to be able to take it a little easier while also making more money."

"Alright, just as long as I can clearly see how all of this applies to me," says Grant, laughing.

Communicating via Web 2.0

"Right, so I usually spend Friday afternoons walking around the building just doing sort of a pulse-taking exercise and I thought I would wander by Hugo's office to talk to him and get his thoughts on improving how we collaborate."

"Right, so is 'pulse taking' what you're calling 'looking over everyone's shoulder?'" jokes Grant.

"Basically, yes," says Moneymaker as she picks up her spoon and idly stirs her coffee. "As I got to Hugo's office—you know what he is like, always different and he doesn't like the sun shining over his shoulder onto his beloved PC screen so his desk faces out toward the window with his back toward the hallway so I could look in and literally watch over his shoulder."

"Okay, rather voyeuristic of you," interrupts Grant.

"I am a CEO," responds Moneymaker with a small flourish of her hands. "Anyway, what caught my attention, though, the thing that made me pause was the way that he was working. He looked like a 1970s-era rock band keyboard player. You remember, the guy surrounded by electronic keyboards and trying to play them all at once?"

"I do."

"He was working with three screens, two connected to his desktop and another to the docking station that he had his laptop in. On his laptop I could see that there was an email window open as well as what I assumed were contact databases, it was hard to see from a distance.

"On the screens connected to his desktop he had another list of contacts opened; there were IM screens opened to probably three or four running conversations that in one form or another were helping him develop sales leads; and on the other screen he had three or four browser windows opened to things such as a marketing blog, one held a Facebook page, another to a site that tracks all sorts of blogs, and another hosted his workgroups."

"What are you doing to this poor boy?" asks Grant.

"I know what you mean," says Moneymaker. "He was in constant motion, but he never seemed stressed by anything that he was doing. He was just fully engaged and plugged into a lot of things at once.

"And you know, the funny thing is that as I was watching him his phone rang, but it wasn't his standard desktop phone, Hugo wanted a special IP phone, which he says connects to everything else he has and does. So when he takes the call a video image of the person on the other line appeared on his computer screen. He told me later that his computer has a small web cam installed at the top of the monitor so the person he was talking with could see him too. And as he started talking he pulled up relevant information on another screen and worked with that during the conversation.

"Then he started working with his instant messaging during the conversation. I couldn't quite make out what he was doing, but he told me later that his instant messaging allows him to know about what his various contacts are doing at any given moment in time. For example, he needed a piece of information, but his instant messaging program told him that the first person he tried to ask was in a meeting at that moment and directed him to a colleague, sort of like when you get a voicemail box and the person says if it is important try talking to so and so. It seems just like standing at the water cooler and having a whole series of quick words with colleagues who pass by to get things done, if you think of it that way its seems more acceptable and less stressful.

"What all of this meant is that he was using his phone and his PC to have a video conference and then he was able to bring others into the discussion through instant messaging and email and even his cell phone if need be. He could bring in an assortment of people into this collaboration on a moment's notice and he could see who was available, in what mode of communication, and make judgments based on the expertise he needed at any time during—I can't really call it a conversation because it was more than just a standard person-to-person interaction, but was more a collaboration with people entering and leaving as needed and according to availability, which Hugo told me is called 'Presence' and is now becoming a standard on these Web 2.0 communications tools."

"So did anyone notice you hovering around the door to Hugo's office?"

"Right, that's all I need is for the office rumor mill to go into action," says Moneymaker, as the ebb and flow of the café and its customers continues to hum around them. "What was funny, though, is that I could barely see his other phone, our standard Vorpal desktop unit. It was nearly covered by papers and I may be exaggerating here, but it could have been covered under a layer of dust for all I know."

"Jane, you've wandered away from how this applies to me..." says Grant.

A New Way to Look at the Web

"Just give me a second. When he finished his call I walked in and asked Hugo what he was doing, if he could show me the things he does as he works. First he showed me the blog that he writes, which is on using certain web applications as marketing tools such as Facebook, Craigslist, and LinkedIn."

"You know, my daughter uses all of those and it used to drive me nuts because she would be instant messaging friends on Facebook and MySpace while she was doing her homework," says Grant. "Then one day as I was reading her the riot act, she showed me exactly what she was doing, which involved a fair bit of playing around, but she was also using instant messaging to talk with friends about homework assignments and Facebook to find people with knowledge about what she was working on."

"How so?" asks Moneymaker.

"Well, if she was writing a paper on the Civil War she would search for content and people, maybe share with friends taking the same assignment through Facebook and just generally seemed able to find everything she needed to know."

"That is interesting," says Moneymaker, glancing out a window for a moment. "Hugo used the term 'The Network of Everything' when I asked him how come nothing ever seems to faze him and he always seems to know the answer to something or assured of where to look. I suppose he knows that what he needs can be found online from either the content on a web page or by being able to ask someone with detailed knowledge directly.

"Hugo was doing the same as your daughter except he was using these things to build connections and networks of collaboration to market our products. His blog interacts with people and is linked to other marketing types, he is involved in a number of Facebook networks, he contributes to a number of wikis, he uses LinkedIn as a resource to find people with particular expertise on any subject, he uses WebEx to connect with his workgroups and hold virtual meetings on the fly, and all of these things could be related to finding and communicating with potential customer niches or with other marketers to gather information…"

"I suppose that's true, but isn't it the weekend, time to take it easy?" says Grant.

"Sorry. If you can't tell, I'm rather excited by it all, which leads to the next thing. David Firehammer, our CTO, used another term, 'Mesh,' by which he meant everyone and everything is now connected. When you put that with the way Hugo and your daughter are working then you see that it's all about their ability to draw together the right people and content at the right time from this mesh. That's where the use of Web 2.0 tools comes into play. If you understand how to use them, then you can understand how to handle almost any problem, which I suppose is why Hugo and his colleagues are so relaxed about the way they work even though they are doing so much. They have the world—the Network of Everything—to draw on for their problems where the rest of us are desperately trying to solve everything with our own resources.

"Well, anyway, I felt that there is something to the way that Hugo works that can be translated to the way that others work. I mean, he may be something of a virtuoso, but it can be shared, so I invited him up to my office..."

"I can hear the rumor mill humming," says Grant.

"Oh, I know. But anyway, I said to Hugo that I was glad that all of this is working for him, but it's not working for me and I have a lot more problems than he does to run the company. So how can this apply to what I do?" Moneymaker says. "So we get to my office, and the discussion starts: if you think of everything that Hugo does as Web 2.0[2], then everything I have been doing would be Web 1.0.

"I have one screen; I only use email to communicate; I don't know about or use all the other forms of communication that Hugo uses; I use spreadsheets to collate my numbers and can't handle the collation of all the other formats that information and content can be provided in; and lastly, if I use the Internet it is to look up a business news site and read from it like it's a newspaper. Oh, and I think I'm smart because I can use Google to search for something."

"Right, so that's the Web alright, it's a super electronic magazine or dictionary or database, something like that," says Grant.

"Yes, that's right! That's exactly what we Web 1.0 people think. Hugo uses Wikipedia because it's constantly changing and updating and I go to Dictionary.com because I think the facts are facts and never change," says Moneymaker, as a loud group of people walks

---

[2] For a very good explanation of Web 2.0 go to: http://www.oreilly.com/pub/a/oreilly/tim/news/2005/09/30/what-is-web-20.html

through the door. Voices and many conversations ring louder as this new group chats among themselves and orders their drinks.

Business Uses for the Mesh

"Ever notice that we drink coffee while the younger crowd drinks lattes," adds Grant, looking at the small group. "Is that somehow part of the same issue?"

"A bit off the point perhaps," says Moneymaker smiling at her friend. "The problem from my point of view is that I need to see more clearly and specifically what the business uses are for all of this because right now I'm feeling distinctly uneasy by the thought that I'm being left behind and that a CEO who can use Web 2.0 is going to beat me. Actually, it was watching Hugo work that made me acutely aware of this because the fact of the matter is that Hugo is far more productive than anybody else in the company and I was witnessing why—he's having more conversations of shorter duration, on demand, and with a wider variety of people using multiple communication tools. And on top of that, he is using other tools, the Web 2.0 tools, the Internet, as well as his PC, and so on to make these interactions even more productive. So when is some sharper and aggressive person going to come along and take my job because they can use and better understand all of these tools and techniques better than I can?"

"Still the classic overachiever," Grant says, "but I'm still having trouble seeing how this is going to make my life easier."

"Hang on, so Hugo stands behind me as I log on to some sites starting with Facebook so that he can show me what this site is all about."

"Sounds like a bit of an intimate moment…"

Moneymaker smiles, and then continues, "I entered the personal information it asked for, which felt awkward because it felt as if I was letting the world know way too much about me and anybody could connect with me. It sort of felt like slowly disrobing in Times Square."

"Come on now, it couldn't have been that uncomfortable for you?" asks Grant.

"No, but Hugo did make the point, which makes quite a bit of sense that this is exactly the kind of information we all share when we meet and start to get to know new people. It's what lets us know if we have certain things in common. Anyway, I started looking around on Facebook. There is something there for nearly anyone and some of these groups, which are networks of people with like interests, contain tens of thousands of members that are looking in and seeing what others in the group are up to. For example, one group dedicated to Web 2.0 entrepreneurs has 30,000 contributing to it.

"Then I looked at a network of U.K.-based technology journalists using Facebook as something of a searchable message board where members can post their own press releases, stories they are working for comment, offer or search for jobs, announce events, or even to just say that they have moved. By doing this they are using this web service as a place for groups and individuals to create working environments that include tools to empower a greater sense of collaboration. You know, I even discovered a community for people who work at Vorpal. I did notice a bit of a generational issue to it in that most of the people on it are much younger, but I started to realize that it could be a very powerful tool for the company's internal operations.

"Hugo also showed me a web site called Technorati, which tracks millions of blogs and I was able to find a blog that discussed the business uses for web sites such as Facebook."

"So it is more than just my daughter doing, or not doing her homework," says Grant.

"It is. For example, I was able to find one blog in particular that reflects my interest and talked about business uses for collaborative web-based applications, including a service called Basecamp. With Hugo watching like he was teaching me to ride a bike, I went to the web site to find out that this service helps companies mange numerous projects around collaboration internally and also externally with authorized partners. I could set it up so that files can be shared, I and others can keep track of who is doing what, the time they are spending on tasks, and track due dates and who is responsible for what."

"But you already do that," says Grant.

"True, but what we have is very different, it's for large projects and is too costly and complex to be used for everyday matters. Also, it's strictly for internal use. By using this kind of a service in sort of an informal kind of way, we can be better at what we do because anyone can invoke Basecamp for whatever they do internally, externally or both, so that we get professionally managed projects every time. With these sorts of tools we can be innovative in the way we work because we can manage more ad hoc situations and events…"

"This is getting to be too much business talk for a Saturday," says Grant, beginning to tire of the topic.

"Right, sorry, but here's where it relates to you. As I worked with Hugo mentoring me along, I started to see that not only could this stuff help me, it could also help us with things such as purchasing, security, compliance, supply chain, HR, and so on. We could establish some of these same services internally in order to enhance not only collaborating with the outside world, but also with each other. We are having a meeting on it next week."

"And this relates to me how?" asks Grant, finishing the last of her coffee.

"Well come on, you can do the same things I was doing."

"You mean go out and find myself a Hugo?" asks Grant with a grin.

"Well, there probably is a web site for that."

"Look, that's all well and good, but my business isn't big enough to be able to afford to have people idling on a computer. My business is much more hands on, but you have just spent quite a bit of time telling me I need to be more innovative about using the Web. Thank you, but maybe you need an internal editor. Let's get going before I have to go back to my little flower shop of horrors…"

"Wait a second," says Moneymaker, holding her hand out to stop Grant from getting up. "You think you have to do everything within your business, and the overhead of hiring more staff makes it seem impossible to be able to afford them. I'm telling you that you should use collaboration to find and share your workflow by getting others to do part of the work that they specialize in. Your role is the customer contact via a physical location while their roles can be any element from making up potted specials to...well, frankly I don't know the flower business very well, but it's about expanding your basic business model of buying mass-produced finished products to resell, into one that buys in services to make up unique products, too. Now do you see why I was so excited?"

Questions for Further Analysis

1) What is Mesh Collaboration and How Does it Differ from Previous Generations of Collaboration?

2) What are the Mechanisms of Web 2.0 and How Do They Support Mesh Collaboration?

3) How is the Increasing Sophistication and Power of Consumer IT Creating Demand for Better Collaboration in the Workplace?

4) What is Enterprise 2.0 and How is Mesh Collaboration Different in the Enterprise?

Chapter 5

Replicating Wunderkind

It has been about four weeks since Jane Moneymaker had her coffee date with Hannah Grant, where she explained how she first came to understand that not only does Vorpal's business model need to go through a transformation, but that her vision for transformation can't really happen without changing the way in which people work.

From watching Hugo Wunderkind work in his office using a number of web-based social networking sites Moneymaker became aware that these tools, which have facilitated Wunderkind's extraordinary productivity and innovation, could also be used by others in Vorpal. If Wunderkind can use these technologies with such great success, why can't they also be used to help support internal operations as opposed to just generating new sales channels?

In the last chapter Moneymaker was just beginning to see the potential for integrating collaborative technologies, but now she and Vorpal are moving ahead to quickly adopt these technologies into the work routines of employees. She has gone from a vision of what could be, to seeing the very real business uses of these technologies.

Two ideas in particular had seized her imagination: the ability to make use of the resources available from the Web—what Wunderkind called the "Network of Everything"—both internally and externally; and the idea that this connected world resembles a mesh where the main challenge is developing the ability to reach across the mesh to find the people and resources that can aid specific actions in a timely manner.

What this represents is a move away from what has come to be described as Matrix Working—individuals working at specific tasks in which they hold specialized expertise for a number of managers via technology implemented within the company—to a different model called Mesh Working, built on the four pillars of Web 2.0—social networking, blogs, wikis, and RSS (Really Simple Syndication)—and relying on using the Web as a platform for collaboration. Mesh Working is also facilitated by the use of communication tools such as handheld devices, web browsers, instant messaging, email, video communication via IP phone, and so on.

The difference between Matrix and Mesh has become clear as Moneymaker considers its use within the company. Matrix Working has played a critical role in helping businesses use PC networking technology to deploy applications in a more effective manner for people and procedures in an enterprise. Mesh Working, on the other hand, is about using the Internet and the Web to extend people-centric technologies into a new generation of capabilities that cover both internal and external people, events and content.

The question that Moneymaker must now answer is how to get her coworkers and employees to think differently and exploit Mesh Working in order to make use of the Network of Everything to find people with the skills, expertise, and knowledge to provide useful information and even answers to complicated and complex issues. Successfully implemented, the limitations of Matrix Working will be replaced with an open global community of almost unlimited facilities connected through the mesh of the Internet with the capabilities of the Web.

However, Moneymaker realizes that pursuing this new form of working isn't just something you can do by sending out a memo with the directive to engage in Mesh Working. Instead, it needs to be explained and learned and the risks and benefits to each approach used by the company need to be understood and managed. Somehow she has to draw attention to the benefits that Mesh Working facilitated by Web 2.0 can bring to Vorpal.

Therefore, she has had Wunderkind, Lovecraft, and Cashtender draw up a document to list the tasks that employees perform, the collaborative Mesh Working approaches used to improve on the execution of those tasks, and the benefits and risks of those approaches.

Tasks	Collaborative Approach	Benefits/Risks
Recruiting	All employees are encouraged to submit names of any friend/colleague they feel should be recruited. Finder's fee is paid if they are hired	Much wider talent pool, Web 2.0 savvy people suggest Web 2.0 talent. More screening is needed of each candidate
Problem Solving	Problems are posted on the Web for anybody internally to suggest a solution	Harnessing the collective IQ of the organization
Supplier Collaboration	Shared wiki with suppliers and blogs with RSS feeds	Ecosystem reacts to real-time events quicker. Full visibility of supply chain
Product Design	Design dedicated wiki	Fast method of iteratively developing designs, but could be susceptible to incorrect information
Internal Best Practices	Internal experts work in external peer communities to develop best practices. These working groups then lead internal focus groups to take new knowledge and integrate it into the business	Expedited development, understanding, and integration of best practices. Time commitment for staff taking them away from existing work

Knowledge Management	A wiki with robust search capability becomes a repository of all the information in the organization, including documents, PDFs, and spreadsheets	Information from any project can be found by everyone
Internal Social Networking	Wikis and blogs on internal and cross departmental issues	Employees can find others with common interests and expertise who they would not otherwise meet, enabling new collaborations
Managing Customer Expectations	Telepresence and WebEx sessions with customers become part of the normal sales and exec relationship process	Frequency of customer interactions drastically increases. Cycle times reduce as information is shared quicker. Salesforce productivity increases as they can talk to more customers each day
Manage Public/ Media Relations	Open Source, web-based blog hosting with RSS feed	Allows company to maintain interactive community around its products and issue press releases as well as news podcasts and video clips in a more automated and timely manner
HR Management	Video conferencing and related tools are enabled by IT at home to reduce travel time and improve home/work balance	Lower building costs as more employees telework. Friendlier HR policies for working parents leading to increased loyalty

To integrate this initiative into the day-to-day operations of the company Moneymaker has added a Mesh Working education initiative into Vorpal's overall change management strategy. Her expectation is that once people understand the possibilities and learn the strategies and techniques, they will become equally excited about the improvements Mesh Working can bring to how well they are able to perform their jobs.

One of the primary means by which Moneymaker is disseminating this message throughout the company is a series of workshops led by Wunderkind. And while understanding these tools and strategies is primarily targeted toward Vorpal's many employees and line managers, Moneymaker strongly believes that leadership must also better understand how they can improve the manner by which they manage their tasks and responsibilities.

"In for a penny in for a pound," which means that if something is worth doing then it should be done completely, has become something of a personal idiom for Moneymaker. Therefore, she has taken the somewhat unusual step of having Wunderkind guide her leadership team through a series of workshops similar to those he has given to the employees, but targeted toward the unique responsibilities of Vorpal's executive and VP-level leaders.

Executive Mesh Workshop

"Alright everyone, if we could please take a seat I would like to get this workshop going so that we can all get out of here a little early today," says Wunderkind in a joking tone with a smile. "I'm not sure who thought holding these things on Friday afternoons was such a good idea, but here we are."

Moneymaker's leadership team is seated around the table and true to form each member occupies their regular spot. The lone exception is Moneymaker, who has given the head of the table to Wunderkind and is now seated slightly off to his right. Though she is removed from her literal position of power, one can feel that even as Wunderkind speaks she has not relinquished control of the room.

"Hugo?" says Moneymaker, causing Wunderkind to turn slightly to his right.

"Yes, Jane."

"In light of some of the issues that have come up over the past couple of weeks I think it would be appropriate to start this meeting doing a bit of a recap as to some of the concerns people expressed during our first workshop," says Moneymaker.

"Yes, that sounds like a good idea," says Wunderkind as he turns to the rest of the room. "We have certainly come a long way since our first meeting to discuss the use throughout the company of what is increasingly being called social networking as well as other collaboration techniques that we are calling Mesh Working. However, I do understand that many of you are concerned that these technologies and related strategies aren't on the same level as our enterprise technologies; that they can't be used to run the company. I agree and would like to stress that what I have been going around the company teaching people…"

"Preaching would be more like it," interjects Frank Cashtender.

A little insulted, Hugo gives Cashtender a slight, cool glance, "…is not intended to replace the technologies and strategies for their use that we already have. Rather it's to enhance how we work and how we all work together, which I think of all that I have myself learned over the past few weeks is the most important.

"I also agree that we need to be mindful of some new issues as we move forward, not the least of which is in the area of security."

"That's right, Hugo," interrupts Moneymaker. "One of my chief concerns has been the possibility of airing our dirty laundry in a rather public way because we have so many of our people online and chatting in these social networks. With such an open door policy we risk having competitors accessing proprietary information for no other reason than that we are deliberately allowing them to take a peek behind doors that some would argue should have remained closed."

"Absolutely, I think that is the fundamental issue that we need to understand as there clearly are inherent risks created by the fact that we are reaching out beyond what have customarily been clear walls of separation," adds Cashtender. "In fact, we are encouraging our staff to seek out people to chat with."

"I agree, Frank," says Lovecraft, "but we're moving forward very quickly on establishing controls in order to achieve the separation to make sure that the things we want to remain closed for our own commercial and compliance purposes behind our firewalls stay there."

"I know, Josh, and what you say sounds good," replies Cashtender, "but we have already had some security issues, which makes me concerned about compliance and Jane's worry of allowing information that could be damaging to our reputation or brand out in the public. I would also add that we have no firm grasp of how to measure the value of these efforts to the company. I mean, if we are accepting that there is increased risk, as it seems that we are, I need to be able to understand and measure that risk both for compliance and in non-compliance areas so that we can gauge gains."

"Frank, I agree that we are accepting some additional risk with this initiative," says Moneymaker, "which really is a new type of risk that has come with our new markets and revenues. We should also remember that the existing business, the brick-and-mortar sales, carries with it a number of risks as well. I also believe that this is something we have to do if we're going to stay out ahead of our competitors and possibly even remain competitive. However, Frank is right in that we need to quantify what *is* at risk."

"Do we even really know exactly who our competitors are anymore?" asks Cashtender. "I don't mean to be facetious, but the fact of the matter is that we have encouraged a much higher degree of collaboration internally and externally. In an effort to be expedient we are doing business now with some companies that traditionally we defined as competitors, if not in direct products, then for a share of the customers' money spent in that sector of the market. I wonder if we aren't blurring some lines between ourselves and other players in the market just a little too far—are we collaborating with people we're in competition with? And now we're talking about opening our systems to these people as well?"

"Is there anything in particular that you have noticed, Frank?" asks Lovecraft coolly.

"Yes, there is," responds Cashtender, sitting forward in his seat. "Let's have a show of hands. Has anyone in this room been solicited or had someone in their department solicited by headhunters that have gained access via our presence on some of these social networking sites we're being encouraged to join?"

Nearly everyone in the room reluctantly raises their hand. Envy can clearly be seen in the eyes of those who don't.

"Frank, I think that I can..." says Hugo, but Cashtender cuts him off.

"Has anyone been approached by a member of the press who has found them via one of these social networking sites?" asks Cashtender, to which a few hands go up. "You see, we are vulnerable to these kinds of issues."

"Hold on there a minute," interjects David Wannamaker, VP of sales and marketing, "we put out a lot of effort in marketing trying to get the press to notice what we are doing. This isn't necessarily a bad thing you know."

"Frank, I believe Hugo was going to respond to you," says Moneymaker.

"Thanks, Jane," says Wunderkind uneasily. "This is true, Frank, that we have had some situations arise, and from the beginning we have been moving forward with our eyes open to the fact that with the advantages we may be gaining there may be a few disadvantages as well. But you know, the attention our employees are receiving works both ways because we're also being approached by people that want to work in the kind of company we're developing.

"However, we have been moving forward on some initiatives that are designed to provide an added layer of security on both a technical and governance side, which I know you are aware of in outline, Frank, but would be worth briefly reviewing for everyone else. Josh, could you describe some of the tech stuff please?"

"Sure," says Lovecraft briskly. "The first thing that I would say is we are now keeping logs on external communications and sessions that exit the firewall so that we are able to build an audit trail in case we need to identify any activity we would want to follow up on. In particular, this would include being able to investigate noncompliance with company policies that we have updated and clarified. Some of you may feel that this would only allow us to take action after a problem has been identified, too reactive not proactive enough, which is an accurate description and valid concern, but we have noticed that since staff are aware of this that we have seen changes in traffic patterns. It's really a case of educating people as to how we want them to behave in the new way we are doing things around here.

"Further, we have just this week been talking with a vendor that may help us to deploy a packet scanning capability at the firewall to search for certain key words or phrases. For example, as Hugo may move on a particularly large sales initiative, the system could scan emails and instant messages for any proprietary information that we may not want escaping past the firewall. This capability would in effect provide almost real-time capabilities to shut off a Vorpal user who is letting slip sensitive information. It also allows us to handle some of the issues on topics such as monitoring to make sure that issues such as personal data won't cross the firewall."

"That seems a little Draconian," interjects Sarah Brown, VP of customer service, "like it's a violation of privacy."

"More Draconian than what would happen if we violate Sarbanes-Oxley or some other personal information privacy law?" asks Cashtender.

"The thing we have to remember," says Moneymaker, slightly exasperated at having to defend this issue again with Cashtender, "is that above all this is more than simply an enterprise IT initiative. If this is truly about enabling people to work the way they choose, with whom they choose, and so on, then we are talking about a very knowledgeable group of people. They are the people, and there are quite a few of them, who we currently trust to make a wide array of major decisions and to talk to an even wider variety of people on the phone or in meetings. We can trust them to talk to large suppliers and customers alike, so why will they be tempted to break their existing and trusted behavior model just because they have some extra channels to communicate through?

"No, this is not an enterprise IT initiative built around our corporate desktop provisioning and applications; it's more an HR issue about how we expect people to behave."

"This brings me to something I had planned to discuss today," says Wunderkind, reaching into a colorful shoulder bag similar to what a bike messenger would carry and producing a folder brimming with papers. "If we could pass these out…. This is the draft collaborative code of conduct that we have been working on for the past couple of weeks. If you all could follow along as I read at least the first page here…"

Draft: Collaborative Code of Conduct

Requirement: To provide guidance that is mutually beneficial and enables the use of collaboration to create value for individuals in the execution of their work, and for Vorpal in achieving its business goals, while ensuring that the management can exercise due control over necessary content and activity where collaboration may jeopardize the commercial activities of Vorpal, in respect of the law, confidential, and/or competitive information, and so forth.

Statement: Whereas collaborative mechanisms have proven to be extremely valuable to the overall ability of the company to achieve its primary business objectives, there is the recognition that these mechanisms come with some risk and a new set of responsibilities to be shared at each level of the enterprise.

As such, Vorpal recognizes the need to establish a standard code of conduct applicable to all employees in order to clearly delineate each individual's responsibility in reference to the creation, sharing, reuse, and editing of content used for collaboration as well as the starting, joining, commenting, or similar activities within communities so that we may maintain Vorpal's high standards of professionalism as we participate in this exciting new media.

In general, this collaborative code of conduct extends the existing code of behavior expected of employees in current situations to new forms of interactions internally or externally using new technologies such as, but not limited to, wikis, blog sites, mailing lists, social networking sites and/or applications, and in any other collaborative format as yet defined that may be created as the Internet and the World Wide Web continue to evolve.

In particular, Vorpal will both implement a Digital Rights Register and publish continuously updated guidelines for the use of Digital Rights Management so that individuals can maintain appropriate control over their content used for collaboration. Vorpal management will use this same facility to ensure internally sensitive documents and information cannot be distributed and used in ways that are inappropriate.

Guidelines:

In all cases, without exception, if any employee of Vorpal is in doubt as to how to conduct or whether to conduct any interaction, they are to seek out their immediate supervisor for guidance, before proceeding. Training in this regard will be maintained and ongoing with a substantive effort to disseminate new information, policies, and practices as they are developed.

It is incumbent upon every member of the Vorpal team to maintain a polite and professional appearance while engaged with collaboration internally, but, in particular, externally in order to maintain the good reputation and strength of Vorpal's brands. In particular, when interacting in a collaborative manner employees are not to engage in any dishonest or illegal behavior, or any behavior that could be construed as such. Further, employees are to avoid any strong or heated disagreements, personal attacks, ongoing arguments, or behave in any other manner that could be perceived as harmful to Vorpal and its brands.

Any press inquiries that may come as a result of chance encounters or other interactions from members of all forms of media must first be presented to Vorpal's public relations department for vetting before any comments, quotes, or information is to be supplied. Further, if an employee has reason to believe that a person they may be interacting with is a member of the media they are to ask that person if they are in fact with a media outlet. The definition of "Media" is to extend beyond the commonly understood forms such as print, television, and radio, to include publishers and content providers to blogs, wikis, and any other format for the dissemination of news and information.

It is strictly forbidden to release any information about any topics listed on the Vorpal intranet site specifically for the purposes of ensuring there can be control over sensitive information generated by events and circumstances as well as those topics already defined. This includes, but is not limited to, identifying information, contact information, or any other personal, professional, or job related information.

Vorpal intends to create an openly innovative and collaborative environment both externally to assist its customers, suppliers, partners, and others in having a positive and enriching experience in doing business with Vorpal, and internally to assist its employees in working in a personally and collectively rewarding manner. As such, employees are asked to participate in the Vorpal communities as they relate to respective job duties both internally—blogs and wikis—and externally such as communities on Facebook, LinkedIn, MySpace, professional blogs, and various wikis. Further, it is the responsibility of managers to notice the use and effectiveness by employees of collaborative and social networking technologies and to encourage and train for effective usage of these mediums.

It is also required that employees maintain a separate online identity to those that they may operate under during their home Internet use. Wherever practical, employees should also maintain a screen name while interacting externally in order to protect their personal information, but not where it could be construed as a deliberate attempt to hide or confuse the truth from a situation where this might be considered sensitive.

Accessing unacceptable, profane, or inappropriate web sites and/or behaving in a similar manner while engaged with collaborative resources internally or externally will not be tolerated or treated in any different manner to the existing requirements for acceptable behavior in the Human Resources manual.

Employees by default accept responsibility for their actions and share responsibility for the actions of those around them, and are expected to not only comply with the written requirements of the Code of Conduct but also to comply with the spirit of the code as well.

"So, there are a few more things here, but this should give you an idea of what we are aiming for," says Wunderkind. "Also, given the current speed at which the world we are talking about is changing, this needs to be a living document that our people can continually access, offer thoughts on with regard to needed changes and updates, and so on. It must be recognizably what they need and not something that is imposed on them at some meeting without continued updating.

It also has to be posted online with other relevant and supporting materials accessible via the company's internal portal."

"Hugo, I assume you are advocating making this into a wiki of some sort?" asks Lovecraft.

"Actually, no," interjects Moneymaker. "One of the other bits of governance we have been working on is delineating those things where an open collaborative approach would work well and where there needs to be a tighter leash. What we need to do is separate the absolute code of conduct as approved rules from a parallel environment where comments and collaborations can be posted. The link between the two will be made in the normal way as management decisions.

"What this will accomplish is to make the collection of information and suggestions continuous, which will aid an equally continuous review of the need to make any updating decisions. This is an important point for developing our understanding of the difference between governance and open collaboration. There are areas where we can't accept giving employees the right to make any alterations to key rules as they see fit."

Mesh Working in Practice

"So to continue," interjects Hugo, "our first working session focused on explaining to people the thinking behind this shift and to bring everyone up to speed on the strategy behind merging these collaborative mechanisms into day-to-day operations. As has been mentioned, we also aired some common concerns.

"Then the second session was run like a tutorial where we went through a number of sites, signed up for some, and then experimented on how they work and how to interact with people.

"For the third workshop we went through and talked about the experiences we have had using these tools and techniques, which is where we were able to identify some of the issues we already talked about. Out of that discussion we came quite naturally to the need for our new collaborative code of conduct. Most of all, this means that people have understood why it should necessarily be respected.

"So today I think it would be helpful if we held a discussion to see how these things will work and are already starting to work."

"If I could start," says Moneymaker, confirming her role as the ultimate decision maker, "we are about to go online with what I would describe as an internal mashup for ad hoc project management. The term 'ad hoc' doesn't sound right when talking about project management, so let me explain what I mean by that. There is something of a new understanding of the 80/20 rule, which is that 80% of what should be managed and structured work on projects isn't. Why? Because the time and cost of setting up and using our current project management application makes it seem inappropriate, meaning that only 20%—our bigger projects—are handled in this manner.

"To add to the issue, we are experiencing a huge change in the projects we are undertaking that can be characterized as smaller and much faster, being done more often, and, in particular, with an increasing amount of external content. In other words, exactly what we should be focusing on doing better at is not in the scope of our traditional tools.

"This means we will be working on these projects with at least an external web-based service that we will pay for as and when we use it and by the people using it. It's based on the new Software as a Service model and allows us to directly attribute costs to the users or at least to their project codes. And because it can be used by anyone who is authorized to a particular project, those increasingly common new projects of Hugo and his colleagues, where we are cooperating with several other enterprises at once, should be no problem. Finally, as the service was designed to be accessed and used in the new online web world, it's also highly secure to the very risks that we see in using our existing applications, which were never designed to be used online in this manner.

"When it is fully up and running I, or any other manager, should be able to assign tasks to various teams and units within the company and then track to ensure they are meeting assigned deadlines. The system also has a reporting mechanism so that when a team hits a milestone they fill out a quick report that is automatically emailed to the supervising manager. If they don't hit a milestone the software notifies me.

"I see this as helping reduce the amount of time any of us spend managing individual projects and, thankfully, reducing the number of meetings that need to be held in order to receive project updates. I also expect that we'll see more use of this being made by individuals to manage their own projects or activities."

"We've been talking about taking this new approach to both manage and test the packet scanning security project that I mentioned earlier," says Lovecraft. "Basically, we're establishing a series of milestones between the supplier and ourselves that need to be met in order to stick to our desired feature releases and overall deadlines for the project. If I know that we may not hit any of them then I'm able to communicate to those involved, even Jane if I need to, via its built-in communications package. It even has IM capability so that we can have conversations in real time."

"How do we know that this information, which could be rather sensitive, isn't accessible by someone logging onto our web site or even the service owner's site?" asks Cashtender.

"Actually, Frank, there are two answers to that question and I will assume you're not asking me why at a technology level these types of services are built to be secure in a way that quite frankly applications designed to be in an enclosed, internal world are not," says Lovecraft drawing a glance from Cashtender. "At a working level access is strictly password protected and the password for each project, depending on the level of security we believe we will need, can be changed at regular intervals. We can also provide a variety of ways to control who can issue a password and more."

"On that point, I would add that perhaps we need to set up some governance to determine if a project meets a higher level of security as well as the kinds of information that can be shared via this new service of yours," says Cashtender.

"That's a good point, Frank," says Moneymaker, "but don't forget that we'll only need this kind of governance for less than 20% of the projects. Mostly, we want to make using the service as easy as possible to ensure we get better management right across the board.

"I would also add that just saying I have this service available isn't going to do anybody any good if we don't use it, which means we will all have to invest some effort to encourage its use, which I think will initially be a common theme for all of these tools. If we're active in using them ourselves we'll create the example that will draw in the less enthusiastic users by forcing them to participate in our projects."

"That's why, if you look at the collaborative code of conduct, one of the points sets out the expectation that employees will adopt these mechanisms," says Wunderkind.

"That's great, Hugo, that way we have a piece of paper saying what people should do, but it's useless without a mechanism to encourage its use," says Moneymaker.

"Right, perhaps we could amend the document to include penalties for noncompliance," adds Cashtender.

"We should be clear about breaking rules and noncompliance for sure," says Moneymaker, "but that's not what this is all about. I believe that there will be no barrier from the younger half of our staff because the fact is that they're already going there with these kinds of tools already. Our challenge is to make them aware of how to use the tools safely. For the other half, well, they're mostly our contemporaries in terms of age and technological proficiency, so we're going to have to make a personal commitment to show that we are garnering effective use of these tools."

"That's going to be a good educational experience for you, Frank," adds Moneymaker with a wisp of a smile.

"Welcome to my world," says Wunderkind under his breath. "Okay, who would like to go next?"

"Well, as I have been trying out your 'Network of Everything,' I have found something that will allow us to enhance how we communicate not only with customers, but also with the media and people in general," says Brown. "It's called WordPress, which is open source software for blog hosting that comes with some very helpful features.

It's RSS feed capable, meaning that each and every time we place a blog on our web site we'll know that a lot of people will automatically be told that there is a new piece. This is even better and cheaper than mail slots and it provides us the opportunity to create and maintain a real interactive community around various topics related to our products. We can get feedback on what our particular views may be on any given topic so that we can change and develop how we think about our products and services in a manner that reflects the thoughts and opinions of our customers and suppliers."

"What exactly do you mean?" asks Cashtender, seeming a bit confused.

"Well, in the case of the media we can encourage our media contacts to link to our RSS feed as opposed to receiving more traditional press releases via email, or, God forbid, fax," says Brown. "We'll be able to provide these people with a constant flow of real-life experiences around the products, from customers, with their thoughts on the products, which would be far more useful than a carefully crafted press release sent out every now and then or left on the 'News' page of our web site hoping for someone to happen upon it. We can also blog about other topics we may not traditionally issue a release about, allowing us to dissuade rumors or generate buzz about our strategy, in short hold a more consistent dialog with the media.

"For customers, it's a fairly similar experience because they are looking for ideas and personal experiences on the topics that interest them, and we can see from other blogs that customers seem to want to add their comments to the discussion as well. The target is to create a highly connected and targeted customer base.

"Also, both Josh and Hugo say that we can extend this by creating wikis where customers that are showing interest in certain areas can interact with the design team, in a wiki, to help develop a particular product.

"One other feature, and this is one that I think will prove very useful given our pace of product and market creation, is a method to create a post, say on the features of a new product or that a product is aligned with some future event, and it will essentially be embargoed until a specific date and time when it will be released to a particular community."

"Is this another example of a service made available on the Web and hosted as Software as a Service?" asks Wannamaker.

"No, in this case it is an application with the software locally installed onto our web server, but because it is open source it's less expensive and more flexible if we want to do some extensions to suit our own particular needs," responds David Firehammer, CTO of Vorpal.

"Since this is open source software, couldn't we just redesign it and take on a greater ownership role?" asks Lovecraft.

"I would call that old thinking," says Firehammer.

"And it would be anathema to the intent of the collaboration we are trying to spark here," notes Wunderkind.

"Not only that, but by being a member of the community that surrounds this software we are sharing a common link; we are all working on creating common business processes that by being common allow us all to be more effective in working together," adds Firehammer. "And, because the community is huge, there is everything we need from blogs and wikis, all the way to whole forums dedicated to getting increased functionality from the software. We simply couldn't replicate this by sticking with our own proprietary version."

"I like this," says Moneymaker. "We're using this software as a collaboration tool with a number of communities related to improving our business on one hand and, on the other, we're also able to work collaboratively to improve our usage of the software, which could lead us to adding more value."

"Okay, I think I understand your enthusiasm," says Cashtender, reclining into his chair, "but I still want to make sure that I keep you up to our commercial requirements."

"We've already got a number of user-developed wikis and we're starting to dedicate some of these to supporting internal operations," says Wunderkind. "Surely there must be someone here who has worked with one of these."

"I have," says Wendy Chiselpenny, VP of operations. "About a month ago I received word that a downstream component supplier, that manufactures electric motors for a line of customized blenders, was no longer going to be supplying those motors. Our vendor called me and said they have been having trouble finding another component manufacturer because these motors are oddly sized."

"I remember talking about this with you," says Lovecraft. "The motors are for a set of mixers that are between what you would find in a professional, almost industrial kitchen, and in a home kitchen."

"Right," continues Chiselpenny, "because of their size, these motors are specially crafted to run at the kind of load that you would expect to find in a home electrical supply rather than the more industrial supply standards found in a larger professional kitchen. The vendor said they had no idea where to find another manufacturer because the specs of what we need are so specialized.

"I posted the problem on one of the wikis that the design team uses, which led to our internal experts concluding that this was not something they could answer and that we needed to access a wider community to help us find a more focused level of expertise. That same day we found a link to a social networking site where we were able to interact with a community of electrical engineers working on how to solve the exact problem of using domestic level supplies for heavier duty motors.

"We contacted them via a published email address for inquiries and they wrote about our dilemma on a couple of blogs they maintain, which led us to an electrical engineer from a company based in Appleton, Wisconsin."

"Talk about six degrees of separation," says Wunderkind.

"I know," says Chiselpenny, smiling. "We supplied this engineer with the specs used by our vendor, which as it turns out nearly match a design his company manufactures for a motor to run air compressors commonly used to power small tools for garage mechanics. This company has seen its market share decline over the past few years because more people are taking their cars to dealers now and because there's a foreign competitor in their market that makes a cheaper version of the motor used by mechanics. Recognizing an opportunity, we're now in three-way discussions to have the Appleton-based company add our requirements to their existing line. So, in a similar manner to what we have done, these guys are finding more opportunities in the market from a wider array of people with a wider variety of uses for their product."

"Couldn't we just go to the foreign competitor and get a bigger discount?" asks Cashtender.

"No," responds Chiselpenny. "The motors that we need have to respond to a wider variety of speeds for the mix settings on the mixers. They also have to incorporate a couple of standards, such as noise level and safety issues related to home power supplies as compared to those found in a large garage or industrial setting. The competitor's motors are designed for one thing and one thing only, which is to power a compressor for mechanics' tools. Also, our volume of orders is so small the overseas company couldn't handle our business affordably as compared to its mass-market business.

"And, Frank, you and Hugo are going to love this, the manufacturer practices Lean Manufacturing so as we find new uses or need modified motors, they're going to be able to scale up the number of production cells to meet our needs. We're also talking with some of the other group companies in Jabberwocky about the possibility of consolidating our more particular motor needs with this one manufacturer so we can leverage our group bulk buying power across markets and products."

"I have to say that my meager project management tool pales in comparison, Wendy," says Moneymaker.

"Well, actually we have arranged all of this as a pilot with the new project management tool," says Chiselpenny, happy to be a step ahead of her boss.

Mashmarking

"Jane? Or rather, Hugo, may I get back to something I mentioned earlier, which never was addressed?" asks Cashtender.

"Yeah, Frank, go ahead," answers Hugo.

"Look, from Wendy's little story and some of the other things we have discussed, it seems as if we are getting value out of these mechanisms," says Cashtender, "but, as we have acknowledged earlier, there are associated risks and I haven't seen how we are going to identify and quantify them against real-world metrics.

"There is also the related issue that, since we don't have metrics, it's hard to tell who's doing something that's business related or simply checking on their fantasy football league.

"These are things we always do even when it is difficult to place a precise value on it. You know, we do all sorts of weird things to increase sales, but you and the rest of the sales department have hardcore metrics that you follow, such as the number of leads that are created, leads that are followed up on, calls of certain types, and so on."

"Well, perhaps this is an exception to prove the rule?" says Wunderkind.

"No, it isn't," interjects Moneymaker sternly. "You're right, Frank. We do need a way to monitor what people are doing and the value we are creating and the best way to do that is to create solid and rational metrics."

"But social networking doesn't easily adapt to that kind of thinking," adds Wunderkind.

"Actually, it seems that people are working on ways of assessing how well they're doing," interjects Lovecraft, as he pulls a copy of a web page from a small stack of papers in front of him. "Obviously this has been something I have been thinking about, as well, and have been exploring internally with a wiki I've developed and externally on a number of sites and blogs. The other day in a network dedicated to web services, I posed this question, which is how do you assess and set metrics for collaboration.

"One of the responses I received led me to a blog posting by a corporate innovation officer based in the Netherlands, which may be a role we would want to consider adding. Anyway, he is promoting the idea of mashmarking as opposed to benchmarking when it comes to measuring a company's performance using collaborative technologies.

"He has published how to try to reassess the characteristics of competitive advantage from mass-market benchmarks on price, delivery time, and all the other usual metrics, into a new generation of comparisons that illustrate how well a company compares in new capabilities for Long Tail markets. Basically, he's looking at how good a company is at answering questions such as, 'Does your company have an ecosystem of business partners outside your vertical market?' and 'Does your company have an open, innovative culture?'"

"Josh, you know I don't like to be the company contrarian just for the sake of being contrary, but that doesn't really get to the heart of what I was saying," says Cashtender.

"No, it doesn't," responds Lovecraft, "but it is a start and it does tell you that this issue is recognizable and being addressed and that we should be working in different ways with others in order to take part in the development of solutions for these types of questions. I think that it would be very worthwhile to correspond with this person and find others in much the same way that Wendy did who could help us create the metrics that we need."

"Josh, what about other measures as to the value of these new tools and strategies?" asks Moneymaker. "Such as reduced travel costs because people will no longer have to be physically in the same place to hold meetings, reduced meeting lengths, or even increasing the number of people who can attend a meeting via video conferencing and then saving a recording of the meeting for future reference. We could also look at how much more environmentally efficient we are, which would be good PR and help us reduce our carbon footprint."

"No, you're right," says Lovecraft. "We could also look at the HR side of this and see how these measures improve job satisfaction as well as reduce complaints that work and travel are negatively impacting people's home and family life."

"All right, Josh. That's another project for me to add to my management tool," says Moneymaker, turning to Wunderkind. "I think we also need to make sure that we have our own experts work with these communities to make sure that we're getting what we need out of the collaborations. In turn, these people can drive internal focus groups that will actually take responsibility for the transformation of their parts of the business where we need to apply the new knowledge that we capture. Can we have something in the works by next week, Hugo?"

"Yes, we should be able to meet that timeframe using the internal collaboration tools we have already implemented," says Wunderkind. "Something we need to develop more fully is the use of video communications. For example, when I answer a call on my IP phone, I am able to also have a video feed of the person on the other line, which means that these conversations hold more value and are more meaningful. Video would be a great way for these experts to hold meetings amongst themselves, reducing the need to travel. They could also record these meetings and save them as tutorials for staff."

"Okay then. Let's keep this ball rolling," says Moneymaker, ending the meeting and sweeping out of the room in a manner clearly meant to express that she is in charge.

Questions for Further Analysis

1) How Can a Culture of Emergent Collaboration be Encouraged?

2) How Will the Role of IT Change to Support Collaboration?

3) How Will Users Be Empowered to Do for Themselves?

4) How Can You Secure Proprietary Information and Maintain Privacy and Security?

5) How Do You Set Metrics for This Level of Collaboration?

Part 3

Scaling Innovation— Solving Larger Problems on a Bigger Stage

Chapter 6

The Supplier Revelation

After what at times has felt like a very difficult journey into new and unfamiliar territory, Vorpal has managed to reinvent its business model to one commonly referred to as an Enterprise 2.0 model.

The payoff for this hard and often frustrating journey is that Vorpal is better able to differentiate its product offering among a number of markets, increasing its revenues. The company is also finding opportunities within the underlying sales support structures to synergistically link together its use of resources and capabilities to increase its operating margins and therefore add real deliverable value to the company.

And Vorpal is not above bringing its suppliers into the process by treating them as if they have a mutual business partnership rather than an arm's length, antagonistic vendor relationship. The end result is a system of mutual value creation as they, too, benefit from increasing revenues and operating synergies from adopting the Enterprise 2.0 approach.

However, these lessons have not yet been translated to Vorpal's sibling companies operating under Jabberwocky, the parent company, and its CEO and chairman, Charles Dodgson.

Among his contemporaries, Dodgson is considered something of a visionary, yet to date he has only noticed the improved financial performance of Vorpal. He doesn't know the mechanisms being employed by Moneymaker to transform Vorpal. Instead, Dodgson believes that it must be the result of running a classically tight ship.

Tilo Costman, the CEO of Power Plus, which is a sibling company to Vorpal within Jabberwocky, has no idea what Moneymaker has done either. As is commonly found in many such groups, there is little that can be or is shared beyond treasury functionality. Power Plus and Vorpal are, with the other group companies, linked by little more than regular meetings of Jabberwocky CEOs and the reliance on an electric motor supplier. At the time of the acquisition of many of the group members, vertical integration was seen as a way of increasing profitability, so Power Plus' Small Motor Division was originally a supplier to Vorpal and other Jabberwocky group companies.

In addition to its Small Motor Division, Power Plus also specializes in manufacturing and marketing electric generators for onsite industrial use as well as for a range of retail applications as a supplement to external power supplies or an for emergency backup power supply.

On its surface, Power Plus appears to have managed to maintain its margins and remain a player in the segment. However, the truth of the matter is that global competitors have eaten dramatically into its market for new generators, forcing Costman to maintain his sales by cutting his prices. In an effort to maintain realistic margins, he has also been forced into round after round of cost-cutting initiatives.

Internally focused cost-cutting and efficiency programs worked for a short while, but the law of diminishing returns makes it harder and harder to carry on with this strategy, so Costman has focused his efforts over the past couple of years on seeking greater discounts from his suppliers. This has driven a similar cycle in the suppliers' businesses of falling sales and losing margins, making it progressively harder for them to respond to changes in the market as well.

Initially, this strategy worked because the volume of materials purchased annually was enough of a lever, but Power Plus' sales have stagnated and suppliers are not feeling committed to offer larger and larger discounts year after year. Instead they are focusing on new customers with growing markets that are able to pay better prices.

However, Costman still believes that he can compel suppliers to continually offer discounts almost as if it were some unwritten law. He is unaware that the rules of the game have shifted, believing that historic relationships and the allure of the once powerful Power Plus brand will compel them to support him.

He believes this even though his largest and most significant supplier has been sending increasingly insistent signals, prior to a meeting at Power Plus' headquarters, that their company may no longer be receptive to Costman's requests for discounts. In fact, senior staff at Cogswell Motor Corporation have come to dread the annual meeting over prices and call-off quantities because it feels more like an annual wrestling match than a meeting of partners.

These signals have fallen on unreceptive ears in the case of Costman, who is unbowed in his belief that as an important customer he is entitled to essentially dictate terms. This becomes clear as he meets with James Hughes, VP of marketing at Cogswell Motor Corporation. The meeting is taking place in Costman's large office and he is joined by Stefan Bieber, VP of purchasing for Power Plus, and a sales director on Bieber's staff, an earnest looking young man named Max Kluge who has steadily managed to rise through the Power Plus ranks.

Hughes and his marketing director Jack Oliver are seated across the table from Costman and his associates. From the moment Hughes and Oliver walked into the room the mood has been tense. Both sides know what is at stake…

The Supplier Meeting

"James, thanks for coming, but look, I'm going to get to the point," says Costman. "You know how this works and the simple fact of the matter is that the pricing you have laid out simply doesn't work for us. I can't even believe that with our long history together you would come to me with this."

Hughes takes a moment to size Costman up. He glances around the office and notices that over the course of their 17-year business relationship the room has changed little. The plaques and awards on the wall behind Costman's desk are the same and reflect only his successes in the mid-1990s. The photos of his wife and children create the impression that they have not aged nor grown with the times. From their hairstyles and clothes it's as if they never made the leap from 1988 to today. Hughes smiles at the thought of Costman returning home each day to an unchanged world from a time nearly 20 years past.

And yet, sitting before him is a thoroughly modern looking man. His clothes establish his station as the CEO and leader of his company, and he obviously is not a technophobe when it comes to the use of technology. His computer is an up-to-date model, there is a BlackBerry sitting on his desk, and Hughes knows from past conversations and working with Costman over the years that Power Plus is savvy to the uses of ERP and supply chain management systems. And though it is relatively unchanged, the room is not uncomfortable nor does the furniture look as if it is 20 years out of date. Rather, the furnishings are stylish and thoroughly modern.

"You know what?" asks Hughes as Costman lifts a graying eyebrow in an almost churlish manner. "I *do* know how this works. This is the annual beat up on the supplier meeting that we have been having for the past few years."

Oliver's eyes quickly turn toward Hughes, as this moment of frustrated anger was not what they had planned for the meeting. Kluge looks almost stunned.

"You can call it what you want," says Costman, leaning forward in his seat, "but the fact is we are one of your biggest customers and if you don't start showing a little more respect by way of your pricing we may have to reevaluate our relationship with your company."

"A year ago, or two years ago, you could have gotten away with that," says Hughes, looking directly in Costman's eyes, "but things have changed."

"The only thing that has changed is that for some reason you think you can come in here and dictate to me," says Costman. "But you know as well as I do that Power Plus is growing and spends a lot of money…"

"That's not true and I'm going to tell you why," says Hughes sharply. "The volume of your purchases with us has been static and even falling over the past three years. When I pulled the numbers up before coming here, last year was your slowest year yet. That says one of two things: either you have a new supplier, which you don't, or your sales are down. Oh, and by the way, that biggest customer claim, forget it. You simply aren't anymore because we have other customers that are growing fast and paying good prices for our products."

"Look, there are very good reasons for…" says Bieber quickly, but he is silenced by a wave of Costman's hand.

Costman's bearing is stern as he opens his mouth to speak, but is cut off by Hughes.

"You also act as if I live locked away in my office," says Hughes. An expression of concern washes over Oliver's face. "From what I have been reading in the press and on more than a couple industry analysts' blogs, your company isn't selling generators so well anymore because you're getting beaten by a major competitor in Korea. So the fact of the matter is that your problem isn't how much I'm charging you for our motor components; your real problem is that you're not selling generators with the specifications, prices, and quality of support that your customers want because your business model is all wrong; it's stuck in the past and you aren't adapting."

"Don't tell me how to run my company!" yells Costman. "We are still a vital and energetic participant in this industry and are more than able to compete…"

"No, I don't think you are because your purchases with us tell the story all too clearly, and, believe me, we watch our market and customers very, very carefully these days," says Hughes, brushing some lint off his knee. "There's no innovation in your products, no creativity in your marketing, and the relationship we have with you is nothing like what we have been building with Vorpal—you know who they are, right?"

"Vorpal?" says Costman acerbically. "Sure, Moneymaker's managed to sell a few more popcorn poppers and blenders, but do you really think she's going to be able to sustain that momentum? Come on."

"So you really have no idea what's going on over there, do you?" says Hughes. "Their model is as good as yours is bad, and, yes, they are sustaining revenue and profitable growth. They have gone through a number of changes over the past year or so, and one of those is working with us for mutual value creation and working with us as a partner rather than just a vendor to be pushed and prodded for yearly discounts. How can you guys be in the same group and yet be so different?"

"There's nothing Moneymaker is doing that I don't already know how to do better," says Costman.

"Really?" says Hughes sardonically. "Instead of trying to pawn your problem off on us, you should go and talk to your sister company. If you'd like, I'd be happy to introduce you to your own coworkers because clearly you never speak to them. If you did, you would know what they have been up to and that they are beating you in every direction."

"That's enough!" says Costman, tossing a folder across the table. "Here's what we're looking for from you."

Hughes looks at the folder, but doesn't reach for it.

"It's not going to work this time," he says. "The fact of the matter is you're mistreating us while you slowly lose ground and we're not going to sink with you. You've been taking advantage of us for years and Cogswell isn't going to put up with it any longer. The prices are realistic and in tune with the rates in today's market—you should get out and go online more to check—and if you don't like it, that's too bad."

"Then we may have to take our business somewhere else if we don't see at least a little more respect," says Costman coldly.

Bieber looks at his boss as if to say something, but thinks better of it and remains silent.

"Then I suppose we're done because I am not going to budge, and frankly, I have no reason to do so," says Hughes. "What I don't understand is how you can be so narrow-minded while these other people in your own group are actually moving with us in new directions and letting us work with them to do some really innovative things."

"I'm doing nothing more than getting the best price for my shareholders, which is good business," says Costman. "If Moneymaker was as concerned for the shareholders as she appears to be for giving your company a handout, she'd be doing the same."

"You know what our offer is, and remember, we have shareholders too," says Hughes, reaching for his briefcase. "I am sorry it has come to this after so many years, but that's history and this is today, and it really is a take-it-or-leave-it situation."

Hughes and Oliver stand and begin to walk out of Costman's office. As they pass through the doorway Oliver asks in almost a whisper what they are going to do if Power Plus declines the offer.

"It will be sad if they do, but we can't afford to subsidize them any longer," says Hughes. "We can sell that capacity at higher prices to those customers we're working with to grow markets. That's our future at Cogswell and we can't ignore it."

"You mean the Koreans?" asks Oliver.

"Absolutely," responds Hughes.

Back in Costman's office Bieber is clearly worried that his boss may have just ended a critical supplier relationship.

"Tilo, you know we need them more than they need us right now," he says. "How do you expect me to go out and generate another relationship with the level of give and take over quantities and call-offs we have with Cogswell and at the prices they are offering. I know you want a bigger discount, but it still is a lot better than we are going to do on the open market."

"He'll be back because he needs us more than we need him," says Costman calmly. "He can't go back to his company and tell his CEO he just ended one of the biggest accounts they have. Either he'll be back or his replacement will be."

Max Kluge, who has remained silent, does know the current market for the kind of components Power Plus has been buying from Cogswell. He is thunderstruck that his CEO could be so disconnected.

Word Travels Fast

A couple of days later Hugo Wunderkind enters Moneymaker's office saying he has to speak with her.

"Hugo, I'm kind of tied up right now; do you think this could wait?"

"No, this is really important," says Wunderkind.

"Alright then, what is it?" says Moneymaker, gesturing with her hand for Wunderkind to take a seat in one of the chairs in front of her desk.

"Well, last night I was in a discussion with one of the people I've met through a big social marketing network. I don't know his name specifically because we both use screen names, but from past conversations I know he works in the marketing department of Cogswell Motor Corporation…"

"Oh yeah," interrupts Moneymaker, "how'd you figure that out?"

"He said once, 'I work for Cogswell Motor Corporation,'" says Wunderkind, smiling. "Anyway, we were instant messaging each other and he was telling me about a meeting he was at with his boss and some representatives of another company. He said the other company was asking for another round of discounts, which would have made the fifth year in a row, and his boss told them to essentially either accept the price on the table or find another supplier."

"And?" says Moneymaker, raising an eyebrow as if to say that Wunderkind should get to the point.

"The discussion became very intense, it really was more of an argument, and they stormed out of the meeting. As a result, my friend says that they are busy reselling the capacity with a load of their newer high-growth customers, and they are really pleased with how it's working out for them. He then wrote, and I have it here, 'It looks like I will be servicing these new contracts if they go through, because the Power Plus contract is on the brink of shutting down.'"

"Power Plus?" says Moneymaker.

"Yeah, Power Plus," affirms Wunderkind.

"How do you know this is true?" asks Moneymaker. "I mean, if you don't even know his name, he could be stringing you along or just gossiping or something like that."

"I know, so I sent an instant message to a friend of mine at Power Plus. His name is Max Kluge and he's in the purchasing department there. He wrote back that not only did he know about the meeting, but also that he was there and it didn't go well at all. He said his boss, Stefan Bieber…"

"I've heard of Stefan, but I don't know him," says Moneymaker.

"…he was trying to convince Power Plus' CEO, Costman, that the supplier seemed like they meant what they said and that if they end the relationship it would be nearly catastrophic for the company; their margins will all but evaporate," says Wunderkind. "Max also said he thought he overheard the Cogswell VP of marketing say as he was leaving the room, that he doesn't care what Power Plus does, they're going to talk with the Koreans because they really want to do more business with some of their new customers, which is exactly what my friend on Facebook said he's leaving to do tomorrow."

"How badly could this one meeting have gone?" asks Moneymaker.

"I don't know, but apparently the Cogswell VP said this was the last 'beat up on the supplier' meeting they were going to do and that 'this is the last time they were going to put up with it.'"

"No, that's not good," says Moneymaker thoughtfully.

"And that's not it either," adds Wunderkind. "Apparently your name came up because the Cogswell guy, I think Max said his name is Hughes, said he couldn't understand why Vorpal is doing so well with its sales and supplier relationships while Power Plus just keeps asking for more discounts."

"Really?" says Moneymaker with the slightest suggestion of a grin.

Wunderkind smiles a bit, "And then Hughes told Costman he would introduce him to us if he wanted."

"So what's Tilo going to do?" asks Moneymaker. "He may be a bit of an old-fashioned sort of guy, but he can't be that stupid, he must realize that he's about to lose this one supplier."

"Not according to Max," says Wunderkind. "He says that after the meeting Costman said Cogswell will be back because they need Power Plus more than the other way around, but obviously that isn't the case. Max said Hughes looked serious and what I heard from my guy at Cogswell only confirms they are going to end the relationship."

"That's bad for the Jabberwocky group so that can't be good for us either..." says Moneymaker.

"That's not all," interrupts Wunderkind. "Max said shortly after that meeting the CFO at Power Plus resigned and there are others who are starting to update their resumes."

"Simply because they may lose a supplier?" asks Moneymaker, clearly stunned by these events. "That seems a bit unlikely, Hugo."

"They figure that Cogswell is going to not only stop supplying at the current rates, but will sell the extra capacity to Power Plus' competitors thus giving Power Plus two new significant challenges," says Wunderkind. "These new players have been out-competing Power Plus in every direction, from price to product specification, and they fear that Power Plus will soon be reduced to living off maintenance streams from existing customers plus whatever sales they can get.

"Also, Max said the CFO likely left, he doesn't know for sure, because he didn't feel secure that the full financial picture of the company is fully understood, which would tarnish his reputation if things get worse."

"You know this will nearly kill us as well, through the side effects," says Moneymaker. "I mean this kind of thing could affect all of the companies in the group."

"If Power Plus fails, aren't we insulated from them to some degree?" asks Wunderkind.

"On one level yes, because we are individual companies without anything to do with each other in the markets and business other than being Jabberwocky group members," says Moneymaker leaning forward on her desk. "However, we share Cogswell as a supplier with Power Plus on a call-off quantity for one critical component. We're a fairly small customer as compared to Power Plus, but because the contract with Cogswell was negotiated at the corporate level by Jabberwocky some years ago, in the days when vertical process alignment to boost margins was all the rage, we still get a volume discount on the motors used in our larger home appliances such as clothes dryers, washing machines, dishwashers, and so on. If Tilo loses Cogswell, it could be a problem for us in the short term at least in finding another supplier and one that could match the price.

"I'm also wondering how all of this would look to other vendors across the Jabberwocky group."

"What do you mean?" asks Wunderkind, clearly concerned by all that Moneymaker was telling him.

"Well, think about it. If one of our companies has managed to dig itself into such a deep hole, who's to say that we won't find that other suppliers are questioning the wisdom of their pricing and supply contracts with the group," says Moneymaker. "Suppliers won't start pulling out on us, but they'll want to reconsider pricing and they may well want assurances that they're going to get paid and may ask for shorter payment terms or cash up front or who knows what else. Our financial model built around the strength of the Jabberwocky group could fall to pieces because Tilo is not looking beyond his office and out into the real world."

"So where does that put us?" says Wunderkind. "It seems like we have to tell someone at Jabberwocky."

"That's true. Tilo obviously isn't going to listen to us," says Moneymaker. "On the other hand, he's certainly cagey enough to figure out a way to counter what we would say, arguing that we don't know his business, the supplier is bluffing, it's all not true, and that kind of thing."

"Yeah, but the problem is the supplier isn't bluffing and Costman doesn't understand or doesn't want to see what is happening around him," says Wunderkind. "Max was telling me that Costman is completely disconnected. He just doesn't get where his company is at right now."

"No, you're right," concedes Moneymaker. "I'll give Dodgson, the group CEO, a call and we'll see what happens. I wonder if he'll even believe that we really do know all about what is happening with Power Plus. He's a relatively old-fashioned sort of person who would think everything is buttoned down internally and wouldn't recognize that's simply not the case anymore. I suppose if he tells me to mind my own business and this ends up causing Power Plus and all of Jabberwocky problems, at least I tried to warn him."

Making the Call

Later that afternoon Charles Dodgson returns Moneymaker's call.

"Look Jane, I'm really impressed by the numbers you are posting there at Vorpal, which is probably the only reason I'm returning your call," says Dodgson. "Normally I don't like to get into this kind of sibling bickering. It's a distraction. So unless this is really important I'd rather you and Tilo work out whatever it is you need to do. You know we have a dispute resolution process for these arguments."

"Well, thank you for returning my call. It must be rather late in Amsterdam," says Moneymaker apologetically.

"It is, but I suppose these odd hours come with running an international company," says Dodgson.

"Thank you," says Moneymaker. "Normally I would agree with you and I wouldn't ever have even called you if this was just the two of us not working well together."

Moneymaker then tells Dodgson what she learned, saying that her information has come via a number of sources, though she does not have documentation to back up what she has heard.

"So all of this is really only one step above rumor?" asks Dodgson.

"I agree that it would sound that way, but I have to say that the source who made me aware of all this is one that I have come to place a lot of faith in," responds Moneymaker. "Look, the point is that not only would my company be affected if Tilo ruins that supplier relationship, but if he is in more financial trouble than he's letting on, Wall Street will find out, which would all but kill our reputation in the market not to mention what it would do to the brand."

"This is true," says Dodgson, softening a little. "I also have been getting an earful from my CFO up here that Power Plus' financial performance has been a bit shaky."

"We also know that Tilo's CFO resigned almost immediately after that meeting," says Moneymaker. "When I look at all of these issues, I guess I am saying that if he really does have a problem, then we all have a problem, and it could cause a lot of harm to Jabberwocky, including the share price."

"So you see this as a group financial issue," says Dodgson.

"I don't like to say this, but, as a member of this group, I don't believe I have any choice but to act like a professional and raise the issue," says Moneymaker.

"So now you have passed this on to me and then I have to do something or I'm the one in trouble for not doing anything," says Dodgson thoughtfully. "Okay, I'm going to do some quiet poking around, but, Jane, if this turns out to be nothing, you're going to be accountable for this. Remember my views on getting sidetracked by playing politics?"

"I knew that when I called," says Moneymaker.

"Cheers," says Dodgson.

Questions for Further Analysis

1) How Has Globalization Changed the Competitive Landscape?

2) How are Business Models Changing in Response to Global Competition?

Chapter 7

Coffee, Collaboration, and Web 2.0: Moneymaker Tells Her Story

For better or worse, Jane Moneymaker has informed Charles Dodgson, her boss and the group CEO, that Power Plus seems to be facing a serious threat in its relationship with a key supplier. In addition, there is quite a bit of comment on the Web regarding Power Plus' position in its market and its ability to succeed and grow. It seems to Moneymaker that the issue is not just a question of facing new global competition, but also one of whether Power Plus' CEO, Tilo Costman, is operating under a business model and mentality more appropriate to the challenges his company faced in the 1980s and 1990s, rather than those of today.

In particular, Costman has placed nearly all of his focus internally on reducing costs without externally examining the larger world around him and how it has and continues to change. He no longer can count on the size of his company, its brand, and its past market positioning as incontrovertible facts that establish the preeminence of Power Plus and its products. New competitors have not only appeared, but have changed market expectations in terms of product specifications as well as price, delivery, and service.

By alerting Dodgson to Costman's predicament, Moneymaker has taken a very big personal risk, but, through her own journey to adapt and learn how to work in this new world, she has become a firm believer in the need for real collaboration to recognize and proactively manage events. By using the connectivity of the mesh and the resources of the Network of Everything, Moneymaker now has access to the knowledge and experience of others to add to her own.

After Moneymaker's tip-off, Dodgson had some of his staff take a look at Power Plus and he has come to realize the company is in trouble and action must be taken. What worries him the most is that the figures being sent to group finance are not telling the full story.

Much of the information he has received has come from his young personal assistant, Jenny Thompson. She is a savvy and ambitious woman who has earned Dodgson's respect over the few years since Dodgson selected her from a pool of fast-track executive candidates. Not only does Thompson understand and deftly handle the politics associated with her position, but she also understands the power of Web 2.0 and collaboration to help her be better at her job.

Though he does not yet understand the tools she uses to do her job so well, Dodgson has tremendous respect for her abilities. He is regularly impressed at the speed she is able to find, assimilate, and act on new information to develop innovative strategies and solve problems.

By using the Web and tapping into a few connections developed through her many social networks, Thompson has quickly been able to assemble an impressive amount of information that paints an alarming picture as to the changes the electric generator and motor market has been through in general, as well as information and comments specific to Power Plus and its performance.

Via more traditional methods, Dodgson also knows that little more than a year ago Vorpal's sales had been relatively flat in the face of spirited competition within the home appliances market. He has watched from afar as Vorpal's financial performance has moved from sluggish to where it is now outperforming every other division in the company. He is a bit sketchy on the specifics, but Thompson has done some homework on Vorpal, too, and has provided her comments to Dodgson.

The seeds of an idea are slowly germinating within Dodgson's mind and he has called Moneymaker to an informal meeting with him in order to discuss what lies at the heart of Vorpal's performance. Rather than meet in his office Dodgson has decided to take Moneymaker to a local café near a local shopping district, which has been recommended by Thompson.

As they walk, she notes to Dodgson the ubiquity of small decals announcing the availability of wireless Internet connections, posted on doors and in the corners of shop windows near those advertising credit cards accepted at these shops, cafes, and restaurants. She has noticed the same trend in Boston and other U.S. towns and cities, she tells him, but the notion of a wirelessly connected world seems so much more profoundly real to her in these surroundings.

Dodgson steers the two of them down a side street and then into a modest-sized café. Moneymaker notices the same wireless decal and gives a small tug on the strap of her laptop case, which is slung over her shoulder.

Collaboration over Coffee

"Jane, why don't we take a seat here, as I believe someone should come round to serve us in a moment," says Dodgson, pointing to a corner table.

Moneymaker sits and places her laptop down beside her chair, which is across the table from Dodgson. It is mid-morning and the café is busy, as a number of young, college-aged people rush to grab a cup of coffee as they are hurrying to a nearby college for class. Among them are numerous shoppers, merchants on break, and business men and women also on break from one of the many offices in the area. In one corner a small group of young mothers sit and talk as their babies gently rock in their stroller seats. At one table a young man works intently on a laptop and at another table a trio of girls smiles as they surf the Web on a laptop one of them has brought to the café. In fact, leaning against two of the legs of their table are two more laptops—one each—acting as a reminder that it is truly a connected world.

Looking around some more, Moneymaker notices that nearly everyone there is either working on a laptop computer or handheld device, or at least has a computer case hanging from a chair or leaning against a table. Seeing all of this activity Moneymaker understands why Thompson selected this café and insisted that Moneymaker bring her laptop to the meeting with Dodgson.

A young waitress approaches the table where Moneymaker and Dodgson sit and Moneymaker orders a latte and Dodgson an Italian roast.

"I'd like that black by the way," adds Dodgson as the young woman wends her way through the crowd of people and tables. "I hope she caught that. Anyway, Jane, thanks for going to the trouble of coming over here from Boston for such a casual discussion. I don't mean for this to be some big secret that we're meeting or anything, but I also don't want to draw too much attention, because the fact of the matter is that I have done some research and you're right; Tilo is in a lot more trouble than he's been letting on."

"I didn't and I wouldn't bring something like this to you unless I thought it was important," says Moneymaker. "I know well enough that you have a lot of responsibilities and the last thing you need is your CEOs to come running to you every time we get into a bit of an argument."

"I know that, but I also remember that you and Tilo haven't gotten along well in the past," says Dodgson.

"That's right, he made a few personal comments about me in public and since then we haven't been very friendly," says Moneymaker, brushing the creases from her skirt.

"Tilo could stand to use a bit more discretion," says Dodgson, looking out the café window as a small animated group of young people passes by. "Not only with regard to you, but also for the company he seems to have monumentally angered. I don't know what Tilo was thinking, but apparently he's made an enemy of his most important supplier."

"I wouldn't know the specifics of the situation," says Moneymaker.

"Well, from what you've told me it seems like you know quite a bit," says Dodgson. "I may not be as much into this web thing as I now know you are, but it didn't take Jenny long to find out quite a bit about all of this. I should also add that it makes me even more uncomfortable to find out how quickly information spreads these days. It seems as if things are quite a bit more transparent than they have been in the past."

Moneymaker shifts uncomfortably in her seat.

"Look, Tilo has essentially reached the limit to what he can do as far as cutting costs and squeezing more efficiency from his operations," continues Dodgson. "He's caught in a tough situation and he doesn't seem to know what to do about it.

"Meanwhile, there's you and what you've managed to accomplish at Vorpal. A little more than a year ago, Vorpal's sales were flat and you were getting some fairly intense competition from low-cost outfits and yet, here you are outperforming every one of the other group companies."

"We're holding our own," says Moneymaker as the waitress returns with the coffee and latte and sets them on the table.

"You're doing more than holding your own, you're doing something that a lot of other people haven't figured out how to do, which is sell a lot more products in the face of increasing competition and even manage to get decent margins," says Dodgson, leaning forward to blow on his coffee before taking a sip. "In my book that's not only the Vorpal challenge, it's the group's challenge, and in particular it's Power Plus' challenge.

"Now, don't get worried, but I also had Jenny take a look at what you are doing at Vorpal and from what she has presented to me there's quite a story here. What is it?"

Moneymaker takes a sip from her latte, then wipes a bit of foamed milk from her lip.

"To start," she says, "we hit essentially the same wall, or at least a similar wall as Power Plus. We weren't growing our market share, and cost cutting and efficiency initiatives, while important, wouldn't be enough to maintain let alone grow our margins. And then we discovered that we could niche market and sell our products in new and unique ways. This is something that has taken hold in a number of business schools, and others who are calling it the Long Tail, which is the simple principle that the overall size of any market is made bigger if you can add into it all the variations that the mainstream product doesn't hit …"

Dodgson interjects thoughtfully, "I have read about this in one of my business magazines, but it was related to the low-cost airline business and how the market for air travel had massively expanded with all their variations in pricing, timing, destinations, even seat locations. I simply didn't see how that could apply to us."

"Well, what we've found is that there is a real market out there among networks of people with shared interests for products that can be customized to that interest," says Moneymaker, acutely aware that though Vorpal may be across an ocean from Jabberwocky's Amsterdam headquarters, it is not an island unto itself. "Each network may be small, but there are a lot of them. In fact, there is an almost infinite market for products when you think of it that way."

Moneymaker goes on to describe to Dodgson how Hugo Wunderkind had discovered the idea for the PopMe! and that it has led the company to create entire lines of customizable products that are offered to customers as web-based services that can be included on any web site as a mashup. She then goes on to tell him about how the company has had to transform its business model from one focused on cost cutting and mass-marketing of products to where the company continually seeks synergistic opportunities and innovative ways to create value mutually by the development of new markets.

Dodgson listens attentively and shows particular interest as Moneymaker talks about how this transformation has also helped bring suppliers and vendors closer to the company to the point where they are real partners engaged in initiatives that create value for both companies.

"So what has really underlined the shift we have gone through is looking at the Web as more than just a static environment where a web site simply advertises a product," says Moneymaker, "but as a tool with which to interact with our customers, who are far more sophisticated in their use of technology than even five years ago, and creating whole new experiences for them around our products. The real secret of this, if you could call it that, is to take the outside world of Web 2.0 technology and seamlessly integrate it within the internal daily workings of Vorpal."

"That's a lot for one company to change in a relatively short amount of time," says Dodgson. "Where did you come up with all of this? Is there a training manual I might have missed?"

Moneymaker pauses for a moment, remembering her initial reaction to Wunderkind telling her that he had been sharing information about the company with people in his various web-based social networking groups.

"No, there isn't a training manual on how to do these things that I know of yet," says Moneymaker. She looks to the group of young moms sitting and sharing conversation in one corner of the café. "Those women there, the group of moms, you could consider them a network of people with a common interest and maybe they are using this time together to share parenting tips such as how to calm a colicky baby. That would be something akin to a traditional approach to collaboration, a formal meeting with an agenda to seek answers to various issues."

"True," says Dodgson.

"But the girls over there, looking at the laptop screen, suppose they're working on a term paper as a group project on calming colicky babies," says Moneymaker. "They have a world of information available to them on the Web that is beyond what they can gain from simply meeting with each other and even the resources of the college. And I'm not just talking about a health-related web site, but blogs and wikis that have links they can follow to other resources focused on the topic of their paper. They can also seek out networks of people with experience dealing with colic on web sites such as Facebook or LinkedIn in order to further broaden the amount of quality information that is available to them."

"I can see how that would be a powerful tool," says Dodgson. "I can also see how this works in the way that Jenny always seems to be able to be a step ahead of me and just about everyone else."

Dodgson looks around the café and with a slanted grin says, "You know, I imagine that she recommended we come here just for the purpose of showing me how these things work."

"But it goes beyond that," says Moneymaker, "to include services such as a wiki hosting site where they can create a wiki dedicated to their project and they can work on the paper collaboratively and with partners from anywhere in the world. Think about how all of that can enhance their ability to write a better paper."

"And you're applying these things to what you are doing at Vorpal?" asks Dodgson.

"Yes," says Moneymaker, reaching down to her laptop and placing it on the table. When she opens it the screen comes to life. "I think you would agree that better information makes for better decisions, so we use all of these tools—social networking and web services—to help us find groups of people with common interests and discover what it is they may want to buy from us."

Turning the laptop toward Dodgson, she points to a web page she has pulled up.

"This is a wiki that we have been working on to help us build an even better book-to-bill system," says Moneymaker. "I have broken the entire process down into a number of smaller steps and we're looking in a rather granular way at how each of these steps could be improved. So this wiki is dedicated to one of those steps and what is happening as we move forward is that those people with relevant expertise are credentialed to participate in the process. And this is a continuing process so that we are gathering ideas and new strategies as they occur and refining them among a group of people working remotely, but also collaboratively much faster than we could if we had to schedule meetings, develop agendas, and essentially go through a much more formal process."

Moneymaker then goes on to show Dodgson a couple of the management tools that she uses as well as show him a few of the web sites that carry Vorpal's services.

"So you can see that here I am, sitting with you in a café in Amsterdam, and yet I have access to most if not all of the work I am doing back in Boston and I can communicate with the necessary people via a wiki or the management tool or email or instant messaging and so on," says Moneymaker. "Using many of these same collaborative tools and social networking opportunities on the Web is also how we are managing to keep our costs down.

"By better knowing what customers want we don't have to create markets around products that we *think* might sell, which is expensive and means we can only hit mainstream markets in order to get enough volume for payback. This also means we would be hitting our low-cost, high-volume competitors head on. The way we are working now means we have a pull effect with virtually no marketing costs. Really, the sales are defined by our increased effort in interactive collaboration with our potential customers, and even our partners, on getting the right product for them into production."

"And your internal core systems and operations are able to support this very agile model you're describing," says Dodgson somewhat skeptically. "It seems to me that you would at least have very real issues with production because of all of the customization and product changes, not to mention increased costs from suboptimal production runs."

"Yes, you're right," says Moneymaker taking a breath. "At first we were almost exclusively focused on getting the sales, beating anyone else to these markets, and we thought we had the production piece to this under control through batch methods. We even found we could charge higher prices for these niche products, so we thought we were covered."

"But there's more than that, right?" asks Dodgson.

"Actually, what we found is that this sales method is a lot more of a change than what we originally anticipated," says Moneymaker slowly as she refinds her train of thought. "And once again we discovered that what we were doing was being covered by a number of business schools. They call it business model innovation. Put simply, it's changing the way the company works, to do business from a traditional model built around internal static procedures to a model built around the ability to react to dynamic change and provide supporting processes and experienced management.

"It's been a huge change and I have worried about doing it and what the impact would initially be on our numbers, but I didn't really see we had any choice in the end or we, too, would have ended up where I fear Power Plus is right now."

"I knew you'd been doing some innovative stuff and to be honest I haven't paid a lot of attention to anything other than the numbers until recently," says Dodgson, rubbing the stubble on one side of his face. "You know how the analysts follow our numbers, and it's been tough recently, though, now that you come to mention it, I did get a question on our last quarter results call about whether we were planning to address our business model.

"Actually, I'd scanned over some press reports about new approaches that mentioned you and the changes at Vorpal, but I guess I just thought that it was business as usual and the PR department doing its job so I didn't connect that there was really something worth looking at.

"The numbers show there's value here, but do you really think these strategies would translate to the other group companies and their markets, or are they particular to what you're doing at Vorpal in the consumer market?"

"Well, it's certainly true, from what I have found out about this whole topic of business model innovation, that some market sectors are changing faster than others, but, speaking broadly, I would have to say that it does seem that these strategies could work in most industry sectors," says Moneymaker. "There is always the exception to prove the rule, but at the heart of what we're doing is using a very powerful force to drive change. Business is about people, and people have changed in respect to how they use technology in their lives, whether at home or at work. We're using a combination of their wish to change coupled with our use of the same technologies to innovate our business model.

"One thing that I read recently, and that really puts what I am saying to you in context, goes something like: Companies don't fail by making the wrong choices, but by continuing to do what *was* the right thing for too long. So really, don't let the fact that you are succeeding today blind you to the fact that you likely will need to change tomorrow."

"Okay, I see what you're saying and I think it helps put the question I received from that analyst into better context," says Dodgson thoughtfully. "It seems like what you're doing could prove helpful across the group, but where it is particularly needed right now is at Power Plus. It seems that more of the same old thing isn't going to work there and Tilo needs some help generating new ideas, new ways of thinking in order to pull the company out of the hole it's in."

"I'm prepared to do what I can, but I don't think Tilo is going to be very receptive to anything I have to say," says Moneymaker.

"Maybe not," says Dodgson, "but look, we've got a chance to do it in an uncontroversial way at our group meeting in two weeks and I'd like you to put together a presentation on what you've done with Vorpal and send out some materials ahead of time to all our CEOs so they know what you'll be talking about. We need to get a discussion going and from that maybe we can get Tilo engaged smoothly."

The Presentation

It is two weeks later and Moneymaker, with the help of Wunderkind, has written and sent a discussion paper to her fellow CEOs at Jabberwocky's four other companies. The paper lays out the key points of Vorpal's new sales and marketing strategy using the Web for the Long Tail niche markets, the effect this has had on revenues and pricing, as well as the transformation the company has undergone to reorganize its business model from its traditional major product release cycles linked by static periods, into a wholly different dynamic and opportunistic organization using new methods to find and utilize expertise and experience in support of the new model.

Realizing both the value and depth of knowledge that Wunderkind has brought to the entire change, Moneymaker has asked him to join her at the group meeting and, he is seated next to her with his laptop open and online. Periodically his fingers quickly move across the keyboard.

Moneymaker also has her laptop with her and it is resting open on the table in front of her with her notes displayed across the screen. Though she is well practiced on what she is going to say, Wunderkind suggested that having her laptop, with a few notes as visible reminders, could prove helpful, to which she agreed.

The room is spacious with three large windows spanning the wall behind where Moneymaker and Wunderkind are sitting. A cabinet stretches across the far wall displaying a number of awards the various group companies have won over the years. Moneymaker couldn't help noticing there are no awards for the most recent years. The other CEOs and assorted assistants are seated around a long rectangular table with the head chair clearly left open for Dodgson, who has just entered the room. Thompson occupies her usual spot, which is the chair next to his.

"Thank you people for being here today and for taking the time to read the discussion paper that Jane has sent around to you," says Dodgson, laying a sheaf of papers on the table in front of him as he remains standing to address the room. "As I indicated in the memo I sent around prior to this meeting, I am rather impressed with the job that Jane has been doing over at Vorpal. Her financials are strong and by all indications the company is looking to have one of its best years yet.

"Therefore, it seems to me that it would be of value for all of us to take a look at what she has done and see if there are lessons that could be applied across the organization. Jane, since everyone has read the paper, could you give us a brief overview?"

Dodgson takes his seat as Moneymaker begins.

"Before I get going I want to say that if anyone has any question please feel free to ask, as I think the point here, if I'm correct, Charles, is to provide this overview as an opportunity for you all to see if perhaps some of the things we're doing at Vorpal would translate to your companies," says Moneymaker, looking to Dodgson for confirmation.

"Yes, we're not going to redraft policies today, but I want to start looking to see if we could make some changes," says Dodgson. "In fact, given the individual companies' performances, I would say that as a group we are going to need to make some changes."

"Okay, as it states in the paper, about a year and a half ago we faced flattening sales across our entire line of home appliance products," continues Moneymaker. "When we dug a bit deeper we realized that the market was still growing healthily, but that the challenge we faced was that we were losing share. We were receiving significant competition from lower-cost competitors and cost-cutting efforts simply weren't going to be enough to drive the margins we felt we needed to achieve even on the sales we were making.

"So we decided to approach the issue from a different angle. If we weren't going to be able to cut costs, then we needed to seek out ways to increase the value of the products we sell. Put a different way, we needed to find out how to make our products more appealing so that people would choose to pay a premium price. In a traditional market this would have been a huge marketing gamble—to launch new specification-rich products and then see if we could persuade people to trade up. Frankly, in the consumer market we are in that's not easy, as most of our products are bought on function and cost. That meant the only way we believed we could grow was by seeking out differentiated niche markets with identified communities of people that would want that particular specification and pay for it."

Moneymaker pauses to see if the room is still following her and makes a brief glance at her laptop screen.

"Traditionally, the difficulties associated with such diversity in markets and products would result in a huge rise in costs from nonoptimal production runs, increased administration, and so on," continues Moneymaker. "The real advance we made at Vorpal was how to simultaneously market and sell across niches, and to manufacture and operate to support this without losing either control of our costs or of our business administration."

"But, Jane," says Lars van Vleck, the CEO of JubJub, a company that manufactures and sells a series of home and garden supplies intended to augment Vorpal's home appliance sales, "I read the paper and it tells me a lot about the results, but it wasn't very clear to me how you managed to connect with these communities in order to carry out the sales. Where is your point of sale for these items? Am I wrong to think it is your web site?"

"I'm sorry, but I deliberately left the details out to discuss at this meeting," says Moneymaker. "I suppose it might be better to say that we have managed to grow and leverage our presence on the Web..."

"So you're offering these things through your web site, but it's a new type of web site?" asks van Vleck.

"In a sense, yes," says Moneymaker. "Of course anyone can access our products via our web site, but as I was saying, we're leveraging a lot of other web sites, some belonging to other companies, some to social organizations such as fan clubs, and some that are called social networks and have been created around these niche communities. For example, sports teams have a number of blogs and web sites dedicated to each team. What we do is offer to web site and blog owners a common API that they can then use to add a page to their site where visitors can customize and purchase a product from us. They like to do this, as it's an additional service they can offer their members and it makes the community and web site even more interesting."

"Well, that's great," says Dieter Mahler, CEO of Bandersnatch, a company that manufactures automobile and large vehicle engine components for the OEM market. "You know, I have an RSS feed from Business Week and about a year ago there was a story describing how BMW is working to offer more personalized cars, which seems to at least have some relation to what you are describing.

"However, after reading your paper, which seemed very consumer market oriented, it occurred to me that the markets you described almost seem to pop up at random and your products must come and go at an equally unpredictable speed. How are you attributing costs to each product before it has essentially come and gone? You seem to be claiming strong margins, but how can you really be sure?"

"The short answer is that we have redefined elements of our P&Ls so that aspects of them can be pushed out closer to the actual products themselves so they can be closely managed by the product managers. This means we are able to feed their very granular level information back as a continuous flow into our financial systems, where they can be managed as to their overall impact by our CFO and CIO," says Moneymaker. "Essentially, we're managing a fast change cycle as information flows to our conventional books in almost real time. In addition, we have moved many of our previously indirect costs—you know, the so-called general sales and administrative—into the same model. Our financial model works at the same speed as the rest of our business now, so we can rapidly assess and correct anything that is moving in the wrong direction."

"That brings up a point I wanted some clarification on," interjects Hubert Claes, the Belgian director of Service Plus, which is the service arm of Power Plus, providing support services for the company's electrical generators and motors. "You must drive your suppliers crazy as demand for a product or material climbs sharply and then disappears."

"Actually, our suppliers have never been happier," says Moneymaker, giving a brief glance toward Tilo Costman, who is sitting across from her and has so far remained silent. "First of all, we are providing them with rising volumes of business and that's always a good starting point. What we have really done is changed our relationship and brought them into the process as a partner. That provides them with continuous information on our sales and production planning, which helps them with their planning to accommodate what they increasingly think of as a high-growth strategic partnership. So, in essence, what we have is full supply chain visibility. We all, and that means our suppliers as well as us, came to essentially the same realization that the future could only get more difficult if we continued to work in almost an adversarial relationship. We tried to get them to offer more discounts and they worked on choosing their markets and customers that would push their margins up. Instead of operating in closed off isolation we all do better in an open and collaborative relationship where we could genuinely work out win-win goals together. It's straight out of the new business thinking of how to gain mutual value creation rather than value destruction out of ignorance…"

Moneymaker continues to describe the processes and changes that have been implemented by Vorpal as the other CEOs pepper her with questions. As the questions seek more specificity with regard to all that Vorpal is doing, Wunderkind provides Moneymaker with information and data that he is finding via a number of resources through his laptop. Occasionally Moneymaker glances down at the screen of Wunderkind's laptop to see that, as usual, he has an Internet browser window open as well as his email and a couple of instant messaging pages. Wunderkind is rarely out of touch with markets, business, and events as he works in his own win-win manner sharing collaboration with his communities to create their own form of mutual value creation.

Before long Moneymaker is reaching the end of her discussion as she describes the crucial internal changes that allow people to be able to work differently, but still connect to the all-important traditional IT systems. She describes the concept of the mesh and the Network of Everything and how this places people at the center of activities. She describes how the driving force is "interactions" to recognize and optimize continually changing situations as opposed to traditional IT being based on repetitive standardized procedures leading to "transactions" to record the business after agreements have been made. So far Costman has been quietly listening, only taking a few notes here and there.

"Jane, may I?" asks Costman eyeing Moneymaker coldly. "This is interesting, what you have been talking about here, and it does seem as if you've developed a workable marketing plan and that you are leveraging your suppliers to better advantage, but the fact of the matter is that you are a relatively small company that sells blenders and other simple consumer goods. It doesn't seem as if anything you have presented here is of value to a large complex industrial company such as Power Plus. We face very different issues that you wouldn't understand."

"I would have to disagree with you on that Tilo…" says Moneymaker.

"Why?" interrupts Costman. "What are you, a $50 million company? Power Plus is around $500 million and by far the biggest financial engine of this company…"

As Costman speaks Wunderkind's fingers move quickly and easily across his keyboard. In a moment an instant messaging window opens on the screen of Moneymaker's laptop. She looks at the message quickly as Costman speaks.

"And I'm not really sure you could even understand the nature and dynamics of the industry I operate in, we face a constant stream of challenges that we are deftly overcoming…"

Wunderkind's fingers bounce from key to key again and in an instant another instant message appears on Moneymaker's computer.

"Also, do you really think that altering the very nature of our supplier relationships is going to gain us any advantage? Think about it, whatever we would show to them by bringing them closer to our operations would be broadcast out to every one of our competitors where we share a supplier in common…"

Wunderkind types yet another note.

"Hugo! That's your name isn't it?" says Costman sharply.

"Yes," says Wunderkind.

"Will you stop that incessant typing!" says Costman. "At any rate, I think, though, that the one area among them all that couldn't apply to us less is the idea that these web services you have talked about are more than a fleeting idea and that I should allow my employees to spend part of their day essentially navel gazing with each other about more innovative ways for us to do business. We build large generators and motor sets for those generators and the proven method for deriving more profit in our industry is through cutting costs and selling more products..."

Wunderkind types one final note.

"I'm sorry to burst your balloon, Jane. It's great you have made a success of your little company, but this all seems to be just a bit too naïve to really be applicable to what we are doing over at Power Plus," says Costman.

In the wake of Costman's diatribe the room is silent. Moneymaker pauses to consider how she is going to respond and glances at the series of messages that Wunderkind has sent her. She then glances at the screen of his laptop and sees an instant message window and reads the last line: "Thanks Max."

"Tilo, thank you for your frank evaluation of what we have done at Vorpal and your assessment of its value to your company," says Moneymaker almost as a slow exhalation. "I would agree that Vorpal and Power Plus, though under the same parent company, are two very distinct operations. Power Plus is a much larger company manufacturing products that are quite a bit different from the blenders and so on that we sell. I would also add that there are some other critical differences between the two of us.

"You're right that we are a $50 million company and Power Plus is a $500 million company. However, last year we were a $40 million company and Power Plus was, well, a $500 million company even as the market is growing around you. It's true, though, that for the time being Power Plus is still the biggest financial engine of this company.

"I would also note that the dynamics of your industry has its differences from ours, but at the heart of both is that we have to sell more products at a better margin than the other guys in order to grow and be competitive. And as you have pointed out, that's complex and becoming more so as the number of factors to contend with seem to get more numerous by the day. Obviously, when looking at how Vorpal has grown, we are managing to connect those dots even though we face similar competitive pressures from Asia and other parts of the world as you. Meanwhile, you're being beaten by global competitors who are providing at least a comparable product at a much better price, and frankly seem to be innovating into new markets with new products, too. And according to one source it doesn't seem likely that you are going to be able to discount your products any more than you already have because your achieved margins are so tight and getting tighter."

Costman looks uncomfortable at first, but with Moneymaker's last revelation he turns toward Dodgson in what appears to be an appeal for him to end this discussion.

"And according to that same source," continues Moneymaker, "you're losing more customers than you're able to bring in and current customers are leaving because your competitors are not only beating you on price, but are offering better specifications, sales support, and all manner of things, which is something you can't afford to do.

"Another difference worth mentioning is that right now one of my biggest suppliers is meeting with my CIO and VP of operations on an initiative that, once online, will add value to both companies, creating an even stronger link between the two of us. Meanwhile, it's become known to us, Tilo, that one of Power Plus' key suppliers is currently in Korea negotiating with your biggest competitor because they are thinking of dropping you.

"The fact is that in every category Vorpal is outperforming Power Plus by every measure even though not that long ago we faced similar, not exactly the same, but similar challenges."

Costman can barely contain his anger any longer as he pushes forward in his chair and begins to speak, but is cut off by Dodgson, who is visibly upset.

"Alright, that's enough," he says quickly. "I've had enough of this between the two of you. You've both had your chance to speak, so cut it out. I'd like you both to stay after we're done so we can talk about what is going on between the two of you.

"Jane, what you have done at Vorpal obviously has value, which is something I hope all of you have taken note of because I think we should start looking for ways to incorporate some of these ideas in our other operations. Perhaps it would even be helpful to have Jane visit and meet with all of you individually to share some ideas. We'll start working on a schedule and putting together a more formal method for information sharing. Perhaps we can start by asking Jane's CIO to set up some form of a corporate-wide web community dedicated to this Mesh Working idea. You can work with Jenny on the details.

"At any rate, let's take a break here for 30 minutes or so before picking up with the rest of the agenda. Jane, Tilo, if you could remain here for a minute."

"Wunderkind sits back in his chair unsure of what to do and looks to Jane for guidance."

"Hugo, if you don't mind, I think I need to meet with Jane and Tilo alone. You can also turn your laptop off. I think you've proven your use," says Dodgson.

The room clears with Thompson leading everyone else out to get coffee. A buzz of conversation follows them down the corridor and the three are left in a strangely empty and silent room.

"First off, I mean it when I say you two better learn how to work together because you each carry too much weight for the group and therefore I will not put up with much more of what I saw today," says Dodgson angrily.

Moneymaker and Costman glance at each other, but there is no sign of reconciliation between the two.

"Jane, I have to say that Tilo is right about Power Plus being a much different company than Vorpal," says Dodgson, "but it seems as if there may be areas where these strategies could be applied."

"Well, every method that we have used at Vorpal has led us to see and understand a broader application of our own specific lesson," says Moneymaker. "It's just a question of knowing where to look. So maybe we could be useful in terms of coming up with some innovations."

"Jane, please understand I operate in a much different sphere than you, with pressures and limitations that you simply can't grasp," says Costman angrily. "I don't know where you came up with this idea about Cogswell going to the Koreans, but the fact of the matter is that I'm going to get those discounts."

"Actually, I'm not sure you are," says Dodgson. "To tell you the truth, I think you've pushed them too far and we need another plan. I also think you need to get some fresh thinking about what that plan could be, Tilo. You can say what you want as to whether or not you need this, but the numbers don't lie. If nothing else, we will get some new blue sky ideas to discuss for Power Plus and I want Jane to go over there and take a look around to see what she can come up with."

"Charles, I don't need any help..." says Costman wearily as he faces the fact that he really doesn't have any other options if his negotiations with suppliers don't deliver what he needs.

"We can't wait until we are on the brink of disaster around here to change anything, but, Tilo, I've made my decision," says Dodgson emphatically. "Even if Power Plus gets its supplier discounts and continues its flat performance, it's bad. But if it doesn't, then it's going to be a crash and we risk losing the whole company, and there is no way I'm going to allow that to happen.

"By the way, Jane, I'd take Hugo with you. He's a sharp kid and I think we could use his mesh of collaborators hovering over your shoulder."

Questions for Further Analysis

1) How Have Open Models for Innovation and Open Business Models Created New ways to Respond to Competition?

2) How Can the Generation Gap Be Closed at the Management Level?

Chapter 8

Core Competencies: The Clues to Transformation

Though her fellow CEOs remain somewhat skeptical as to whether Moneymaker's strategies would prove useful to their companies, she has managed to win over Charles Dodgson, Jabberwocky's group CEO, who believes that the results being posted by Vorpal make it at least worth exploring using Moneymaker's approach elsewhere.

Most importantly, he has taken an active role in helping Moneymaker gain access to the inner workings of Power Plus, where Dodgson sees the most immediate and compelling need for innovation and transformation. True to form, Power Plus' CEO Tilo Costman continues to insist that he can resolve the issues his company faces by continuing with strategies that worked well for him in the 1980s and 1990s. During a flurry of emails and personal appeals, Costman has tried to either prevent Moneymaker's visit or limit her access to his company.

However, his appeals have only served to convince Dodgson that Moneymaker needs to take a good hard look at what is happening at Power Plus. Further, Moneymaker's use of the Web has uncovered quite a bit of information related not only to the changes within Power

Plus' market, but also the fact that, as the company's growth has been stagnant other companies are succeeding to significantly grow market share. With his concern for Power Plus at a heightened state, Dodgson has made sure to use his authority to guarantee Moneymaker access to any area or resource controlled by the company.

He has also assured Moneymaker that she will be able to operate independently of Costman while at Power Plus. To this end he has sent an open email to Costman's direct reports explaining the initiative and asking for their support and cooperation with Moneymaker.

For her part, Moneymaker is intent on looking in detail at the company and seeking out what its core competencies may be beyond simply manufacturing electric generators and motors. She has the first hints of an idea developing as the result of her research on the Web, but she needs a better, more granular view of the company and its resources in order to develop the best outline for a plan based on all that she has learned of business model innovation.

We pick up the story as Moneymaker is making her first visit to the Power Plus headquarters. Traveling with Moneymaker is Hugo Wunderkind, who has proved to be a valuable asset to Moneymaker. He also has several friends at levels in Power Plus more directly connected to the real operational issues being faced. In particular, there is one in the marketing department who has come to admire Wunderkind and Moneymaker's efforts at Vorpal and has indicated he may have some ideas to help the company out of its current predicament.

Moneymaker and Wunderkind decide to be diplomatic and start their visit in a relatively low-key way by touring the company's production center, rather than its executive headquarters. They meet Power Plus' VP of operations, Erik Strauss, in the vestibule for a group of small offices located just off the factory floor. The offices and vestibule are elevated in such a way that the manufacturing lines can be viewed through a large bay window. As Strauss enters the room he approaches Moneymaker and Wunderkind, who are standing by the window watching the production floor.

The Factory Tour

"Erik, thanks for agreeing to meet us down here," says Moneymaker, introducing herself and Wunderkind. "I'm not sure if you remember, but we were sent to the same Lean training seminar in Detroit a few years back."

"Oh sure, yeah I do now, I thought you looked familiar," says Strauss a bit nervously.

"I remember you because I was amazed at how quickly you caught on to the Japanese phrases that were used to describe everything. I did wonder at the time if you are familiar with the language at all?" asks Moneymaker.

"No, not Japanese," he says uneasily, "but prior to that I had been to quite a few Lean training sessions because we've really embraced the Toyota Production System here as part of our efficiency and cost-cutting efforts over the past few years. You could say that I had learned the language of Lean. In fact, if you look out the window here you can see that we have divided the floor into three distinct manufacturing lines."

Moneymaker and Wunderkind look out the window into a huge open space that is filled with a variety of machinery distinctly laid out in three discernable production lines.

"How come only one of the lines seems to be operating today?" asks Moneymaker, jotting a note in a small notebook she is carrying.

Strauss glances at the notebook in Moneymaker's hand and pauses for a moment, unsure of what to say.

"Look Erik, I'm not sure how much you have been told about my visit here, but the bottom line is that I'm really depending on you to be forthcoming to the questions I'm asking," says Moneymaker. "It shouldn't be any secret to you that Power Plus is in some trouble and what I'm here to do is to try and help find a way out of it so we can get this company back on track."

"Frankly, the only thing that I've been told is what Tilo said, which is that he seems to think that he is being punished for some reason," says Strauss. "But I have to say that most of us at the managerial level, and probably the guys down on the line by now, heard about what happened with the Cogswell people, so it seems obvious that there are some serious issues."

"Well, listen, Erik we only know each other a little bit, but hopefully from that one experience you may have figured out that I'm something of a straight shooter, so I give you my word that whatever you tell me stays with me, none of it goes to Tilo," says Moneymaker, looking at him earnestly. "I give you my word because if Power Plus hits trouble then we will all be in trouble, too. I'll be standing on the unemployment line right next to you. Okay?"

Strauss looks at Wunderkind trying to decide on his reaction.

"She means what she says," Wunderkind says, smiling.

"Actually, Hugo, you and I have a friend in common, his name is Max," says Strauss.

"Oh sure, yeah, I haven't actually seen Max in person in quite a while," says Wunderkind. "I was hoping that we could meet up with him at some point."

"He wants to see you as well," says Strauss. "It seems he feels the same way, too, so if you two have time we could certainly stop by his office later," says Strauss.

"That would be great," says Wunderkind, checking his BlackBerry for any messages with one hand and tapping his fingers of his free hand on the case of his laptop, which is slung over his shoulder.

"Alright, your question was?" says Strauss.

"Thanks Erik," says Moneymaker, betraying only the hint of a smile. "Only one of the lines seems to be operating and from the looks of the pace the workers are taking it doesn't look as if it is going all that fast."

"The fact of the matter is that we simply don't have the orders to keep the lines running," says Strauss. "Every now and again we hit a bit of a spike and it seems the busy days are back, but then just as quickly it fades away and we're down to just the single line. There were actually a couple of weeks this past summer where we didn't even have enough work to keep the entire line up. We called each Lean cell in as they were needed."

"You're kidding," says Moneymaker, "I knew things were slow, but I had no idea they were that slow. Do you have any idea what the issue is? I mean, is there some ancillary issue that is causing a sudden decline in Power Plus orders, something related to your administration, sales, marketing, or whatever?"

"No, it's nothing like that," says Strauss. "I just don't understand it myself—especially with the number of very large retail outlets being built throughout Europe and North America, which have created even more opportunities within our market."

"What do you mean?" asks Moneymaker.

"Each of these very large retail outlets needs to have continuous power in order to stay open," says Strauss. "Think about what happens at your house if the power goes out in a storm. Then think about what would happen to a few hundred people shopping in a store and the lights go out. And not only that, but most of these stores rely on refrigeration to keep perishables fresh, so even losing power for an hour or two could ruin a store's quarter because they operate on such tight margins."

"So your generators and motors are their backup power?" asks Moneymaker.

"Well, at this point someone's motors and generators are their backup power," answers Strauss. "What I don't understand is why it's not ours. We made that market years ago when these retailers first started building these stores."

"Yeah, right," says Moneymaker thoughtfully as this confirms her preliminary research. "So there really isn't any issue on the demand side of the equation then."

"I don't think so, and actually from what I hear in the trade the demand for these products is up and it's not only from large retailers using these things, but a lot more industries, too, because not only do they need a continuous supply of energy for health and safety reasons, but with the growing amount of high-tech gear they carry they really need to ensure their power supplies," says Strauss. "Then, of course, there are the more traditional uses for motors and generators, such as for industrial plants and so on."

"And yet, with this industry in something of a boom the floor here is operating at less than one-third of its capacity," says Moneymaker.

"The truth of the matter is that these things, while large and relatively complicated pieces of machinery, aren't so complicated that it takes an extraordinarily high level of expertise to build," says Strauss. "We build the best machines on the planet because we've captured the best and most knowledgeable workforce of any company and have invested quite a bit in keeping their training as ahead of the curve as is possible, but the problem is that our competitors, especially Chin-Gu, which is located just outside of Seoul, South Korea, are producing a comparable product at a much lower price."

"What are the main differences between the two products?" asks Moneymaker.

"Really, it's the price, but also our generators and motors have a longer lifecycle and require less routine maintenance to keep them operating optimally," says Strauss. "The Korean products run well and get the job done, but they require a bit more maintenance and service. The problem for us is that we've tried making the sales pitch that you get a better quality machine built to higher standards from us, and that means lower overall maintenance costs, but the upfront purchase price difference is more than many people are willing to pay—especially as they are only working with a budget for the purchase."

"Is there any other difference?" asks Moneymaker.

"Well, they're both broadly comparable on the basic specification, but ours is better if you take a close look at the operating performance, such as fuel consumption under max-load conditions, and that sort of thing," says Strauss. "We have tried to add more features to increase differentiation, but then our competitors jumped right past us and offered sets of customization kits so you could choose features you wanted and only have to pay for those."

"Thanks, Erik, that's interesting," says Moneymaker, looking at Wunderkind. "Do you think we could get a look at how the lines operate and the Lean cells work?"

"Right this way," says Strauss, opening the door and holding it for Moneymaker and Wunderkind. At the bottom of the stairs leading to the floor, all three put on hard hats as they walk from one manufacturing station to the next.

"As you can see, we really have six lines, though we consider it to be three because we manufacture the motor and generator simultaneously on each of the three lines," says Strauss. "The idea is that we can hopefully cross-pollinate knowledge sharing so that individual employees can be switched from building generator assemblies to motor assemblies depending on where the greatest need is. There is also the idea that we could add a bit of customization to the product by being able to add certain features to either the generator or its companion motor and build the two in parallel."

"Did it work?" asks Wunderkind.

"At first it did, but we were quickly matched by the Koreans and we still were losing out to them based on price," says Strauss. "You see, it kind of comes down to that song, you know? 'Anything you can do I can do better.' We can change up our manufacturing processes or add certain features, but at the end of the day our competitors can match those efforts and still beat us on price. It always comes back to price."

"Maybe, but isn't price normally set by what a buyer chooses to pay for what they value?" asks Moneymaker. "But you said they can't beat you on expertise?"

"Right, over the years we've built up what I think is an unmatched level of expertise around our in-house manufacturing teams and, so far, we've managed to keep them here," says Strauss. "One of the reasons for that, and I'm going to brag a little bit here, is that when we were building our Lean system I structured each cell so that it could act as its own leadership team. Rather than have one manager with all of the knowledge in his head, the team has the same level of training, and if you'll look over here…"

"Where?" asks Wunderkind.

"There and there and over there," says Strauss pointing down the line to each cell's workspace, "you'll see protected computer stations connected to an intranet where we keep notes on past issues, online build manuals, and a few other helpful items."

"So you've been doing more to automate and innovate on the line…" says Wunderkind, but is interrupted by Moneymaker.

"But what Tilo has been missing is the need to innovate on the business model," she says thoughtfully. "It seems that Tilo really doesn't understand the direction you are moving in or the business needs to be moving in."

"No, down here on the floor, we've been way out ahead of everybody else here," says Strauss. "That is, except for Max. He and I have been working on these kinds of things essentially on our own."

Moneymaker looks to Wunderkind, "Well, it seems as if Tilo's evolution and ability to innovate doesn't embrace this part of Power Plus."

"Tilo?" says Strauss. "He pushed hard against these changes for a long time because he was worried that if we skilled up and placed our in-house knowledge in our workers' hands, it wouldn't increase their value, but it *would* increase their cost by making the teams more expensive in terms of payroll and training costs, which it did, but as I said, we are the best at what we do. We just don't seem to know how to make that count anymore."

"Erik, there seems to be a number of crates near that one workstation, the ones with the Japanese lettering on them," says Wunderkind. "What are those for?"

"Those are called intelligent controllers, which is a controlling panel that is installed between the generator and where it links in to the installed power grid for whatever application the generator is used for, whether it's as backup power or supplemental power," says Strauss. "They are the brains of the system that senses the power dropping off as it starts to fail and kick-starts the next generator of a set that is ready to come online and pick up the power. Once the generator is online the controller keeps it running and monitors the power levels so it can overcome any fluctuations in the power grid supply."

"You mean so that the generator is essentially going full-throttle all the time?" asks Moneymaker.

"No, not really," says Strauss. "Basically, you want the generator to be able to respond to whatever the power need is inside the building, whether it's a retail or industrial application. You want it operating just enough, but not too much. For example, at an industrial site the power needs for an assembly line will ebb and flow depending on the nature of the work being done at any given moment in time, so you want to make sure that the supplemental generators you're using essentially throttle back or even shut off as power usage ebbs so you aren't using more diesel than you need, but you also want the generators to respond when power usage surges."

"How smart are these devices?" asks Wunderkind.

"What do you mean?" responds Strauss.

"I mean, can they be integrated into an IP network or are they just a mechanical lever like the gate valve on a water spout?" says Wunderkind.

"Well, no, electricity doesn't really work that way, but yeah they can be linked together over a Local Area Network," says Strauss.

"How do you mean?" asks Moneymaker.

"One example would be at a large industrial site," says Strauss. "You would need multiple generators operating at the same time to provide enough power in total, and that means you need to keep track of what each one is doing from a centrally located control point. That control point can be programmed to, well, for example, if power usage is ebbing it will reduce the output of each generator in a preconfig-ured pattern so that rather than have all of them running at some percentage of capacity, five out of ten are at capacity, the sixth is at some percentage of capacity, and the rest are essentially not running. Then, as power usage climbs, the sixth is brought to capacity, then the seventh, and so on. And all of this would be controlled over the Local Area Network."

"What about in a retail application?" asks Moneymaker.

"In that scenario they would likely be for backup power," says Strauss. "If the external power goes down in a storm, or something, you want there to be only about an instant between when the power goes down and the backup system kicks in. There is what we call 'bridge power' that will fill the gap between the power loss and when the backup system is engaged, but these things happen very quickly. You also don't want all of the generators to go online immediately at the same time, otherwise the surge would overload the system and cause worse problems, so they have to go online in a controlled and synchronized manner. As I said, the controllers are the brains coordinating the bridge power and the backup system as well as synchronizing how each generator powers up, and they do it in a way that is virtually unnoticed by the people in the store. It's nothing more than a blink."

"How many other manufacturers of these controllers are there?" asks Moneymaker.

"Other than that one Japanese company there really isn't anybody else," says Strauss. "As far as components go, the requirement and the technology is a kind of standard across the industry, and about 15 years ago that one company beat out the competitors on price. They also added some functionality to them that the other manufacturers around that time didn't think to do."

"Do they have a monopoly on these things?" asks Moneymaker.

"Not quite a complete monopoly, but virtually every generator used in the world has that controller on it," says Strauss. "Also, as I was saying before about our teams in the cells, they are fully trained on the use of these controllers and know probably more than anybody else about how they really work out in the field."

"So that means you have all of this expertise captured in your intranet in machine form so you can use a software program to make necessary decisions in real time?" asks Moneymaker.

"Obviously, where else would we keep it?" answers Strauss with pride. "Also, that isn't all the data contained in our intranet."

"What do you mean?" asks Moneymaker eagerly.

"Some years back we set as a requirement of our engineers that they record everything they found out about the controllers and how they interacted with the generators in an artificial intelligence database before they would go home for the evening," says Strauss. "Adopting this took some work because the engineers at first didn't like having to perform this one last task at the end of the day, but after about eight years we now have the largest database of knowledge on how our generators and the controllers work together in the field of any other company in the world."

"That was a very insightful move to have made," says Moneymaker.

"Erik, do the field service engineers at Service Plus have access to this database while they're out in the field?" asks Wunderkind.

"No, they don't," says Strauss. "Tilo let us do the investment to build this part, but he balked at the cost of making it available outside the firewall. He said the engineers could look up whatever they needed when they got back to the office anyway and if they had to go back to the customer it was an opportunity to bill the customer for more time and materials."

The First Hints of a Solution

Strauss takes Moneymaker and Wunderkind through the rest of the line and then to the company's warehouse for a brief visit. Afterward he drops them off at the office of Max Kluge, Wunderkind's friend and fellow marketing professional.

"Max, it's good to see you, it has been a while," says Wunderkind.

"Yes it has, you look well, and hello," says Kluge, reaching his hand out to Moneymaker.

"Max, this is Jane Moneymaker, our CEO at Vorpal," says Wunderkind, making the introduction.

"Yes, of course, hello, I've been hearing a lot about what you have been doing at Vorpal from Hugo," says Kluge. "Of course, it's all very visible on the Web too, where there is a lot of praise."

"Well, thank you, Max, we have been very busy and Hugo has certainly played a significant role in the changes we have been able to introduce to the company," says Moneymaker.

The three of them take a seat in Kluge's small, but comfortable office.

"So did you go down to the line?" asks Kluge.

"Yes we did," Moneymaker says, "and it was quite a bit quieter than I thought it would be. That was shocking, but what really grabbed my attention was that the warehouse was full, nothing seems to be moving out the door at all."

"Most of those are cancelled orders that were made anyway," says Kluge. "Before I continue, Hugo says that I can talk candidly with you?"

"Yes, I need to find out the facts of what is going on here and the only way I can do that is if people are open about sharing what information they have," says Moneymaker.

"Okay, well it should seem obvious by now that we aren't doing very well, but I suspect that we are doing worse than we have been letting on," says Kluge. "Around here, the rumor that I have been hearing from my colleagues in accounting is that our CFO left after the meeting with Cogswell because he finally was fed up with warning Costman about what's happening. Apparently Ferguson, Thomas Ferguson was our CFO, had been pushing Costman to warn corporate in Amsterdam that the business has not been doing very well—as you saw when you were with Strauss—and is at considerable risk, but Costman kept overruling him. After the meeting with Cogswell, well, Ferguson just couldn't see how he could stay without ultimately having his reputation and career ruined when eventually the trouble Power Plus is in becomes known. He was just tired of playing games."

"If Power Plus is in as much trouble as it seems then I guess Tilo is just trying to buy himself a little more time," says Moneymaker, thinking out loud. "And that would explain why he's been getting upset about a lot of things; not just me coming to look around, but I suppose he also needed to make a real breakthrough with his main supplier's pricing, hoping that might balance the impact of reporting, finally, poor sales to Dodgson."

"I've also been hearing that he's been trying to do the same thing with all of the suppliers," says Kluge. "But we have also heard that they have nothing left to give and are getting more and more nervous with the situation we're in."

"So if we don't come up with a plausible plan by the end of the quarter things are going to get a whole lot worse for all of us," says Moneymaker dryly. "Well, good thing it's the beginning of the quarter and we've got some time at least."

"Right, and I guess Ferguson simply lost faith in the whole situation, so he left," says Kluge.

Moneymaker pulls her little notebook from the satchel she has been carrying and jots down a few notes. Wunderkind gives Moneymaker a slight smirk at her actually writing notes. He has been making his notes directly into his smartphone while also keeping an eye on email and what is happening with the rest of the world.

"Max, you had mentioned to me the other day that you had a few ideas," says Wunderkind, looking at his smartphone.

"Yeah, I do," says Kluge, looking at Moneymaker. "I've been following what you guys have been up to at Vorpal and, as Hugo will tell you, we have both been very active in a number of marketing networks and communities so when I heard you would be coming down I started doing some hunting around for ideas, some things that maybe we could do here. I've got some preliminary thoughts, but it's too early to make any form of meaningful presentation to you. In a couple weeks I could have the outlines of something for you."

"Hugo and I have been working collaboratively on an internal wiki I created at Vorpal to pull together research we have been doing because I wanted us to come in here with some idea of what is happening in the Power Plus markets," says Moneymaker. "We can give you access to the wiki and the two of you can work together to speed things up, because, right now, I don't think we have two weeks. It's got to be more like two days to get some things identified.

"One thing in particular is an idea I have been developing on the intelligent controllers that Erik showed us."

"You and I may be on the same line," says Kluge. "I don't know how much Erik told you about those things, but for a long time now those controllers have come with more functionality than people in the generator world realize. In fact, the design changed some years ago and today hiding in that box is a fully functional PC. This has intrigued me for some time."

"Yes, that's interesting, and good to hear with what I have in mind," says Moneymaker. "Max, I think it may be best to bring you to Vorpal so we can discuss these possible opportunities in more detail. It's got to be no later than the beginning of next week because we don't have time to wait any longer than that. If you're anything like Hugo you won't mind working the weekend because I have to make a report to Charles and he's impatient too…"

"Mr. Dodgson, the group CEO?" says Kluge as the full enormity of the situation sinks in.

"Yes, Mr. Dodgson, and it can't just be a dire forecast," says Moneymaker. "He will want some proposals, too, so we have to provide some ideas for a way out of this situation."

"What about Costman?" asks Kluge. "I'm not sure he'll want me running over to Vorpal even for a visit. We have a warehouse full of product that he wants sold by the end of the quarter, you know."

"I think we can make this work," says Moneymaker. "Just sit tight for now and get your ideas sorted out and in a workable form for next week."

"Alright, but listen, I think it would be helpful with regard to what we are thinking if you spent at least a little bit of time at Service Plus, which is our service arm," says Kluge. "I think that would be very important."

"That was already on my itinerary," says Moneymaker.

Seeking Clues at Service Plus

The next day, after Moneymaker has spent a busy evening online monitoring and interacting with her collaboration requests to make sure Vorpal remains on track, she and Wunderkind are shown around Service Plus by its director, Hubert Claes. The tour of the facility doesn't take long and soon they are led into Claes' office, where Moneymaker begins to ask him a few questions.

"So, I hate to admit it, but we really were something of a sleepy backwater for Power Plus," says Claes. "Things for the most part work well. We bring in a good amount of money each month through our annual support contracts, which we recognize as revenue monthly. It's a great business because Power Plus' products are so vital to running our customer's businesses that they almost always purchase a service cover.

"However, Tilo has been all over me lately to make more, so we're trying to grow our business by supporting products for other Jabberwocky companies, which is something I would like to talk to you about before you go, in connection to Vorpal. We have pretty low overhead, just key part stocks, and we can always top them up if need be from the main Power Plus warehouse. We do need to make sure our service engineers are kept up to date with training, but that isn't much of a problem as Power Plus hasn't changed its models for quite a while. Don't forget, a lot of our cash comes from yearly service contracts, so it's a steady earner."

"Do all customers renew on time?" asks Moneymaker, needing a bit more detail.

"No, some are late and some decide to take the risk and not renew at all because they think they can fix things if they have a problem," says Claes. "However, these generators are complicated combinations of mechanics and electronics and you need an expert. So we end up getting called out for emergency service when the line is down, which means that the customer learns the hard way that the cost of downtime to their business is many more times the cost of the annual service contract.

"Not only that, but we often then find out that 30% of the generators we have to fix are old and actually past their recommended deployment life and this is what caused the failure in the first place. In these situations we invariably patch them up and recommend they upgrade to the latest models, so you could say that the service team creates their fair share of new sales leads."

"How do you think the service engineers are perceived by the customers?" asks Moneymaker, "just as people who fix things or is there a more strategic role they play?"

"Oh, it's definitely strategic," says Claes. "These guys see the customer more often than the Power Plus rep, who is often only there when there's the chance of picking up a purchase order. It's not that they don't care, but they are paid on monthly sales so that's all they can do. Our engineers are paid on customer satisfaction metrics and, as a result, they build up a trusting relationship with the customer and often find themselves recommending new units or upgrades, which are then taken up with Power Plus.

"It's sort of a solutions-led sales process, which leads to more product sales down the line and greater velocity for business value creation. Mind you, I'm not sure how much Tilo recognizes what we do. Half the time he's telling his reps to take Service out of the proposal, thinking that we're making the quotes too expensive."

"What would you say your biggest issues are then?" asks Moneymaker.

"The biggest cost I have is coordination of the right combination of people, parts, and tools to hit the service call-outs within our contracted times," says Claes.

"How is that coordinated?" asks Moneymaker.

"Which aspect do you mean?" asks Claes.

"Just generally speaking, as I am trying to get a picture in my mind," says Moneymaker, "and as I learned on the tour there are a lot of parts and more than a few specialized tools involved, not to mention determining if there is a service engineer available in the right location with the right training. You tell me it's simple, but it seems to me there is a lot to make this work well."

"Well, we try to do as much as possible around routine maintenance visits, which reassures the customers that they get value for money from their contracts, and in these cases the people can be scheduled in advance," says Claes. "We package up the service kits with the tools and materials they are going to need and send them to the job site ahead of time. The real problem is when we get emergency call-outs. That's tough to handle, yet it's also when we really have to perform. If we do badly that's the one time we are at risk of losing the customer through nonrenewal of their contract with us. The trouble is, we generally have no information to go on as to why the unit has failed, so we have to guess or get there and assess what the issue is before we can organize the service kit for repair."

"Does the customer ever do the diagnostics of why a unit has failed for you?" asks Moneymaker. "And by the way, if they don't renew with you, who gets the business?"

"Sometimes, when it's a fairly straightforward issue, they can use a local service agent for the actual engine unit, as an example, but it's more likely that they will consider a new parallel unit from a competitor, as they pay a lot for reliability of service and our timely response," says Claes. "For example, we had an industrial customer about a week ago tell us that they were receiving an error report on their main console. When we got there and plugged in diagnostics it turned out to be the intelligent controller at fault, and that's not something any local servicing competitor can deal with."

"But didn't you have to call in the company that manufactures that component or at least replace the whole unit?" asks Moneymaker.

"No, they are a huge volume supplier based in Japan and, as the units are programmed uniquely before dispatch for each individual manufacturer, it isn't really practical for them to provide any field service," says Claes. "Of course they would like us to pull it out and replace it as a complete unit, but it's way too expensive for us to do that on a fixed-price service contract. Anyhow, we know really everything there is to know about those controllers. The hardware isn't likely to fail; it's usually in need of a soft reset and maybe some local adjustments to the set up codes. I imagine Erik over at Power Plus told you about the training initiatives he has been running over there?"

"Yes he did, in some detail," says Moneymaker.

"We've been partnering with them to make sure that the training his people receive parallels what our guys get," says Claes. "We also have a wealth of knowledge on the components and equipment that attach to our generators and motors too."

"What do you mean?" asks Moneymaker.

"Well, to enhance the service that we offer, and really to just be more practical, we train on and work on the equipment made by other manufacturers that attaches to our equipment," says Claes. "We can't just be Power Plus–centric to the pieces we make in the generator package. The customers expect the whole system to work, and that means the engines, cooling systems, backup engine systems, everything, and to do that we have to understand the entire system that our products feed into."

"Erik also mentioned that line workers in each cell also have access to an intranet as the way to catalog and share information on particular orders and the work they do in general," says Moneymaker. "Do you have access to this or do something similar to that?"

"Well, not exactly, but we do keep good records in a database" says Claes. "When our technicians return from the field they write up a report on what they found and that gets logged into our database, but we don't have access to the Power Plus database in the field."

"How functional is your database and can they access it from the customer's site?" asks Moneymaker.

"It's good, though of course it could be better if we were allowed to spend some money on it," says Claes. "We can search for most things, though it would be nice to extend it to more topics, but our real challenge is getting information into the database, because it can take some time as the technicians write either paper copies or send reports from the field via email and those have to get fed into the system. Of course, it gets worse when it's holiday times or we are very busy."

"And I guess those are the very times when you need it to be up to date the most," says Moneymaker. "Alright, well thank you, Hubert, for hosting us. I know you've been busy and I appreciate that you took time out of your schedule."

"Well, it's no problem," says Claes. "After our last group meeting I did a little poking around of my own on the Web from home to get a sense of what you've done at Vorpal and even took a look at some products. I'm still not exactly sure how it would all relate to what we're doing, but something seems right about giving the customer what they want."

"Thanks, Hubert," says Moneymaker, smiling. "I have a few ideas percolating, but I need to give them a bit more thought. I'll be in touch."

Moneymaker Makes Her Report

It is a week later and Moneymaker has filed her report with Dodgson. The two of them are meeting in his office.

"This is incredible, I had no idea things were this bad at Power Plus, it's a disaster scene over there," says Dodgson. "I have to say that I was so overcome by the first part of your report that I spent a lot of time on the figures and the impacts across the group. I confess that I understand the second half and I certainly get the main ideas and the numbers, but do you really think it can be done?"

"Yes, I do believe that Power Plus is capable of undergoing a change similar to that we have made happen at Vorpal," says Moneymaker. "The markets are definitely there for us to hit. It's all a question of how we hit them. It won't be easy, but I believe the basic elements that we need are already there."

"Alright, Jane, I need you to run with this," says Dodgson. "I can't rely on Costman pulling off his supplier discount moves and I don't think I can even trust his reported numbers, which is something else I will be addressing with the group CFO. We need a recovery plan and that means I need you to develop this as a plan that we can present to the board and everybody else. We have to do this, as I can't see how we can ignore the impact this is going to have at the end of this quarter. We don't have much time."

Moneymaker pauses and for a moment is lost in thought.

"Okay, but I'm going to need some good people as resources to make this happen and you're going to have to keep Tilo out of my way," she says.

"Don't worry about Tilo," says Dodgson grimly. "I'm reassigning him until we know just how bad this thing is. He'll be out of everybody's hair until we're ready to make our report and present your plan to fix things."

"And the people I need?" asks Moneymaker with one eyebrow raised.

"Jane, if we don't succeed with this the floor will fall out from underneath us all," says Dodgson. "Whoever and whatever you need, just tell me and I'll personally make sure you have it."

"Okay, to start, there're two people at Power Plus that I need to pull out and get over to Vorpal as soon as possible," says Moneymaker, "Max Kluge and Erik Strauss."

"You've got them immediately," says Dodgson, writing their names on a notepad. "Now if you'll excuse me I have to give Tilo a call."

Questions for Further Analysis

1) How Have the Challenges of Creating a Strategy Been Transformed in the Modern Marketplace?

2) What Are the Roles That Need to Be Played in Order to Execute a Program of Business Transformation?

3) How Can Innovation Be Supported from Within?

Chapter 9

A Plan for Transformation

It is now a month since Jane Moneymaker was handed responsibility for developing a plan to rescue Power Plus from the predicament it is in. Moneymaker has worked diligently with Hugo Wunderkind as well as with Max Kluge, a marketing director for Power Plus; Erik Strauss, VP of operations for Power Plus; and with Josh Lovecraft, CIO of Vorpal, to develop a plan to radically shift—really transform—Power Plus' business model.

As the team moved forward with its work, Moneymaker was also able to bring in Thomas Ferguson, Power Plus' former CFO, to help consult in their deliberations. As the plan has been developed and fleshed out, Moneymaker was able to use her influence with Charles Dodgson, the Group CEO, to have him encourage Ferguson's return to his post as CFO and join her team.

Once formalized, the plan was sent out to Dodgson for his review and then out to the board members and the CEOs of the various sibling companies. A formal presentation was set and Moneymaker with Wunderkind, Kluge, Strauss, Lovecraft, and Ferguson are seated almost as if on a stage in a relatively large room at Jabberwocky's headquarters. The audience is composed of members of the Jabberwocky board and the company's CEOs. The atmosphere is somber. Conspicuously absent is Tilo Costman, former CEO of Power Plus.

Dodgson signals that it is time to begin and Moneymaker opens the meeting...

Selling Innovation

"It has been a while since we have all met," says Dodgson, "but as you all know the marketplace continues to get tougher as globalization presents us with more competitors and products, usually with a strong price advantage. We face some particularly difficult challenges with Power Plus that could have profoundly dire consequences for the rest of the company. As you know, we have been working on a plan to pull Power Plus out of the situation it is in, which has been sent to all of you in outline form to familiarize yourself and be ready for this session. This is your opportunity to question the originators of the plan and at the end of the meeting I will ask for your support to implement it with all due speed."

There is a slight murmur and a few heads nod as Moneymaker takes a moment to assess the reaction of the room.

"Good morning, I am Jane Moneymaker, the CEO of Vorpal, where we have successfully implemented an approach, similar to what has been outlined to you, to transform our business in the face of nearly identical market pressures to those facing Power Plus," says Moneymaker. Mr. Dodgson asked me to lead an examination of Power Plus to see whether a similar initiative would work there, too."

"Perhaps I should start by adding that more detailed specifics will be drawn up by the working groups we will be forming should you decide that this project should move forward," continues Moneymaker, "but for now I wanted to outline the general approach we are working under.

"The plan for Power Plus is to more tightly intertwine its subsidiary Service Plus into the Power Plus trading name in order to bring together the two sets of skills. The goal is to create a vehicle to transform Power Plus from a product and support services business to a business with a smart energy services offering. The emphasis of this new offering will be on high-value managed services as opposed to the commoditized generators where prices in the market will continue to fall in the face of low-cost competitors. After a period of transition, the new company will be titled Energy Plus and offer end-to-end energy management services.

"Based on the existing expertise that both Power Plus and Service Plus already possess, we can bundle both our service offerings and products that we produce—the generators and motors—and if it suits us, those of our competitors, too, to meet unique customer requirements and to fit their infrastructure environment. Our charging mechanisms for this are flexible and can be tailored to the circumstances that fit the customer's preferences.

"The key to this approach is to remind ourselves that our customers want reliable, sustainable power supplies and not generators. Currently a generator is a distress purchase made on cost grounds. Whereas we plan to replace this with services focused on delivering what they truly want and need, which in turn is a value they are prepared to pay for. What this means is that we will be changing our model from charging for the products to charging for delivering the business outcome that the products were purchased to deliver. The mechanism that allows this transformation is called smart services.

"Critically, the means for initiating what are commonly known as smart services already exists within our current Power Plus business as an untapped capability in the so-called intelligent controllers used ubiquitously by us and nearly all power equipment manufacturers. What allows us to exploit it is the expertise developed by Power Plus and Service Plus engineers in their search to try to differentiate their products by adding more features. An approach we can now recognize as of limited appeal given that a generator is for many of their customers a cost-based purchased.

"We propose to develop our own software that will enable the controllers to be both accessed remotely over the Web and to add more controlling and monitoring functionality. Then we will use our intellectual property to deliver remote services to our customers to enhance the value that our products and our competitors' products deliver to the customer's energy management problems. This is something that could not have been done until recently, but we now have the ubiquitous availability of Internet connections, localized wireless connection services, YouTube-style digital video interactions, and most importantly, the hardware in the controllers themselves has become a standardized PC chip set that we can load software onto. This can be done remotely without the need to touch any product physically. In other words, a zero touch solution affording us massive scaling possibilities.

"Effectively, we are offering a level of service and control as if the customer had a full-time Energy Plus employee onsite. We can remotely monitor the usage of the generators and motors within any environment—whether it is emergency backup power at large retail sites, supplemental power at an industrial site, or anything in-between. Think of it as a way of franchising our intellectual property over a low-cost channel, the Internet. The effect will be radical in terms of our margins as services that used to be delivered by engineers traveling to customer sites are increasingly delivered by software on a machine-to-machine basis.

"These smart services will allow us to proactively maintain equipment, manage energy usage, consult on how these assets are configured within a particular application, and a whole host of other professional services placed around the generators and motors in order to help a user optimize and improve their use of this equipment. Maybe we could even extend our services to cover the negotiation and supply of the whole electricity supply, as deregulation in some countries would allow us to take on this role as well. We can also aggregate data so that customers can conduct benchmarking of network and application performance by industry vertical and market segmentation.

"We're moving away from selling energy generation components as our primary value proposition to one where we're selling integrated systems and solutions—we're going to be delivering at a new level of service level agreements, which will be based more on business requirements than our current service contracts that are based on simply maintaining a product. This means that Energy Plus is going to be able to walk into any requirement, to any plant manager and talk to him about how we can work with him to solve a number of his problems by better managing his energy assets—we are going to make his life easier and his energy infrastructure run more efficiently. Therefore, a deal with us means he carries less risk and gains a far higher value from his investment, so he is going to easily realize the business value of working with Energy Plus. Most importantly for us, though, is that once potential clients recognize the value of what we are offering, they will be more than happy to pay for it. Leveraging the data into more personalized services enables us to achieve breakthrough customer intimacy that can scale through life-like consultative platforms such as telepresence.

"Smart services are a new service delivery paradigm, one where we can get into the market early and build the foundation for enabling a highly differentiated and customizable service delivery experience for customers to enhance the value of our products and open a host of sales channels servicing competitors' products.

"The team has laid out the basics in the pack we have given you."

Moneymaker pauses for a moment to scan the room. All eyes are on her. There is silence. On the wall across from her is a screen with a PowerPoint slide displaying the highlights of her presentation so far.

**FROM COST PURCHASED PRODUCTS
TO BUSINESS VALUED SERVICES**

▶ Redevelopment of Intelligent Controllers to provide necessary
capabilities

▶ Smart services create genuine customer intimacy through allowing
continuous assessment of the customer's requirements, which in turn
creates the feedback to develop new services to offer them as solutions
for commonly recognized requirements

▶ Remote delivery of professional services leverages the expertise built
up by Power Plus and Service Plus from years of experience in the use
of generators for standby power solutions

▶ Combined, this equates to a transformation in which we will move from
products and traditional break/fix services at pricing levels largely
outside our control—due to a number of low-cost competitors—to being
able to capitalize on Energy Plus' and competitors' installed base to
deliver a high level of services that meet genuine business issues and
can be understood as offering value in the delivery of customer's
business outcomes

▶ The margin to deliver these services will be significantly higher as
they franchise their intellectual property over a low-cost channel —
the Internet

Figure 9-1. PowerPoint highlights of Moneymaker's presentation[3]

Moneymaker draws a deep breath and concludes her presentation by saying, "We have the opportunity to redefine the market again, just as we did when Power Plus led the industry by being the first to add an intelligent controller to its generators. This breakthrough placed Power Plus in a leading position that it held for quite some time. However, the market has changed and these changes are beyond our control. Rather than resist them, we can now adapt by rethinking

[3] Glen Allmendinger and Ralph Lombreglia, "Four Stages for the Age of Smart Services," *The Harvard Business Review,* October, 2005, online at: http://harvardbusinessonline. hbsp.harvard.edu/b01/en/hbr/hbr_current_issue.jhtml?issue_id=s8703stg&x=13&y=5

what technology can enable and using these capabilities to deliver a product that offers our customers customizable solutions to the issues they face—a product that they need and will want to buy."

Controllers

Moneymaker presses a key on her computer and a new PowerPoint slide appears.

Energy Management in a Networked World	
From our research and the collected experience of Power Plus and Service Plus, it is apparent that many companies—especially industrial manufacturers—do not view their electric generators and motors as more than simple devices unable to provide increased value to the company. However, networked and web-aware intelligent controllers have the potential to radically recast this perception. Key to understanding how this is so is gaining some understanding of what these devices can do:	
Status	Capture and report on the operation, performance, and power usage of individual motors and generators as well as the entire system of generators
Diagnostics	Intelligent controllers will enable self-optimization of the generator as well as allow an engineer to remotely monitor, troubleshoot, maintain, and in some cases perform repairs
Upgrades	Networked and web-aware intelligent controllers will allow for remote software upgrades improving on or adding new functionality
Profiling and Behavior Tracking	Intelligent controllers will allow for monitoring the behavior of individual generators in order to provide customers with an enhanced view as to the level of performance gained from specific generators and motors
Replenishment and Commerce	This function will monitor usage and generate purchase orders or other transactions as part of a managed maintenance program
Logistics	Energy Plus will be able to proactively optimize service support systems required by engineers prior to onsite visits resolving supply chain issues in these instances

"Now, if you all would turn to page eight of the white paper titled "Energy Management in a Networked World," you will see a brief list of what we believe are some of the functions networked controllers can do and why the idea of smart services is such a powerful one…" says Moneymaker.

"Jane?" says Malcolm Winterwood, a British member of the Jabberwocky board, with his right hand held up.

"Yes Mr. Winterwood," says Moneymaker cordially.

"I've read through this with some interest and I know we need to think pretty radically right now, but I have to wonder if this isn't wildly ambitious," says Winterwood. "I mean, we don't have any of these smart services competencies; it's not the business we're in and it seems as if this is far beyond our core competencies. Surely we should first concentrate on getting the basics at Power Plus right and then we can think to try this."

"That's pretty much what Tilo Costman, the CEO at Power Plus, has been doing," says Moneymaker, "and it's fair to say there is little that could be done in that direction because, after the past few years, which have been devoted to cost-cutting and efficiency initiatives, there is little left that could turn the situation around. Similarly, if it were possible to sell their way out of this with the same products in the same markets then it would have happened by now, after all the efforts that we know have been made. You said 'Think radical,' well there are really only two options: a dramatic downsizing to suit the current conditions, but that wouldn't last for long either as we look at the market and competition; or start to change the business model in the manner I am suggesting.

"Remember, though, but we do have service as an existing competency as well as an understanding of motors and generators, controllers, and the equipment and systems they connect to. In other words, we're not talking about creating new intellectual property, we're suggesting we leverage the intellectual property we already have."

"If I may," says Strauss, VP of operations for Power Plus, raising his hand to gain Moneymaker's attention. "At Power Plus we are recognized for building the best generators in the market; that's what our brand still stands, for even if the current cost of those products isn't acceptable. To do this as a matter of policy we have sought to have the most knowledgeable workforce of any other company and have invested a lot of time and money in keeping our people's training ahead of the curve.

"And this training includes detailed knowledge. I would even go so far as to say intimate knowledge of how our products work, based on information from the controllers, which are the central enablers for the smart services we would provide."

"I could add to that, too," says Kluge, of Power Plus, "the company that manufactures the controllers a few years back switched to using standard Intel PC-based motherboards rather than the previous generation of specialized chips. We realized this, thanks to Erik and his team, when we were looking into how to add product features that we hoped would differentiate our existing products. Most potential customers weren't prepared to pay for the features, so we shipped generators with extra capabilities in the intelligent controller, but locked out so the customers couldn't use them. I believe only about 10% of our customers use or even really know about this, but it's there in all the sets we've built over the last few years."

"But that doesn't tell me how we add smart services to our core competencies," says Winterwood, aware that execution is the real issue.

"You're right, and if this meant having to set up a huge field operation then it would be difficult," says Moneymaker, "but the whole point of this approach is that we use the Internet and the Web to remove that problem. We bring the work to the Power Plus and Service Plus site and the workers, using the network. We have core people and the competencies to handle this approach as we have a strong base of knowledge and expertise on generators and motors and even on the equipment and systems these pieces of equipment connect with and feed into. We even have a database of how generators and energy are used in various industries plus billing, contract management, and other IT systems. What we need to do is rework how we use these assets into an interactive and proactive set of capabilities we can use with the new real-time data and event-management information from our connected intelligent controllers.

"Already we're pretty sure that we know more than anyone else about this potential market. It's just that we have never seen the value of this information and how we can use it to create a very different kind of business opportunity. The real issue is to understand this and grasp the opportunity to be the first in the marketplace to bring these things together and create a new set of customer expectations.

"The graphic on page five summarizes this."

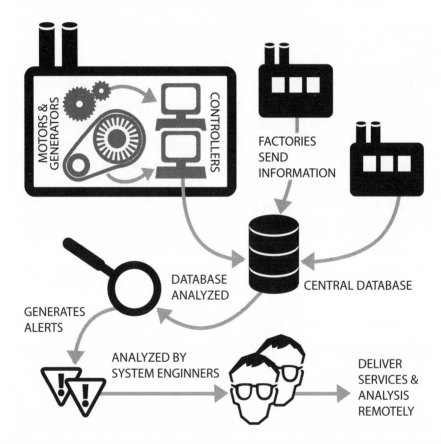

Figure 9-2. Smart Services

"As to everything else, we have learned at Vorpal the best way to handle aligned aspects, that are not core to the proposition, is to work with partners for whom it is their core business. We're already looking at a couple of companies that could help us accelerate getting a comprehensive offering established for Energy Plus.

"Really, what I'm talking about is supporting this initiative by creating a virtual services platform using the Web and the knowledge of what will become an ecosystem of strategic partners built around the Energy Plus brand. The goal should be to add as many value-adding service propositions as possible. It's all about working differently—collaboratively—which is something that some leading enterprises have been developing over the years. Wal-Mart, for example, has rethought its whole relationship with suppliers using technology that started with a massive shared database running through to RFID tagging. It's not about hierarchical power, it's about shared empowerment to optimize and maximize reactions to every event and opportunity. We can do the same to change Power Plus into Energy Plus by making use of the expertise and gaining the capabilities of partners.

"So to answer your question, we are able to build a foundation that never existed before. It's not using IT internally to cut the costs of administering the enterprise's system, it's global change brought about by a new generation of technology—the Internet, the Web, and most of all, people. Products, standards, open source, systems integrators, and most of all, our own people can provide everything we need.

"We don't *have* to invent this infrastructure and architecture for ourselves, we can stick to the core competencies that we have identified and bring in partners, people who are interested and excited by the idea of mutual value creation and who have the experience and proven capabilities to provide that missing piece of the puzzle. And this is something we have done at Vorpal with a great degree of success, which is leveraging the Web to allow for a mesh of collaboration among partners, customers, and our company."

"But really, Jane, it seems to me that the value is in the tangible product," interjects Daan Bleeker, a Dutch member of Jabberwocky's board. "The generators and motors are real and physical entities—I can touch them and build them and work on them, they are the literal product. With great respect, IT has never delivered the kind of value you're talking about. Sure we need it, but to build a business on it?"

Moneymaker presses the key on her computer to change the Power Point slide, which is a two-by-two matrix diagram. "Let me show you the diagram that helped me put into context the nature of what we had to change at Vorpal when we were struggling to determine how to transform Vorpal's business model into what it is today, which I would add has helped us grow revenues and margins by very respectable double digits. Take a close look at this: In the bottom two boxes cost is the justification for the decisions that are made with the business side of the company on the right dictating what it needs from the IT side to reduce its operating costs. IT is on the left, essentially working to achieve the goals set for it by the business side. The closer these two sides are to each other then the better the alignment between IT and the business. I should also add that this bottom left box represents traditional IT operations and from the bottom right box comes the driver for ERP, SCM, CRM, and all of the systems used to help the company record and manage various transactions.

Who is the decision maker and what is the basis of the decision?

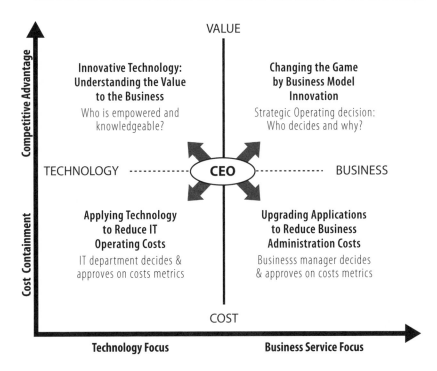

Figure 9-3. Adapting to New Decision-Making Roles

"Look at the upper right box; this is about creating value through more sales, larger market share, better margins, all of the things that we strive to do in every company across the group. And this at the top left isn't about IT as we know it. It's about all of the new technologies of the Web that we have been talking about. On the right we have the business side able to find those new markets and on the left we have the technology that enables finding those markets and acting on those markets. But get this, the direction as to whether it is business or IT driving these things is reversed as compared to the bottom two boxes. Rather than a business need dictating what IT needs to support, here in the top it's the people who understand what technology can do pushing toward business managers to propose what this new IT can do for business.

"At Vorpal it was Hugo who recognized what the technology could do, and here at Power Plus it's Max and Erik. Think of it as the development of industrial electrical supplies 100 years ago. That shift led to the creation of a market that Power Plus was able to enter and thrive in, which is little different from where we are today with these new technologies creating a new market for what will be Energy Plus."

The room is mostly silent as the various board members and other attendees consider the diagram and the point it illustrates.

"Jane, I can see that we have technology creating a new market," says Dodgson, "and if I take what I think your diagram is meant to mean with regard to the top two boxes, this change is not about IT as we know it and the people who have recognized that will now be allowing IT to take a new role to drive changes in the top left-hand box, to the business side of the company in the top right box."

"Yes, exactly," says Moneymaker, relieved to have made her point.

"Okay, that should help put this discussion in perspective, but as to Daan's question," says Dodgson, "I think we need an answer as to what the tangible product is. Is it really no longer the generator?"

"Not anymore, not for us," responds Moneymaker firmly, "which is not the same as saying we will no longer manufacture and sell generators and motors. Think of it this way, the physical product that customers need for their infrastructure is the generator and the motor, but due to changes in the market and the entrance of low-cost competitors that can produce these assets at a lower cost, customers quite frankly don't want to buy *our* generators, at least not in the same numbers as in the past. To react to the changing market, Power Plus has done what would have been the right thing even a few years ago, cost-cutting and efficiency improvements, but the well has run dry. The company will continue to slowly wither if we continue to do what was right for too long. This is a hard and immutable fact.

"However, after the work that our team has done over the past couple of weeks—the work of business model innovation—we have identified a product that fits within the company's core capacities and has value not only for Power Plus—really Energy Plus—but for the customers as well. I want to reinforce this point—what we are proposing is not just a value proposition for Energy Plus, but is also a value proposition for its customers and the partners we bring into the ecosystem. And that product, as we have explained, is superior energy management. All of our research, which, by the way, includes culling comments from existent Power Plus customers seeking advice on how to get more from their generator and motor sets and who have also offered to pay for such a service, but anyway, all of our research clearly shows that this is a solution that customers want.

"We will deliver this solution by using the collected expertise Power Plus already has—and we will aggressively continue to grow that expertise—to solve energy management problems with a fresh set of technology tools and competencies to interact with customers and provide these services in very innovative and meaningful ways.

"So the product is our skill and knowledge—the unique ability to add value to a client's power infrastructure by helping them better manage these assets."

"Jane, is there a similar model that you are basing all of this on?" asks Winterwood. "This all sounds promising, but if there is no tangible product there must be examples of tangible results."

"Well, let me put it this way: there have been very similar disruptive changes in other industries, forcing companies to go through a similar period of business model innovation," says Moneymaker. "The best example that I can think of is what has happened with cell phones over the past few years. The actual phone, which has been the traditional *and* physical product, is now the enabler of developing a relationship with the customer, where the true value is created by the network services of each competitor around the ability to make a call—you know, 'Can you hear me now?'—as well as sending text messages, retrieving email, going online, the ability to upgrade the software in the phone automatically via the network, and a growing number of other services.

"So, yes, there may be a *physical* product, but it's hardly the main value proposition for the provider *and* the customer as well as any other partners in the ecosystem such as software developers and so on. The main value proposition is the service the customer purchases, which is why you see these companies practically giving the phones away. They want to make getting their phone in a customer's hand as easy as possible so they can build a services-based relationship.

"Looking at what we propose to do by creating Energy Plus, we will view the generator as the enabler of the relationship, and this includes not just the generators we manufacture, but those of our competitors—any generator can facilitate that relationship, which is going to be a very close and intimate one with each and every customer based on services the customer defines as having value to them because this is also where the value lies for us and our partners."

"Are you proposing we essentially give our generators away?" asks Bleeker.

"We are here today because we're worried about tight margins on each generator and motor that we sell," says Moneymaker. The intensity in her voice builds as she speaks. "In fact, to sell them at all, in the market as it is, we have to sacrifice price, but if we focus our core value proposition on the services instead, it almost doesn't matter what we charge for the physical product because we are going to make our margins, our profits on the services. I don't mean to belabor the point, but it is an important one: The generators are our phones, so getting them into the market via very competitive pricing acts to seed the market for our services. The Koreans may be able to beat us on price for a generator, but, if they do, that's alright because we can still sell high-value service contracts—high-margin for us, the customer, and our partners—on competitor's equipment *and* our equipment."

As Moneymaker has been speaking Wunderkind has been keenly eyeing his computer screen and then passes Moneymaker a note rather than send an instant message, which would appear on her screen and then the projector screen in front of the entire meeting.

"And we can go beyond monitoring generators and motors to other assets related to a company or industry's infrastructure needs," adds Moneymaker, after glancing at Wunderkinds brief message. "Think of it this way, initially we would be providing monitoring and services for backup power, but there is a lot more than that to the use of energy and, given the current pressures for Green, think of the opportunities. Using the knowledge and infrastructure we will create we could build up our services to add additional layers beyond just power usage and functionality to include every aspect of energy provision plus associated systems such as cooling, air humidity—the composition of the entire environment. Once we have established our basic connectivity services we can continue to enhance them via strategic partnerships to cover whatever the customer wants to bundle together. We would even get into providing design services for large infrastructure installations so that smart services—our smart services—are embedded in the building plans.

"I know I have drifted from the original question, but the point here is that there is room for growth, a lot of room, which simply doesn't exist in our current business model."

"You've started quite rightly by talking about the value this new model would have for customers, but could you provide a clearer picture for us on what it will mean to Jabberwocky?" asks Charlotte Lewis-Carol, a member of the board's audit committee and consequently very interested in the hard reality numbers can provide.

"Jane, I can take this one," says Ferguson, Power Plus' on-again-off-again CFO, as he leafs through a few papers. "Some aspects of monitoring have been around for a while, but only in a few places that can afford a dedicated line and the current highly manual management, but it does give us some real examples to use as a basis for doing the numbers.

"Under our delivery model, which is based on using technology to handle things remotely at a scale that would otherwise be unachievable, and for less cost to ourselves, we are going to enter what has been a high price market as a price leader. In other words,

172 · *Mesh Collaboration*

the customer's pricing expectations are high and our costs are low relative to the market.

"Further, using existing data on installations we estimate the lifecycle for a well-maintained generator to be in the range of 10 years, depending on usage and environment. So when looking at the 10-year lifecycle of the generator we estimate our services will provide additional value to customers in the range of six to seven times the original purchase price of the asset. So when we look at this from the customer's perspective, the cost of enabling their assets with our services is going to be fairly trivial when compared to the value derived from their investment in our services.

"What all of this means is that when we look at our actual costs as compared to the value generated for customers by our services and their price expectations, we will get a better return on our current Service Plus contracts by charging for more value delivered and cutting our own costs at the same time—we are going to be able to make very good margins.

"However, this is really just a pessimistic base to build on. The expectation, once we are up and running with this, would be to add to each contract a whole range of unique services, which we expect to be relatively price insensitive. We have provided some examples of expectations, but the course we are recommending to the board is based on no more than the base-level service. Even at this level we should do very well."

Remote Delivery of Professional Services

"I think at this point if we could turn to page 25 of our paper," says Moneymaker, interrupting Ferguson for a moment. "You will see a relatively detailed explanation of the model we're proposing for the remote delivery of these services, which I'll let Thomas continue with as I believe this is the direction he is heading."

"Yes I was, thank you," says Ferguson happily. "As I know all of you like to see costs well managed, I expect us to be able to cut the current operating costs of our traditional Service Plus model in several ways. Obviously we can cut down on the travel and visits for routine inspections via a remote services delivery model, but we also believe the increasing amount of information we have will enable us to be a lot smarter about how we allocate the onsite service visits that are required. As this is the most significant single cost factor, this is hugely important.

"Again, with more information we can be far savvier as to the types of parts and distribution of those parts because we are going to be smarter about knowing the behavior of the devices. Finally, we are going to know for the first time ever exactly when a generator has kicked on and is running in real time. We will actually know exactly how it is performing in real time and under real conditions, allowing us to plan changes in services, routine, and preventative maintenance that are directly related to the actual use of the asset.

"So, when you look at the biggest costs to Service Plus, you can really say they are created by our uncertainty of what is happening and the events that this leads to. With remote management we expect to really get a grip on this."

Ferguson looks around to see that people are nodding positively. In this moment Josh Lovecraft, Vorpal's CIO, sees a chance to add to the team's argument.

"The really great thing is this whole remote aspect even works for us when we want to upgrade the functionality to cover new things we are learning to watch for or even the range of services we are offering the customers," says Lovecraft. "Because we have remote access we will be able to download software upgrades to the devices. If we do eventually get to the point of needing additional hardware devices, such as sensors to monitor for fumes, dampness, temperature in the rooms, and so on, these can be added with links back to the upgraded intelligent controllers hardware during routine maintenance visits by our technicians as they are needed."

"One last thing that I would add," says Moneymaker, "is that the target customers for these services are facing their own challenges related to maintaining and growing their margins in the face of fierce competition. Think about a company such as Wal-Mart that offers grocery items and is competing to be the low-cost outlet. We will be able to approach them with a solution that would equate to real and significant value for them. As at Vorpal, this model isn't just about creating value for Energy Plus, but for everyone that we interact with, which builds intimacy and loyalty."

"Jane, if I hear you right, you're saying that all of this is dependent on our using one brand of controller," says Richard Murphy, the American CFO of Jabberwocky. "Two questions: won't that limit the segment we could market our services to around this particular controller; and second, isn't this a risk factor around the stability of their business and market?"

"No, because the company in question and the intelligent controller itself, fitted to all the mainstream generator manufacturers' products, are already something of an industry standard, but mostly because we are already talking with the manufacturer to bring them in as a partner," says Moneymaker. "The fact of the matter is that they are more than willing to work with a company that will be creating a market for building up the functionality that can be placed within their controllers. They too had the vision to see that these kinds of services would be coming down the road, but as their business is high-tech, high investment microchips reliant on high volume, it's not going to be part of their business model. Because they see our initiative having value for them, the company has hinted it may be willing to offer funding to develop this idea as it will ultimately lead to more sales of chips across the whole of their market."

Still a bit skeptical, Murphy pushes Moneymaker by asking, "If the company that produces the controllers has had the vision to foresee these services, surely somebody else is already doing this or working to bring it to fruition?"

"Other companies have thought of smart services," says Moneymaker, "but from the research we have done, and again we have been using mesh collaboration to develop this information and access experts in this area, but the research we have done shows that none of them has moved very aggressively on it, or even at all, because they don't know how to position their business for it—they're just about shipping volumes of gear out the door and see that as their singular value proposition. You could think of it as their success making them blind.

"You see, expertise is not the only barrier to entry here. You need a completeness of vision, which ironically we have gained as the result of Power Plus' problems in the market. Also, these other companies that have thought of it think they have to do everything—build these services from the ground up, which we have learned from Vorpal is a fairly blinded vision because there is the ability to create an ecosystem of partners to build the full offering from."

"I would add to that," interjects Kluge, Power Plus sales and marketing staff member, "by saying that for many business people it's difficult for them to even realize that this is now possible because they don't even know that the technology exists with which to create these types of business models. With Energy Plus we are going to lead the way because no one else in the standby power or consolidated energy services has figured out what the business model would be for these kinds of services. So we, Energy Plus, will lead because no one else is seeing what we see nor do they have the experience of using the Web as a platform to build new business models, which has been gained by all that Vorpal has done."

"Don't forget," interjects Moneymaker, "that the basis for the value of this offering is the combination of the business model, the low-cost channel, and the intellectual capital we have developed over nearly 100 years in this industry. If you think of it another way, if any of our competitors wanted to do this they would have to have started 40 or more years ago, but, as we all know, for the most part they are really very new to the industry."

"So what do we say our Energy Plus business model is built on when financial analysts ask questions?" asks Murphy.

Moneymaker signals Kluge that she will take this question.

"Well, we have discussed that the actual product is the services that are attached to our generators and motors or to other manufacturers' generators and motors," she says evenly. "The overall point to that, and one we can explain in a way that will make the analysts more than happy, is we will use this model to provide a personalized form of customer intimacy to each and every customer, based on their unique energy consumption needs and patterns, their collection of assets, and the unique way in which the controllers will be configured. This personalized experience will be provided in the form of a contract, customer by customer, with an SLA guaranteeing the end-to-end performance of the total energy network."

"Can you point to an example we could use?" presses Murphy.

"Absolutely, Google," says Moneymaker smiling. "Google is more than just a search engine, in fact, when you consider its many services and ability to learn and customize the user's experience based on past usage, Google is a mass personalization machine that can place a uniquely targeted ad in front of each user for each transaction every time. They have created the ultimate Long Tail and are giving the best personalization experience, and, as we all know, they are making great profits by doing this. In fact, they suck all of the profit from the ecosystem because they are the ecosystem. So then, I would ask, what is their service? Is it being a search engine or something much deeper than that? This is exactly what we are proposing to do with Energy Plus; we will be doing something quite similar by creating both personalization *and* intimacy with our customers. I suppose that if you wanted a snappy marketing one-liner you could think of us as 'Google on Steroids.'"

"So, Jane, tell us what you really think," says Dodgson, getting a laugh from the whole room.

Moneymaker smiles and continues, "I would add, too, that the really big capability that we have perfected at Vorpal, which is the icing on the cake for all of this, is the work we have done to perfect the use of mashups. Right now we can take any combination of web-based presentation information and integrate it together in whatever way we choose. Every single customer or collaborative partner we bring in can have their information presented to them however they choose."

Moneymaker pauses for a moment, almost as if she is offering Dodgson the opportunity to make another joke at her expense. However, Lovecraft uses the moment to add another point.

"So, we effectively have our very own global marketplace to operate in. And all of these groups will essentially have a dashboard that allows them visibility into the inner workings of these various generators, and they will be collecting…"

"No, remember they will be receiving data, which is a critical element to our security assurances and our own protection of our assets," interrupts Wunderkind, aware that security will be a serious issue for the marketing of these services.

"Right, they will be receiving data and that data is telling them if the equipment is functioning properly and so on," says Lovecraft quickly.

"Jane, I like what I have seen so far," says Hubert Claes, director of Service Plus, "but I'm wondering how we would charge for these services and how we would sell these smart services, as we clearly have to find new customers. The truth of it is that our current sales rate for getting contracts on new generators being sold is not good because customers think we are expensive for what they get. Surely this is going to be costly? And as a second point, how do we get started? There's a big difference between what we do today and what you are proposing for tomorrow."

"Thomas, can you handle that one?" asks Moneymaker.

"We are still developing a price portfolio for the services because one of the things we are going to do is offer what you could think of as an à la carte menu of service options with a related cost structure and corresponding SLA, which essentially places our skin in the game," says Ferguson. "This will allow us to offer a much more customizable experience for the customer, and it will also allow us to add additional service layers as we move forward and become more sophisticated in our service products.

"The whole point is it makes for a much lower entry point for the customer to sign up for as an initial service level. And, as we know the industries where standby power is definitely a requirement, we think the right combination of service price and value offered by cold calling will get a high rate of business. Also, it's worth remembering that once we start this it will be a big talking point in the generator standby power market so we can also expect the mesh effect of Web 2.0 to work for us as well.

"As to your second question, you're right, it will be difficult to move from a break/fix service structure and contract model to an energy management and smart services model in one quick action, but this is the goal, this is where we want to go. And as it is a destination for us, we have broken that journey down into smaller manageable segments with the first being that we are going to embed monitoring into our existing Service Plus platinum contracts and begin promoting the value.

"We can expect these customers will be more appreciative than others to the value of the new services we're offering. As they already have top-end service contracts they will also likely be those who appreciate the need for stronger energy management. As a group, they should be ideal for testing the first release of our new services and that will allow us to quickly build up our business case for the offerings. We should be able to manage to migrate monitoring and services into other contracts by leveraging off the references of these customers."

"Don't forget about utilizing Web 2.0 communities as a customer intimacy tool and a sales tool," breaks in Wunderkind. "If we see older installations, we can recommend an upgrade to a more efficient model or a consolidation of equipment or a redesign of the infrastructure. For those companies using competitors' equipment, and even for those with Power Plus generators, this is a whole family of services, some changeable and some really just sales support. But, the research I have done and what I have learned from some experts on Green operating indicate not just the need, but also the desire for such services. Companies are spending a fortune on power and ancillary operations, especially with the increasing cost of fossil fuels, so the savings we can generate will be too powerful to ignore.

"Enhancing that pitch will be the use of video-based conferencing tools and our virtualized remote expertise resources. A sales rep will be able to go on a site visit to a qualified prospect and will be able to include specialized experts related to not only the product set, but also the industry, and, as we grow to scale, will match geographic location and culture the company operates in. Enabling this will be real-time telepresence capabilities.

"This will not only save on travel costs, but also increase productivity and add to the personalization of the sales process.

"Lastly, and this is very important, as we grow and bring in more partners to expand our capabilities and offerings we will be able to leverage off of their brands and reputation as they will also be engaged in their own marketing efforts around these services."

"You've said we already have some expertise and knowledge," says Ada Weber, the German CIO of Jabberwocky, "but if what you say is true then we're going to see more of the Jabberwocky group companies shifting to being services-based companies and looking to becoming global operators, which leads to the question of how are we going to grow our bank of expertise and the technologies that underpin this change?"

"Traditionally we would have built out our physical infrastructure and grown the company's capabilities via a series of IT projects," says Moneymaker, "but with Web 2.0 and SOA that's not the way we should go. We can do this fast and light by using the approach we have championed at Vorpal. You are very welcome to come and see exactly how we have done it, but it's all based on accepting the fact that many of our staff today are fully IT literate and used to using Web 2.0 in their social and home lives. We have provided the environment for governance and enablement with direct expense attribution."

"What about security?" asks Weber. "Won't potential customers be concerned that their data could escape our system, especially through our partners, not to mention any intellectual property we, our partners, or customers have?"

"Security is already a very big and important issue for everyone," says Moneymaker. "Our customers understand this too, but there is a big difference between the security for the traditional applications around commercially sensitive information and the kind of data that come from a generator report on its oil level. We refer to the two types as Transactional—traditional IT—and Interactional—our new world where value is created by sharing—and treat them very differently. But that's no reason not to deploy all the usual security controls—encryption, certificates, validation to authenticate data streams, and so on—and governance will be enforced between all stakeholders.

"It's also important to note to our customers that all the data is being transferred by them, not taken by us, since it is an opt in model not an opt out. At all times the customer is giving us the approval to see the data and we in return will give them a guarantee that we will firewall it; protect it and not let it be accessed by any other customer or company. Similar systems are already in use by defense companies to allow networking companies to monitor their network and provide services. These guys, above all, are paranoid about security. After all, it's their business."

"There is also the bottom line, too," breaks in Ferguson. "There will be a balance between remaining nominal security concerns and the value of the services, which are not nominal."

"Are there any other revenue streams that you see for these services?" asks Weber.

"The only limit is our imagination and what we can do with the technology," says Moneymaker. "That said, we have been looking into using this data to measure how a company is doing as compared to peers within their market or industry. It's a very rich benchmarking opportunity with data on a very detailed operational level that we could offer.

"We could then enhance that benchmarking data with a consulting offering to show them what we have discovered in the process and the things we believe could help them improve what they are doing.

"Think about the money people are spending on benchmarking services and here we would have data that is far richer and customized to the customer's particular experience. *And* no long surveys."

"Couldn't we also aggregate that data and use it to make better solutions?" asks Weber.

"As long as we have agreement from the customer, but like I said, we are only limited by our imaginations and the technology, which itself is fairly limitless," says Moneymaker.

"I'm worried about the potential for getting competition in this new market before we have really got a payoff," says Murphy. "Suppose we are successful: What's to stop another competitor from seeing what we're doing and entering this market by essentially stealing our model?"

"It is a real possibility," says Moneymaker. "But we have been doing research on this point with a couple of consultants and a few other qualified experts, and the long and the short of it is that as we move forward we would be adding layers of new capabilities, which creates increased value and intimacy with the customer. This in turn would add to our competitive advantage in that the logic behind our operations would be hidden from sight from competitors, though shared to a degree with partners, and our use of the Web and other software products would enable the company with a high degree of agility.

"We have also gone out with a presentation on a few sales calls to clients that are long-time customers, and they expressed a willingness to sign a nondisclosure agreement. All three customers were open to becoming pilot customers in the near term and to sign on to our offer if they like what they see. My experience from working in startups has taught me that if you can get pilot customers that easily then you have probably got it right. I would also add that, as I have mentioned earlier, we have some customers essentially asking for this service because they have recognized a business need for it in their own operations long before we did.

"Above all, though, is speed, speed to change, speed to grab opportunities, speed to take a commanding market share, and speed to continue to develop and shape that market faster than competitors can. So we need to look at this shift not as an endgame in and of itself, but with the realization that we are in a world of constant change and by building in agility, layers of services, customer intimacy, and so on, these things will be very powerful competitive weapons for us."

Moneymaker looks around the room to see that most people are reading the proposal intently and not a hand has gone up.

"Alright, thank you Jane for coming in with your team and laying this out for us," says Charles Dodgson. "These were excellent questions and I think we are ready to move to the next step with this in executive session with the board. I need to ask you and your team to leave us now so the board members can meet together. Thank you."

A New Role for Moneymaker

As the team leaves Dodgson walks over to Moneymaker, where she is packing her things into a satchel she uses as a briefcase. He pulls her aside a bit, away from where the others may hear him.

"Jane, you have done an excellent job," he says. "I know we've got some more to go over, but this is good, very good. I have to get it by a formal vote of the board, but that shouldn't be a problem because I think everyone here understands the hole we're in and the need to make a positive change in our business model.

"So look, we're going to need someone to head up this effort at Power Plus, someone who has experience with this level of transformation, who knows how this is going to work on the front office and the back office. You interested?"

Moneymaker smiles, "You bet."

"You understand this will make you CEO of Power Plus, which will be our biggest company and comes with a whole new set of pressures and responsibilities as we transition from Power Plus to this new model?"

"I sure do," she says smiling.

"Good. Wait for a formal announcement to say anything, but keep your team together, they're good too."

Questions for Further Analysis

1) What Are Smart Services and How Are Smart Services Implemented?

2) How Does the Central Repository of Data Used in Smart Services Delivery Create Value?

3) What Business Models Are Enabled by Smart Services?

4) What Are Value Networks and How Are They Related to Smart Services?

5) How Do Smart Services Help Create an Ecosystem?

Chapter 10

Fighting to Change IT

After Moneymaker presented her plan to the board and the CEOs of the various Jabberwocky companies, the board met and formally approved her proposal to bring together the capabilities of Power Plus and Service Plus to create Energy Plus, initially as a new division within Power Plus using a very different business model. The primary function of this new division will be to start the creation of a smart services operation offering high value energy management solutions. In addition, the start of Energy Plus coincides with the need for a broad range of enterprises to adopt a more responsible attitude toward the more efficient and effective use of their energy producing and consuming assets.

The smart services solutions offered will also allow Energy Plus to move outside its existing customers and take advantage of the installed base of Power Plus competitors as well. Energy Plus' mission is to create and redefine the market around its approach and smart services, thus allowing it to gain both rapid revenue growth and high margins.

It is an ambitious gambit, and one that faced a number of questions from the board, primarily because the plan relies on a number of new technologies and business models of which board members were totally unfamiliar. It is also one that, if successful, promises to turn a critical corner for Jabberwocky, which faces similar challenges across all of its manufacturing businesses.

So far, Moneymaker has received significant interest in the initial smart services offerings and a few companies have promised to sign up for paid pilot projects. The team is sure from this and other feedback that companies want this kind of solution. The team has already been made aware of customer queries regarding extending the services provided in their solutions and is receiving support from the supplier of the all-important intelligent controllers. Now the question is how will Energy Plus deliver on the concept and the promises made.

There is a lot riding on Moneymaker's shoulders, but, to her credit, she has managed to collect a team with a number of complementary skills that is as committed to this project.

Back at Vorpal, Wendy Chiselpenny, VP of operations, and David Wannamaker, VP of sales and marketing, have been appointed joint CEOs to free Moneymaker to tackle her new role. Both Chiselpenny and Wannamaker are enthusiastically looking forward to driving ahead and perhaps even outdoing their former boss at this new game.

The first challenge Moneymaker must overcome is resistance thrown up by a few of the leaders and managers at Power Plus who must now adapt to an entirely new business plan. They are naturally reticent as they meet with Moneymaker and Josh Lovecraft, CIO of Vorpal on loan to Power Plus, for the first formal meeting to discuss the transformation toward Energy Plus.

Overcoming Staff Resistance

"Okay, I think we're all here, so if we could shut the door and get down to business," says Moneymaker as Lovecraft gets up from his seat and closes the door to the conference room.

Seated around the table are Lovecraft and Moneymaker, as well as Martin Gerhardt, CIO of the newly created Energy Plus, who has brought along Elaine Lamfort from his IT department for her technical expertise. Thomas Ferguson, now returned to his role as CFO of Power Plus; Erik Strauss, VP of operations for Power Plus; Max Kluge, recently appointed director of marketing for the company; and Hubert Claes, general manager of Service Plus join the meeting as well. Strauss, Kluge, and Claes are familiar with the plans and are committed to its success.

The room is spacious, with what Moneymaker has referred to as the "ubiquity of wood paneling" that seems to be something of a conference room staple. The table itself is a long oval with a number of chairs, though the current group is only using a few and is seated at one end, with Moneymaker taking the end seat. On one of the walls that runs the length of the room are a series of photos, starting with a handful of the company's original manufacturing facilities. These photos display the initial growth of the company early in the 20th century, as it was among the first to recognize and enter the market for electric generators and then became a defining force within that market. The remainder of the photos display the continued growth of the company throughout the years.

The last photo is an aerial shot of the facility showing how it looks today. It is an impressive facility, shadowed only by a handful of nearby manufacturers. Along the opposite wall is a row of three large, wood-framed windows that face out toward a beautifully landscaped walking area for the company's employees.

In all, the facilities reflect and are a reminder of Power Plus' former stature as the leading manufacturer and marketer of power generators and motors.

"Later today we're going to hold a much larger meeting with the company's employees. There we will begin to lay out the groundwork for implementing the plan adopted by the board of Jabberwocky," says Moneymaker confidently. "As this is our first formal meeting, I wanted to hold something of an open discussion with you, in order to hear some of your concerns and begin to provide the detailed information you will need as we move forward.

"I know you're all basically familiar with the outline of our plan—to initially position Energy Plus as the leading provider in energy management services, using a business model based on smart services, reliant on a mixture of new technology and existing Power Plus expertise. We need our new Energy Plus business to bring about a return to the growth of revenues and margins formerly experienced by Power Plus, to compensate for the problems with the existing business. The intent will be to transform Power Plus over a period of time into Energy Plus. We know that there is a lot attached to the Power Plus brand, especially within the company, but, if we do this properly, we should be able to attach the heritage and positive attributes of the Power Plus brand to the new Energy Plus.

"For all of this to work it is important that you all know that I want you to always feel that you can be open and honest with me. I am not here to act as a parent. I am ultimately responsible for what goes on here, but, as Josh and anyone else at Vorpal will tell you, I consider the people I work with as professional peers. Success will require us to reach new levels of collaboration, which requires open and honest communications."

"Jane?" says Elaine Lamfort, director of IT.

"Go ahead, Elaine."

"Well, I have read through a transcript of the meeting where this plan was first proposed and I know you fielded a few questions along this line," says Lamfort, "and I understand that we are going to leverage our internal expertise and knowledge resources to provide these services, but the fact of the matter is that you are calling for the use of a number of new technologies that we know nothing about, and we certainly don't know how to do remote monitoring and all the things you're talking about around the intelligent controllers and smart services."

"I never expected you or the rest of the IT team to know about this," says Moneymaker somewhat matter-of-factly as she has answered this question a number of times over the past few weeks. "Your role, to date, has been to support a manufacturing company with the applications chosen by the business to drive down costs for internal administration. For the entire history of this company—starting at first with business-related machines and then on to what we commonly think of as business IT—you have only been asked to do essentially one thing, which, as I said, is to support the internal administration of the company. I don't know the full extent of your particular professional experiences, but in many companies the professionals in the IT department rarely if ever have the opportunity to update themselves on what is happening away from the world of internal IT systems. Many of them, of course, are aware of what is happening with the Internet and the Web, but as far as taking what they're using at home and applying it in their work life in new and innovative ways, the opportunities are far and few between. This is because what I describe as the bureaucracy of business administration has been closed to those kinds of changes for a number of reasons. The lone exceptions are when employees are able to find the space to create these opportunities for themselves almost in secret.

"Well, that is going to change. The new technologies and strategies they facilitate don't really have anything to do with IT, as it is commonly understood within a corporate context, because it's a new wave of technology that, once integrated into the company's operations, gives users much more of a say in how it's used than the IT department. Perhaps you remember what happened when PCs first started to appear in the business world. It was a user-driven evolution because it was easy to see how to use a PC to enable users to do their jobs better. It didn't take long for departments to see the value of networked PCs. And as they integrated this concept, and it became a staple of the business world, data center managers didn't have the view necessary to be able to see the shift this brought about in working practices. Either that or they simply ignored it. However, managers were eventually forced to rethink working practices across their businesses and refocus from computing to the much broader concept of information technology, IT. The focus then became all about using IT to support and align to business value, you know, better run and manage administration of what are primarily internal business concerns.

"Well, we have reached a new shift, except this time we're not going to wait until we are forced to make changes, because everything in the business is becoming disconnected. This does not mean we're tossing aside our existing IT systems. The commercial back office logging of transactions and making sure that everything is properly recorded is a necessary component of the business and IT's role within the business. But we also need to make sure that this is no longer the limiting factor to business change.

"I know this is a long explanation, but yes, we are going to provide all of these new things—the remote monitoring, smart services, web-based working, and so on—because we won't succeed otherwise. So it's up to you to decide what your role is going to be. Either you work with the expertise that we're going to develop and adopt in order to be part of this new way of working, or, you can remain with the existing IT systems that you are comfortable with and just accept that you are not going to be responsible for every bit of technology in the way you used to be. Power Plus has to adapt or it will die. That's something that everyone at Power Plus needs to understand and decide whether they're going to use their experience to be a valuable part of this transformation, or to block it, which I can tell you right now will not be tolerated."

Lamfort shrinks back and looks toward Martin Gerhardt, the CIO, for some support. Gerhardt betrays little in his expression and looks away, having seen how firmly Moneymaker handled Lamfort's question. Moneymaker looks at him intently, but says nothing directly to him.

"And I would add that the reason why you people hold the positions you have is because I believe you have the ability and experience that Power Plus needed in the past, which means that you have the necessary expertise to make the transformation to Energy Plus work," says Moneymaker emphatically.

"That seems like a rather broad pronouncement," says Gerhardt quickly. "Could you provide a bit more of a concrete example of what you mean? It's easy to imagine a new wonderful world, but what exactly are you asking from us as a contribution?"

"In essence it's simple," says Kluge, anxious to support Moneymaker. "In order to make more money we have to provide more value. The idea of how we derive that value has changed from being centered on manufacturing and selling what is exclusively a physical product, to products that will increase the value of the physical device for our customers. Think of it this way, a company purchases a number of generators to provide supplementary power to, for example, an industrial manufacturing facility. By doing this they are solving the immediate problem, which is the need for a steady supply of electrical power to run the machinery. They are also introducing a whole host of complications such as: how does an individual generator fit within a much larger environment; how to keep it working properly; how to optimize its function; and even more. And all of this pulls customers away from what their core value proposition is, which is the manufacture of *their* products. So, we can derive value by offering a total solution that solves all of their generator and electrical supply problems and allows them to be free to focus on the things in their business that create value.

"As a sales person, I have seen many times that this idea reflects something that a great many people want in a great many different contexts. For example, for some people car ownership is the ideal, but for many others they need a car, but they don't want all of the additional problems that come with ownership, so they lease the use of a car so that maintenance, financing, and everything else is bundled into one contract with a predetermined and fixed monthly fee. They are willing to pay to simplify their lives so they can be free from the complications of ownership and use their time to do things other than worry about a car. It's worth money to find a way to make sure we don't have to deal with these complications. This is what we offer our customers—freedom from the complications of ownership so they can go out and focus on making money."

"So we are going to rent our generators with support contracts attached?" asks Gerhardt facetiously, which draws a stern look from Moneymaker, but Kluge quickly responds.

"Of course not, Martin," he says sharply. "They are still the owners of these assets, but in a sense you could say that, through our services, we're going to be the owners of the complications that come with these assets and use our expertise and knowledge, supported by a number of new technologies, to turn them from a liability into a value proposition for us, the customer, and the ecosystem of partners we are going to create."

Moneymaker smiles a bit as she sees the intensity behind Kluge's remarks.

"We know that the current situation here at Power Plus is due to a changing market, which is the result of the entry of low-cost, volume suppliers with products that meet customers' basic needs," says Moneymaker. "What's missing in the market, however, is expertise and the knowledge on how to get the most from investments in these physical products; to optimize and manage their use. This knowledge and expertise, our assets, are not easily mass-produced or delivered to a particular location. We need to focus on the larger solution that all of these cost components fit into, and make use of them to drive our own business selling the value of energy management.

"It's also important to position our services to support the entire lifecycle of those products, the generators and motors, within the total picture. To do this, we can and will partner with other businesses, which will work as long as we own the unique aspects of the remote management capabilities, as well as the ability to provide the tailored presentation of information back to the customer."

Providing the Whole Solution

"So we come in once the equipment has been installed and offer this service to those customers?" asks Gerhardt.

"That is one scenario, but in our model the market and the revenue can begin even before the generator's lifecycle begins and even before the facility it's going to be installed in is constructed," says Moneymaker. "We will guarantee the business value that is created by the system as a solution and people will pay for that because we will lower their risk, increase the reliability of their systems, and solve problems for them that are unique to their industry, their usage, or even the environment the generator operates in.

"For a company installing their first system, or replacing or upgrading an existing system, it's a complicated one-off activity for them to find specialists to handle the various elements, coordinate them all together, and finally take responsibility for the resulting system working as intended. We can change that dynamic by using our knowledge to establish the necessary partnerships, the expertise, and the method, by using a number of collaboration tools to do this repeatedly and efficiently. It simply won't cost us as much as it would cost the customer to do this on their own, and the reliability of the result will be driven by our feedback from all that we already know and understand about the use of these power systems."

"Where would those specialists come from?" asks Gerhardt guardedly.

"What I am talking about is building a new consulting capability that is advisory in nature," says Moneymaker. "This will be staffed by experts in the energy management field who will meet with customers, review their business plans, look at their current layout of generators and equipment, and then deliver an architectural blueprint of the long-term vision for energy management. This has huge value for the customer so we will charge for it, but of course it will also influence their future technical requirements and purchases toward our portfolio of solutions—a grand multiplier effect."

"And we will have all of this capability up and running by day one?" asks Lamfort sardonically.

"No, we won't be able to do this as comprehensibly as we know we want to," says Moneymaker. "It will take some time, but eventually we will have the experience to be able to provide customers with an approved architecture that has been tested in the field."

"But, Jane," interrupts Ferguson, "we need to make the point that our strategy is not to become a services company, because consulting services hold much lower margins and if it grows too strongly it will dilute our overall margins."

"They key to doing this right," breaks in Lovecraft, "is to have close collaboration with a range of new partners. What we want is to do a limited number of direct engagements ourselves to learn the tools, techniques, and design architectures that make advanced technologies successful, but then increasingly do future engagements with our ecosystem partners so we transfer the knowledge to them with the intent that once they understand it they can offer these advisory services themselves. That way we can scale the model throughout the industry and control our margin mix at the same time, while protecting our core intellectual capital.

"So our partners are essential to the whole model, but we can't just give each of them a separate set of instructions and let them work on their own. There has to be coordinated collaboration. Our secret is that, because the collaboration can be done remotely via the Web through video collaboration and other technology tools, all of the stakeholders—the customer, us, the engineering company, the architects, installers, and so on—will have access to the BIM—Building Information Model—and can easily share our expertise, our intellectual capital, to help the customer better build and support the equipment and services. We can help them get it right faster and more accurately time after time."

"Alright, that all sounds great," says Gerhardt, "but how are we going to do that? I mean, you have got to be kidding here. I've been supporting a manufacturing department and a call services center and all of these other transactional systems, and now you're asking me to build and install what would essentially be a network to monitor generators in real time, which will require a high degree of reliability and connectivity so that we can even provide these services. This system you are asking for will also have to co-exist securely with partners, adapt to a number of IT environments, and be maintained in other companies' factories. Is that what you're telling me?"

"Yes, this is exactly what I'm asking your team to do," says Moneymaker rather flatly. "The point here is that I want you to think about the role of our IP network not just as a set of transport pipes that sends data efficiently in the company as well as out to suppliers. I want you to think of it as, in effect, an intelligent platform that we can use to change our business processes. I want you to migrate it to a robust and secure infrastructure over which we can deliver a wide range of managed services internally and to our partners on demand and with predictable performance characteristics.

"The capabilities of our network, such as 100% availability, security, response times, and not least of all the services that will run across it will become one of the key value propositions for our partners. This is the Power Plus Inside concept that we talked about at the board meeting. Once we offer this capability our partners will then create their own services to run on top of the network and offer them to end users."

"Hold on, Jane," interrupts Gerhardt. "If I'm a partner, how do I feel about this? After all, a lot of the partners that I deal with already offer some form of limited monitoring and consultancy services to their customers, nothing on this scale of course, but they do have some capabilities. Won't they consider this to be competitive?"

"No, I don't believe so," says Moneymaker, "because this model will improve their profitability and increase their average contract size. We'll be using smart services to do, via machine-to-machine technology, what others do today with expensive specialists that the customers have to recruit, train, and recertify every year. And as we know, the move from supplying the power equipment to energy management will significantly increase the addressable market for the partners' services, which they will wrap around this core data. This is not a direct versus indirect issue. That's the old-world way of looking at your channel strategy. It's a collaborative model built on mutual value creation that combines the best of what we do with the best of what our partners do, packaged as an end-to-end energy management solution for the customer.

"The high-level point I am trying to make here is that we have to recognize a number of things. The first is that Power Plus and our partners have to change in order to not just compete, but to survive in what has become an ever-changing landscape against lower-cost competitors. The second is that in order to do that we have to reevaluate and define what the company's core competencies are. And the third point is that we *have* to understand what new technology is doing to provide new capabilities, and use this to create a new business model.

This means recognizing that we are in a connected world and that with the Web, and particularly Web 2.0, we can work differently, and that means collaboratively. So working with traditional partners and attracting new generation partners, with archetypical expertise in a chain of innovative collaboration that includes the customer is critical to creating our new value model."

"I think, too," adds Lovecraft, "that it's important to make the point that we don't have to invent everything for ourselves because there are a lot of tools that already exist that can be put to a business use. Think about how people are using the Internet and the Web at home in new ways to connect with people, make purchases, gain access to information to make decisions, and so on."

"Actually," says Kluge, avoiding eye contact with Gerhardt, "there are a lot of people here already making use of these technologies to help them in their work and because they aren't using IT's applications they don't tell them about what they are doing. It's really based on using the network as a platform to access and deliver any service that any of us want to make use of."

Building a Business Architecture

"Thanks, Max," says Lovecraft with a bit of a smile before turning back to Gerhardt. "So your job is not to think of your role as being the owner, builder, and operator of everything. Your job and our job is to work together to create an enterprise architecture for the collaborations, processes, and procedures needed for our business model and then to decide on who will provide the various elements. We never expected you to be able to build the entire system. What you are going to do is become great at creating partner relationships with people who've already gone out and made a business of building the kind of stuff that we need."

"Not to oversimplify it then," says Gerhardt, his mind is obviously turning over the points being made, "we're going to outsource for competencies we don't already have, but we won't be losing control."

"I suppose that would be one way to put it," says Moneymaker.

"So our value chain in IT is changed," says Gerhardt. "It's no longer just the existing applications, servers, PCs, and network operating to support the existing internal administration of Power Plus. It's also the extension of a whole range of new services to support the offerings of Energy Plus as well as the ecosystem of partners that underlie these smart services—the remote interactions, the collaboration chains, and everything else that might be needed, underpinned by a new set of enabling capabilities at the network level."

"Yes, exactly," says Moneymaker, "and you can think of it as a mutual value creation model because by providing these services we are creating value for Energy Plus, the customer, and our partners."

"So could you just sort of play this back for me, the elevator pitch?" asks Hubert Claes, general manager of Service Plus, mindful that he will need to play a key role initiating sales on these services.

"Yes, of course," says Moneymaker. "It would go something like: Your company is facing growing competition and needs to focus its efforts, resources, and financing on its core activities to succeed. Energy Plus is able to assist you by taking over the responsibilities for the provisioning of reliable power supplies at the right cost to suit your unique requirements in return for a regular monthly fee.

"If challenged, then you can add our credentials of the experiences gained over many years as the market leader in building and maintaining generators. In addition, you can add that we provide a centralized control center staffed by the most expert engineers, who are in regular contact with the systems on your site so they can monitor and make decisions proactively to maximize responses to any situation. We have the ability to bring to you by our remote services the rarest resource in the market, which is proven expertise that can help you support and enable your business."

"So, what you're talking about is an IP-based platform for collecting and then transmitting data to a centralized repository where it can be analyzed, interpreted, and turned into customer specific advice?' asks Lamfort.

"Put like that, then yes," says Moneymaker, "that's the underlying technology, but we are talking about making the network so much more than simply a connection and transport capability. The network is a business platform for the delivery of a very rich portfolio of services, data, voice, video, and more used by everyone in the world. Because of the ubiquity of the Internet and the Web, used as the network platform, it will be, and already is the one asset that touches everything that we will use to deliver our new services into the marketplace.

"The operations center is our real unique capability, both in terms of the people manning it, the technology we will use to collocate, locate, and use people with expertise; and the way we will use partners, mashups, and more to produce unique value."

"But all of those partners of yours out there will work for anyone," says Gerhardt. "What's to stop, say our Korean competitors Chin-Gu from doing this as well?"

"The key thing here is not that we will always be the only company with this vision," says Moneymaker. "Others have smart people working for them too. It's that we already have the knowledge—the intellectual property.

"Look, we've been in this business for how long now? One hundred years? In that time we have built up an unrivaled source of knowledge on how our products, our competitors' products, and an overall energy management system should work. Nobody else has this; it's one of our biggest assets and we've been walking past it every day without noticing it.

"And as we move forward we will add to this knowledge with a detailed understanding of every plant we work in and of how every device adds value, which will be kept in something of a black box inside of our company. This will form a kernel of proprietary intellectual property that will grow, which we can use to improve our products, our architectural recommendations, making offers for up-sell, and keeping tabs on how companies are doing.

"We will also stay ahead of competitors by constantly using the base we are developing to support the next release of new services that will both extend and lift the value of our offerings. The continuous up-sell angle is really key. It's not just break/fix; it's not allowing things to break at all, as well as advising on when and how to change our products to meet the customer's particular targets that have been set. We can look at the efficiencies, costs, reliability, and any other aspect, and we can provide proof of our recommendations with our benchmarking data. We are providing them with a proactive service to maximize their energy infrastructure."

"But even this is just the beginning," interjects Strauss, VP of operations for Power Plus. "With the breadth of our understanding of energy management building up across entire industries and countries we could provide very rich benchmarking information that can be used to help all of our customers know what they should be targeting in their own businesses. We will also be working collaboratively with our partners via a web-enabled platform so that they can improve on the services they offer to us. If we do this right, they will want to stay with us as their most successful partnership."

"All of this, the services are going to have to mesh with our other IT systems, the transactional ones, aren't they?" asks Gerhardt.

"Absolutely," says Moneymaker. "One of the very important lessons that we learned at Vorpal as we added the customizable product services to our business model is that all of the front office differentiated services have to be properly aligned with the back office systems that have to support them."

"Right," says Ferguson. "To start, we're going to essentially have one service offering, but very quickly we're going to scale up to where we offer something of an à la carte menu of services from which customers can choose those that would provide the most value to them. I have had the opportunity to see how this has been achieved at Vorpal and I must say it has been a real eye opener to me as to the other benefits this can bring.

"We are going to take a new approach to using Service Oriented Architecture to not just act as a technology integration tool, but to become the business process integration layer joining our existing transactional systems with the new interactional services we will be deploying. All of our internally oriented ordering, billing, contracts, service requests, support activities, and so on will be integrated with the externally oriented web-based services. We will have to take into account that these systems will have to assimilate to a certain degree with the customers' and partners' and that means we will need to understand and adopt various open standards.

"So to kind of sum it up, what we have to achieve is a fully integrated, but open environment achieved by using a loosely coupled connection of devices, networks, and business processes designed at the level of business integration."

"Okay," says Lamfort sitting back in her chair accepting that her future has been laid out before her.

"I'd like to step away from that for a moment," says Gerhardt. "Just tell me who is going to be in charge of this because right now I can tell you I can't handle this with everything else I'm running."

"I asked Josh, our CIO at Vorpal, to join us here for a while to help us get started," says Moneymaker. "In addition we have Max here who can add specific focus to the efforts from his existing work and the use of Web 2.0 and mashups. In the development of the actual products, Erik Strauss already has the team that has been working on the intelligent controllers over several years. We will also have the support of the manufacturer of the controllers own people."

"And we can count on making the best use of all these people because we are not limited to the time that they spend onsite here," says Lovecraft. "We'll gain a number of efficiencies. The first being that we'll no longer spend as much on travel nor lose those work hours to travel time. It's also important for us to understand that these technicians are not going to be limited to one central location. Because we're working through web-based collaboration we have full access to anyone whenever we need them; even to participate as a virtual team if need be. Plus we'll be able to really use repositories of knowledge and experience in some very new ways."

Owning Security

"I know I've been rather quiet to now," says Claes, "but what about security? This has been discussed previously, but with all of this data flying around how can we assure customers they are protected?"

"To start," says Lovecraft, "there will be a number of automated security controls as well as strong governance around those controls enforced through Service Level Agreements with all of the stakeholders. But also, this *is* a core competency of Power Plus' IT department as well as those of the partners and customers. We all understand the security issues that are related to data transport and internal systems security, you know, firewalls, encryption, certificates, validation, shutting down denial of service attacks, these are all known to us. We have done this as it relates to use of the Web for everything from sending email to file transfer, so we will leverage off what we already have."

"Also, one of the points that we will hit on as we make these sales," adds Kluge, "is that it is a data transfer initiated at the customer's end. It isn't us or our partners pulling data from them nor do we have access to their existing IT network. It's just a broadband connection."

"And what about the data stored in our centralized warehouse?" asks Lamfort.

"This is where the SLAs come into play and the use of strong governance," says Lovecraft. "The customer will want us under contract to ensure that the privacy of their stored data is protected and that it's used for solving problems, optimizing the use of the equipment, better informed, future product decisions, and so on.

"But having said all of this, security concerns will be critical to the market and our partners, so I'm suggesting that we get some experts to conduct an end-to-end security assessment; not just what we have today, but in terms of the environment and capabilities we want to build going forward to ensure architectural integrity and resiliency."

"You know, Jane," says Ferguson, sitting forward a bit, "there is one issue that I did want to bring up, which I don't think has been fully explained, and that is the incredibly brief lead time that you have set to achieve some fairly important and challenging milestones."

"Yes, I want us to start selling against these services now and I know that five months seems…" says Moneymaker.

"Five months!" protests Gerhardt. "That isn't nearly enough time to even get more than the outline planning and feasibility studies done."

"What I was going to say," Moneymaker says, giving Gerhardt a sharp look, "is that I understand that doing things the way you do them now you won't be able to do this.

"What you have to recognize is the fact that within this new collaboration model people will have to get used to working in a much different way—it won't often be in-person meetings and conversations and you won't have all of the information you need at your fingertips and many times you will responsible for some things that you don't immediately have the resources for because the need for information and the associated tasks will cross functional boundaries because IT is going to be far more embedded within the business. Working this way will mean that work will get done faster and we'll accomplish objectives quicker, but it also will take some getting used to. I suppose you could say that one of the reasons Tilo is no longer here is that he was resisting this change, but the fact of the matter is that working in this way will become the norm. I'm sure of it and we need to accept and embrace that now."

Leveling Hierarchies

"If I accept that," says Gerhardt cautiously, "then I and the other managers in this company will have to accept that the people underneath me are going to operate in ways that I don't always have control over, which sounds like a very chaotic situation to be in."

"There is some truth to what you're saying," says Moneymaker, "and fully implementing this concept requires making some changes to what have been rather inflexible institutions, such as traditional corporate hierarchies and siloed functions. One of the things that I have tasked Josh with is developing a way to manage these issues."

"So far, Jane," says Lovecraft, "I and the people I'm working with on this issue are working on an idea to create cross-functional committees consisting of representatives from a number of departments and levels within the company. Each of these committees will be charged with goals such as services creation, services deployment, operational agility, and so on, which all require the mating of different disciplines in order to achieve the desired outcomes, so these teams will help break down the barriers to interaction.

"Each committee would meet as and when needed in person, but also through Web 2.0 communications technologies, which includes the use of video. Overseeing these committees would be an executive board, which would essentially be the management team that you are leading, Jane. The board would review progress, set top-level policy, and make investment decisions to facilitate each committee's progress.

"I believe this is likely the best way to make the pace of change much more rapid and give very good visibility to senior management."

"Josh, I think you're right about that and this is something we will need to move on very quickly," says Moneymaker. "If we do nothing else today, I think that would be a very good piece of progress to move this project forward."

"With all due respect," interjects Gerhardt, "this is one more initiative on top of many that we are going to have to bring online in a matter of months. The reality is that we cannot do this in that time frame; we can't even do the necessary studies."

"I am not going to spend six months and have 20 meetings talking about what we think we might need and design it all inside out," says Moneymaker forcefully. "We and others have learned that lesson already. We will change from the outside in, driven by our customers and the market. We are going to move forward, learning by doing what works and what doesn't, which is exactly what we did at Vorpal. Remember, you don't have to support 100 companies the first day, just the five or six pilots we have managed to get. Then we create a playbook for how we and our partners will scale this, perhaps using more than one partner for each function to protect ourselves."

"But Vorpal is a much smaller company and the changes you guys were able to bring about happened over a longer period of time," says Lamfort.

"You're right," counters Moneymaker, "but there is one piece to this puzzle that we didn't utilize there and that is the power of these partnerships. This time we're going to work with partners to deliver the adaptable platform and IT architecture and use them to manage it as a set of services. The beauty of this approach is we have no huge upfront costs or commitments; we pay for what we need when we need it. Call it Software as a Service, if you like to use that term—who knows what it will be tomorrow—but what it really means to us is we will have the speed and flexibility to do what is required for as long or as short a period as it is needed."

"But what about the ERP systems?" asks Lamfort.

"Just a moment," says Moneymaker, raising a finger. "We are not going to handle everything in detail right here today, but one comment I can make about that is you need to use the Web to get up to date with what our in-house ERP vendor has been doing because you'll find that they offer a full set of SOA integration capabilities for their products.

"If you don't think you can work within this model there are two alternatives; one that the board has already voted against, which is allowing the company to slowly be eaten away until there is nothing left but to go work for somebody else. And two, leave now and go work for somebody else. It's time to decide, right here and now."

"Well, this is completely new to me and I would say to the industry as well," says Gerhardt, "but this does take me away from being something of a cost-driven ERP jockey to being on the leading edge of a new enterprise that may actually make us all some money. Let's see if we can make this work."

"Thanks, Martin," says Moneymaker. "I understand this is a lot to do in a short amount of time, but I believe we can make it work and when we do the payback will be to more than just Jabberwocky, we all will see some reward for our efforts.

"Now then, let's start issuing some specific assignments to get the ball rolling..."

Questions for Further Analysis

1) How Does the Role of IT Change to Support a Smart Services Ecosystem?

2) What Skills Must IT Departments Develop in Order to Support a Smart Services Ecosystem?

3) What Obstacles Will Most IT Departments Face Adopting an Ecosystem Approach?

4) What Other Industries Have Adopted Smart Services Through an Ecosystem Approach?

5) How Does All of This Affect the Core IP Network?

Chapter 11

Owning the Ecosystem

Power Professional

"Is Energy Plus the future of Power Management?
Power Professional magazine profiles the rise of the dominant
player in the energy management industry"

A couple of years ago industry analysts and insiders had written
Power Plus off as the victim of a bygone western manufacturing era.

Once the leading and most highly respected manufacturer and
supplier of generators and motors for the industrial and retail power
generator market, Power Plus had lost market share to a new generation of low-cost global competitors. At one point the company seemed
near extinction, as analysts predicted that Power Plus would cease to
be a competitive force within the industry, becoming at best a brand
label for low-cost units manufactured by other suppliers.

What a difference two years can make. In the wake of the early
retirement of the company's CEO, Tilo Costman, Jabberwocky brought
in Jane Moneymaker, a relative newcomer with little experience in
the industry. However, Moneymaker has earned a reputation as an
innovative and daring leader, after taking Vorpal, a sibling company

to Power Plus under the Jabberwocky group of companies, and transforming it into one of the largest online sellers of customizable home and kitchenware in the world. As she assumed the role of CEO for Power Plus, a number of industry analysts cited her initial successes at Vorpal as something of a fluke; an aberration dependent more on luck than anything else.

Ignoring these comments, Moneymaker moved to quickly create Energy Plus, a new division with a very different business model to Power Plus' declining generator and motor manufacturing and sales business. The new business unit was to offer remote monitoring and power management services for the company's generators as well as for generators manufactured by its competitors. But soon the company broadened its offering to include Green services, which include reducing fuel usage and optimization of end-to-end power management.

The result has been to create one of the strongest brands in this new segment of the power generator and motor industry. In fact, Energy Plus has recently been named by *Market Review Magazine* as the year's most innovative new brand as hundreds of outside suppliers are using the company as a platform to offer their services and products in the market. The company has also won a series of awards from Green advocates and industry associations. The success so far has also translated into a 15% increase in the Jabberwocky share price.

"When I came to Power Plus," says Moneymaker sitting comfortably in her executive office, "the world was flattening fast and Power Plus was in danger of being steamrolled by faster, more agile Asian competitors. I quickly realized that we had to transform the company by using the skills we had gained at Vorpal to engage in a substantive process of business model innovation."

The result was the development of a smart services offering underscored by a new business architecture that integrates traditional and new forms of technology, business processes, and the network as a platform for the delivery of what has become a rich portfolio of services.

"The Web is essentially the basis for the platform we have created," continues Moneymaker, "because it is the one asset that touches everything and everyone—customers, partners, and of course Energy Plus—to deliver services to the marketplace.

"Underlying this architecture," adds Moneymaker, "is an equally different architecture and provisioning model for IT support in order to deliver this new and more complex business model. This includes the use of Software as a Service (SaaS) to replace a number of internal systems with web-based third-party managed alternatives; the creation of a unified communications system consisting of voice, video, and data to facilitate real-time collaboration and sharing; cross-functional committees that have broken down traditional hierarchies to facilitate faster information sharing across the enterprise; and the aggressive use of Web 2.0 to aid in the company's agility by allowing employees to quickly gather information and solve problems.

Getting Started

Though Moneymaker admits that her plan for Power Plus was far more audacious and bold than what she had done with Vorpal, she was confident that her analysis of the situation was correct and her proposed solution the right choice.

"What we realized," she says, "is that there was a real desire on the part of our customers, and even the customers using our competitors' generators and motors, to be free of their generator purchasing, servicing, and operating issues. They wanted to instead use that time and energy to focus on what their core value propositions are, which is producing and selling products or running their retail outlets or whatever else is their core business."

Therefore, the newly created Energy Plus quickly moved to change its offerings. Instead of only selling products, Energy Plus offered a service that would take ownership of these issues and their solutions via remote delivery of services from a centralized control center composed of engineers with a high degree of expertise in power management and asset maintenance and optimization. These engineers are in constant contact with power assets located within the customer's facility in order to monitor and make decisions proactively.

"Our sales motto, which is something that has developed over time," says Moneymaker, "is 'When it comes to end-to-end energy, we'll manage it—guaranteed.' What this means is that we offer a very unique SLA where we guarantee our highly personalized services and, in effect, the business outcomes. We are completely joined in partnership with each of our customers and as such have quite a bit of skin in the game." After creating a basic level of service the company moved with what analysts are describing as lightning-quick acuity to enrich the offering by leveraging its business and technology platform to add additional partners and their products and services. The result has been to create an ever evolving and expanding product portfolio where customers can pick and choose the services that best match their needs. These services are layered on top of the company's basic level offering as a completely flexible menu of options that allows every customer to design exactly the service support that they need.

"What we have done," says Moneymaker, "is to create an open standard and open source technology platform that is provided to customers with a basic level of service at a relatively low subscription cost. Because the dashboard is open to other companies, they are able to create new services based on our technology as the standard and add these offerings to the many options available to our customers."

According to Francois Roux, an analyst for the French financial services firm TLBN, "She was very savvy in what she did. She was the first in the industry to see that there is real value not in the devices themselves, but in solving problems and optimizing their use for the asset owners."

Further, because the feedback and insights the company receives are personalized to the unique energy consumption needs, patterns, and assets of its customers the company is better able to identify high-value services for its customers.

"The model they are following could be thought of as a web-based Wal-Mart," says Roux. "By provisioning these services from an ecosystem of partners, the company is in effect buying on behalf of the customer and using their requirements to decide what and who to bring into the offering. The net effect is that they have created a Wal-Mart–like brand and reputation for low cost and high quality."

Moneymaker adds, "For us this means we can be creative as to how we define the services and products while not actually owning the things that will fulfill them. We are the owner of the customer's power problems *and* the solution, but not every piece that is put together to create the solution."

Building the Moat

According to Andre Renault, a professor of business model innovation at the Easton School of Business, the real value to what Energy Plus is doing is by owning the connections between the applications and between the applications and the customers.

"By being the provider of solutions directly to customers as well as being the owner of this very adaptive network platform, Energy Plus is the fulcrum, the center of an industry ecosystem," he says. "If one service or solution loses popularity or saturates the market it doesn't matter to Energy Plus because they are always going to be the source to the customer of the next generation of applications and solutions. The clever part is the way that they bring the ecosystem of partners together to comprise an integrated value network where each partner knows its role and value to the other partners."

Therefore, by being the first to market, gaining early relationships with key partners to provide capabilities the company did not posses nor wanted to build for themselves, and then by creating and owning an adaptive network platform capable of providing a rich portfolio of services the company has defined itself as *the* source point or connecting point for energy management services within this space. In short, they have created a fully functional integrated value network that they now own.

"It's a moat, they've created an economic moat," says Dennis LeClerc, an analyst for Toronto-based NA Financial, using a term first coined by Warren Buffet. "They have been able to create and maintain a very durable model for competitive advantage over the competition that will protect its long-term profits and market share, really market dominance, from any entity that decides to challenge them."

Taking the analysis a step further, Roux says that Energy Plus has created a business model that would be hard for any other company to come in and replicate.

"There are the partners, the dashboard, the fact they were first to market, the network platform, the ever growing number of services and increasing quality, and on and on, making it very difficult for any competitor to match what Energy Plus has done in the market," he says. "How is anyone supposed to compete with that, much less even enter the market and try and take over this very rich ecosystem? It's like eBay in that eBay was the first to market and then very quickly built an ecosystem around itself severely limiting the ability of anybody to compete against them successfully."

A Few Challenges along the Way

Though the company has been quite successful at this new offering, there have been a couple of challenges. In particular, the company moved so quickly to market and developing partnerships that it failed at first to spend enough time on creating a standardized model and method to smoothly integrate new partners.

"We needed to better delineate roles and ensure the partnerships were aligned around shared objectives," says Moneymaker. "There simply was too much ambiguity within the initial agreements, creating some confusion."

For example, sales activities were being replicated, pricing expectations in a number of instances were unclear, and there were inaccurate product expectations between Energy Plus and a few partners creating some confusion as to what to expect by customers. There was also the issue of clear ownership and management around each entity's intellectual property as well as the intellectual property that would be created as a result of the data collected by the services.

These realizations in turn led to Energy Plus recognizing the need to make sure partners realize that Energy Plus is the owner of the end-to-end solution and as such represents an opportunity to its partners.

To address these issues the company needed to create a set of policies for establishing partner agreements (see sidebar).

Policies for Partner Agreements

According to Jane Moneymaker, CEO of Energy Plus, the following represents their view to avoiding future issues with partner contracts SLAs[4]:

- Establish ahead of time the markets that Energy Plus will pursue with partners

- Identify each company's core intellectual property and determine how it will be licensed and protected and the roles and limits of allowing other entities (partners and customers) access to internal systems. Once ownership of IP is determined, create definitions for and contractual agreements around creating mutually owned intellectual property around collaborative efforts

- Agree not to build competing offerings before beginning a partnership with strong accountability

- Determine risk profile of a partner based on the amount of resources, risk, and accountability they are willing to put in

- Align sales and marketing models when it is relevant to do so, identify sales support requirements and who is responsible for each, and establish pricing and licensing guidelines

- Customer support—Energy Plus, since it is the closest to the end customer, is the first point of contact and the face of the offering. However, an established process for smooth handoffs and visibility for incident handling are critical. For example, should a partner-supplied service or component fail, the complaint is received by Energy Plus, but then transitioned to the relevant partner and resolved in a manner that is seamless to the customer

[4] R. "Ray" Wang and Merv Adrian, "Avoiding Failure in Technology Partnerships: Twenty-One Questions Every Technology Partnership Should Answer," August 22, 2007, published by Forrester Research at: http://www.forrester.com/Research/Document/Excerpt/0,7211,42640,00.html

Further, to address the variability within the many services as well as prevent substandard services from appearing within the offering, Energy Plus has worked hard to guarantee the quality and capabilities of these services and partners. The heart of this effort is the company's partner certificates, based on three levels—Gold, Silver, and Bronze.

"What this initiative has done," says LeClerc, "is to not only differentiate the products offered by partners within the ecosystem, but to add market value to these offers. These are also branded with a logo so that partners earning the highest level of certificate, which is Gold Certified, can put that logo on their website and literature, earning them credibility within the market as well as marketing development funds from Energy Plus. All of this sits inside the ubiquitous Energy Plus logo that is now commonly recognized within the industry."

A New Way of Selling

Energy Plus is also pioneering a new way of selling its products into the marketplace.

"Well, I wouldn't say it's exactly new as it is being used in other industries," notes Moneymaker, "but we're using a technique we call Smart Marketing."

Currently, when a sales representative goes on the road they carry with them a laptop, which is in and of itself a very powerful sales tool for the company. Because Energy Plus' unified communications system is a web-based network, sales representatives are able to access and communicate via voice and video with any of the company's many service engineers with expertise relevant to the customer's unique needs. This allows the company's experts to do more than solve very sophisticated energy management problems for customers; they are also able to remotely help generate new customers for the company and just as importantly create new pull-through for the value network partners, too.

Moneymaker's Smart Marketing takes this system a step further under a three-part strategy. Prospects can be targeted based on their sophistication in using technology. As an example, those who already have IP network-based telepresence technology can be contacted and asked to take a 15-minute conference from an energy management specialist.

If the prospect agrees, they are connected via WebEx to an Energy Plus sales specialist to talk with the prospect about what Energy Plus could do for them and by using screen sharing capabilities the sales specialist can demonstrate live how it all works. Additionally, customer testimonial videos can be played over the system so the prospect can see and hear from similar companies what the Energy Plus advantage is. At this point a service engineer with experience in the prospect's specific industry and issues can be brought into the discussion to provide a high-level view of the company's services.

In the third step, if the prospect agrees to allow Energy Plus to install a small probe into their network the company will give them a 30-day trial of the basic level monitoring service for free. It's at this point that the field sales representatives get involved—when they have a qualified prospect that's willing to do a trial—which is a very efficient model compared to the rest of the industry.

"What we gain from this," says Moneymaker, "is to very quickly gather web-based information that we can use to determine how their system is configured and if it is an optimal configuration; assess how well it's running; and then make a few suggestions on how to better tune it. We also offer two hour-long sessions of personalized consultancy with an engineer who will talk them through changes they can make to increase their overall energy management."

Moneymaker goes on to add that these sessions are delivered via web-based video and are like the customer having their very own in-house specialist on demand with technical information specific to the customer's site.

"We want to make this as easy for the customer as possible with little or no upfront cost," says Moneymaker. "Once we have shown them the savings we can provide and convinced them that we are going to completely remove their energy management issues, they can see that our business model is based on mutual value creation for the customer, our partners, and Energy Plus."

Looking Forward

Moneymaker is nothing if not ambitious.

The company realizes that in order to maintain its dominance within the ecosystem it has created it must strive to stay ahead of the curve and anticipate the needs and desires of its customers as well as potential points of entry for competitors.

"One of the things our sales reps have consistently been hearing is that our customers simply want the responsibilities and problems of energy management to go away, but, on the other hand, their requirement for reliable power supply is increasing," she says. "We are currently looking at integrating a higher value-added service for our top-level offering where we would actually purchase and take ownership of the assets outright as part of an agreement to manage the customer's energy consumption and energy needs for the life of that asset. In for a penny in for a pound is the thinking behind it."

Roux says that he has heard some mention of this newest initiative from a few of his contacts close to Energy Plus.

"This may put them even further ahead of the game than they already are," he says. "Energy Plus is guaranteeing the business and can even charge for the cost savings they are able to create by using their knowledge and expertise to optimize the performance of the assets. They also would be able to continue to sell value-added services on top of that. For its part, the customer gets these assets off their books, significant savings, and optimal performance without making any effort."

LeClerc adds that he has become aware that Energy Plus is working at moving up the value chain to the component suppliers for the various generator brands.

"What I have been hearing," he says, "is that Energy Plus is considering submitting the tech specifications for its network to an open standards body in order to create an industry forum with component suppliers to encourage them to adopt Energy Plus' standards to enable these manufacturers to design more intelligence in their devices."

And as if that isn't enough, the company is on the verge of releasing an application using a widget that can be displayed in Google, Yahoo!, or Facebook personalized pages so customers can have a scaled down dashboard on the homepage of their choice on their work or home computers.

"Why build your own client portal when they are already using Yahoo!, Google, Facebook and so on," says LeClerc. "Just deliver functionality into the customer's environment. Actually, rumors are rife in the industry that this is the prelude to an aggressive launch by the company of a broad set of consumer energy management services aimed at optimizing household energy bills."

When asked if the rumors are true, a spokesperson for Energy Plus refused to confirm or deny this, saying only that the company does not comment on future offerings.

"I think that's the obvious next step," counters LeClerc. "This is a huge multi-billion-dollar emerging market and they must be looking at it. Consumers are very Green conscious nowadays and this would be aimed directly at that sweet spot. In any event, the bottom line is that Moneymaker is taking the company's value proposition and continually taking it a step further."

Conclusion

In talking with Moneymaker it becomes instantly clear that she is animated by how far the company has come and the myriad of opportunities that have been opened up by her efforts. What was once considered a dinosaur in a cost-based industry is now the new and youthful up-and-comer with a strong value-based business model and a killer brand.

"I suppose the big message is that what we are doing," she says, "the changes we have made, and the transformation we are going through is not about a short interlude to handle a difficult period in the market or world economy before returning to business as usual. This is about changing the way you work now, and then constantly evolving your business. We're not planning an end game, we're in a world of constant change"

Asked if this is just a simple story of a turnaround at a sagging generator company or something with much larger and wider implications Moneymaker pauses before responding.

"There's nothing here that would only work in the energy industry," she says. "Everything we have done, the changes we made, the way we've used the new Web 2.0 tools, and the way we've harnessed the Internet to our advantage would work for any company in any industry.

"This is about reorganizing what the flattening of the world means to your business model and then having the courage to radically innovate and turn that flattening to your advantage. If you don't start having a culture of constant change and optimization and innovation; continuously looking at new things to drive your business forward, then you will be blindsided at some stage and it will be the end of you. At Energy Plus we recognize that, so for us this is just the beginning. There's more to come…just watch this space."

Questions and Analysis

While the preceding fictional story provides a strong illustration of the points this book is making with regard to Business Model Innovation, Web 2.0, and related technologies and strategies, the following sections will take the points discussed above and place them within a real-world context.

These questions and subsequent answers are not meant to provide the definitive prescription for how these concepts can work in your business. Rather, they are designed to provide further analysis and clarification and pull the many points raised above from the realm of the fictional into real life applications.

As such, we hope that you will read on and use the following to spur further consideration and discussion so that you may take these ideas and find innovative ways to apply them to your business.

Chapter 1 Questions and Analysis

Revenues Up, Margins Up, Costs Rising, Profits Flattening

Question 1: Overview of Mashups and Mesh

The first book in this series, titled *Mashup Corporations: The End of Business as Usual*, begins innocently enough with Hugo Wunderkind, a marketing manager for Vorpal, discovering, almost as if by accident, that there is an online market for Vorpal's popcorn popper among fans of football teams.

Basically, he garnered the help of a friend to build a web application that would allow users to select a team emblem or image and then render that image onto the side of a popcorn popper.

After placing this small experiment on his web site and spontaneously receiving orders for customized poppers, Wunderkind came to learn that there might be the potential for growing sales by marketing customizable products via the web as a web service.

Web Service Explained

Web services are standard approaches, often supported by an open Application Programming Interface (API), that allow the capabilities of one company's web site or internal system to be accessed and used by another web site or system by connecting directly to the underlying technology. Simply stated, a web service refers to application-to-application communication and interaction when the two application owners are distinct organizational entities and may be spread across the Web.

A common example of this would be using Google Maps on a web site, such as one for selling homes and land, where users could see a map or a satellite image of a property they may want to consider purchasing. This web service (Google Maps) is providing a web site owner with an added function, increasing the value of the user experience.

In our story of Vorpal, the company is allowing web site operators to access Vorpal's service—customizing and ordering popcorn poppers and other home appliances—by making its API available for use by them. Vorpal is able to quickly and easily build sales channels that facilitate numerous customized product offers to targeted communities of people and the web site operators are able to enhance the user experience that their web sites provide.

The net effect is to add additional channels to a market as well as create additional markets and a targeted range of products, all of which increase revenues and by their specialized nature should command premium pricing.

As a prelude to this book, *Mashups* examined the many changes Vorpal had to make in order to take advantage of this very exciting and new sales and marketing opportunity. Primarily, these changes were as much cultural as they were IT related and revolved around the need to redefine five key relationships in order to achieve the business goals laid out by Moneymaker:

- Between the company and customer-focused innovators inside and outside of the company in order to harness the ideas and energy of both to improve the business, its products, systems, and processes

- Between the company and its customers by bringing customers closer to core business processes in order to allow the services to work properly
- Between the company and its suppliers in order to strengthen the connections between the two in order to work more cooperatively to provide the products in a timely fashion to customers
- Between the IT department and the rest of the company in order for IT to better support employee initiatives (for instance, to better align IT to business objectives), as well as how innovation can be better facilitated at a more rapid pace while protecting critical data
- Among IT professionals within the company in order to gain the most from new capabilities supported by technologies such as Service Oriented Architecture (SOA)

To put this in the current jargon of business schools, by making these changes Vorpal had innovated their business model in order to gain access to new revenue streams.

Business Model Innovation

We will describe what we mean by business model innovation in the next chapter. However a brief explanation here would be helpful.

Business model innovation refers to the process used to differentiate a company and its products within the marketplace by finding new and innovative ways to market and develop products. Within the context of our larger discussion, business model innovation is about taking advantage of the Internet and the Web to enter into new markets (such as the many niche markets Vorpal is working in) with new and creative strategies by rethinking the company's business model.

As we enter our story of Vorpal in this book, the company has taken its success with the PopMe! and extended it to nearly all of its other products in order to enter more and more markets with an ever-growing combination of customization choices, which enabled a very wide array of customers and related communities to personalize their products.

The result is that sales are growing and people like Wunderkind and other members of the sales and marketing team are moving very quickly to create new markets and product combinations. However, the internal systems and processes that have been created for a mass-market model are unable to keep up with the dynamism of the many niche markets and customizable products broadly described as the Long Tail. Due to this, the company is fragmenting at a number of stress points—between the traditionally operated so called back office and the newly added dynamic functionality in the front office, as well as among the systems and processes within the back-end structure—putting at risk its gains from the Long Tail.

The Long Tail in Brief

Essentially, the Long Tail is a sales method enabled by the Internet where customizable products are introduced to relatively small niche markets. In aggregate, these niches add up to a very large market. By contrast, most companies sell into the mass market. Under this model they sell a few products into a very large and broad market. The Long Tail involves leveraging the Internet to sell many products to many small markets that when added together can mean much greater sales than the mass market.

We could describe the last book as looking at externally facing processes and systems that had to be developed in order to act on a Long Tail sales model and allow the company to interact in this very new way with numerous web sites and customers. As such, it is about applying new techniques—SOA and mashups—that changed a number of important relationships and had a lot of business consequences.

This book is focused more on the internal changes that are made necessary by the company's adoption and generalizing of its Long Tail sales: How do you change the internal world so that it runs efficiently and connects with the outside world?

Question 2: Who Owns What as You Transform the Role of Technology in Your Business?

One of the major challenges as Vorpal undergoes this transformation is to understand and make clear who owns what roles within this new structure. In the old IT, the roles, as they relate to who makes what decision and why, are clearly understood by Moneymaker and everyone else within the company. However, as they have added a whole new layer of technology with very different functionalities for the business, over the top of the existing IT services, there has not yet been a clear delineation of how decisions are to be made and who is to make them.

The point should also be made here that this focus on sales opportunities and revenue as a driver of business activities is normal. What has changed is the way that technology has become an integral part of accessing new markets. Value-based decision making and deployment is now conflicting with cost-based administration of the business through IT.

One of the key issues that Moneymaker and her team must resolve is how decisions are made with regard to the new IT and business landscape, and who owns what roles. As we consider these two sets of technologies—transactional (traditional IT and business uses) and interactional (newer technologies and business uses)—it is helpful to visualize them as two boxes with the new as a box over the old; this is the bottom row of Figure Q1-1:

Who is the decision maker and what is the basis of the decision?

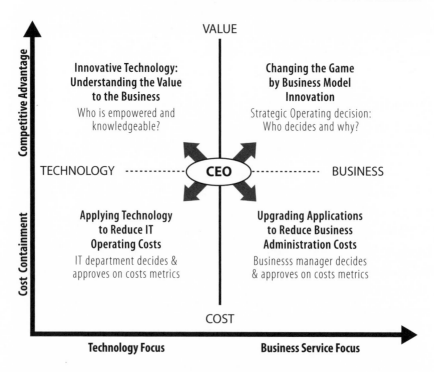

Figure Q1-1. Allocating Roles in the Long Tail

When we look at traditional IT, the primary reasons for its use are to automate a number of processes to record and manage business transactions as a means to create efficiency and cut costs. In this regard, traditional IT is primarily used for cost containment.

The bottom row has two sides because as companies seek to better use transactional IT they are doing two things. The first is they are using technology to reduce IT operating costs, which is a decision made by the CIO and the IT department and approved on cost metrics created by these players. Technology-focused cost-containment is the lower left side of the quadrant. Within this context the CEO, Moneymaker, could decide that the company needs to reduce costs in its IT department. Therefore, Moneymaker knows she has to go to her CIO and the manager in charge of the IT department to make the decision as to how best to do that. The CIO would perhaps respond by saying the company should virtualize its servers, and he would have created a cost model to show that the investment would be earned back in a certain period of time.

The second cost containment use is to upgrade applications in order to reduce business administration costs. This is the lower right side of the quadrant. A business manager is in charge of the decision and the decision is approved based on knowable cost metrics. Within this context, Moneymaker could turn to the CFO and ask Cashtender to cut costs. Cashtender could reply that upgrading Vorpal's ERP system to react to new business requirements would do the job. Moneymaker knows that Cashtender understands the basis of the decision, which is the new business requirements, and that he can build a cost model to support that decision. Cashtender would then work with the IT department and the CIO to find and integrate an appropriate ERP solution.

Within this second scenario, you have a decision that is based on a business need—better managing the company's financial records—that also relies on the IT department knowing how upgraded financial tools would integrate within the current IT landscape. This model represents a business requirement driving an IT decision. As such, it is the alignment between business and IT, and it is broadly known who owns which role within the process to make such a decision.

In these examples, when Moneymaker is looking at the bottom left box of our graphic she knows she is looking at technology and cost, and that she is talking with the CIO and the IT manager about making strategic decisions to reduce IT operating costs. When she is looking at the bottom right box she knows decisions made here reflect upgrading transactional applications in order to reduce costs, and she knows who would be driving that decision and the role that IT would play to support that decision.

Now, when we look at the top row—the newer technology landscape—we can also separate this into two boxes.

As Moneymaker, the CEO, wants to find new business from the top right box the change in the business model is often threatening to existing business operations, managers, and their budgets. The top left box then is about understanding new and innovative technologies that could create new business opportunities.

The problem for Vorpal, though, is that it is unclear who occupies the top two boxes in the graphic and is therefore responsible for making decisions and developing a value model or business case for those decisions so that benefits can be allocated and there is clear visibility between this top layer and the transactional IT environment that must support and record the sales.

Moneymaker knows that as she looks at the top left box she sees Hugo Wunderkind taking advantage of the Web and other technologies to create new business opportunities. As he does this, Wunderkind is also driving the need to understand and create structured new business activities and models that must become part of the Vorpal business and that includes the need to make alterations to the business side (the top right box) in order to execute on those sales. Orders must be received; products must be produced, packaged, and shipped; sales noticed and recorded; and so on.

There is something of a role reversal here because, rather than a business need driving a related IT decision, technology is driving the need to change the way the business model works. However, making this work is going to be very challenging for the company because, unlike in the bottom two boxes, there is no clear owner of what decisions are to be made, or how they are to be made and then supported by a cost model and integrated within the rest of the company's systems.

Other questions that must also be answered are: Who is going to drive business model innovation? And, who is going to work out the value and allocate its direct and indirect costs to the business as it enters these new markets and follows a Long Tail sales strategy?

As it stands now for Vorpal, Wunderkind is driving the need for innovation on the business side by making IT-related decisions in order to differentiate and sell products—without constraints or clear delineation as to how various decisions within these two boxes should be made. Until roles are clearly delineated and allocated by Moneymaker, tensions within the various operational areas of the business are going to start appearing.

For example, Wunderkind is using all sorts of different techniques and technologies to understand markets and sales opportunities better, which is distinct from using an enterprise IT desktop. He wants to use technology to personalize his interactions, as well as his understanding of what the sales opportunities are, in a very different way from merely logging and recording sales and expenditures.

However, Lovecraft is going to be concerned by Wunderkind's use of technology because in his role he has to ensure the company's systems are secure, that IT costs are under control, and so on. So he is going to want to rein in Wunderkind to conform to the conventions of traditional IT approaches. Wunderkind will resist because traditional tools and approaches will inhibit his freedom and flexibility to create differentiated product offerings and market opportunities.

On the other side, Cashtender, the CFO, is struggling to reconcile how all of these new products and markets affect indirect support costs for things such as the call center, manufacturing, supplier related expenses, and other back office services used to support sales. As Wunderkind and Vorpal push from the top right box, adjustments must be made in the top left box, so that Cashtender can properly allocate all of the costs and better manage the financial picture.

However, the roles, with regard to who makes what decisions and why, in these top two boxes, have not been clearly allocated by Moneymaker because these roles are very new. The key point that business schools make in describing this is the need for a business model change to embrace and address all of these issues.

For example, when looking at the top left box it is clear that Wunderkind has a role in making decisions related to the use of technology to create value, but so too does the IT department and the CIO, to ensure that requirements such as security, IT costs, efficiency, and so forth, are met as well. It could also be said that many CIOs realize that they should be playing this role and are frustrated by their currently constrained role around cost reduction in the existing business through IT.

The upper right box will also have to be populated in order to assure that not only are differentiated products being created and sold, but also that they contribute real additional revenues and profits. Further, these sales will need to be captured by the transactional IT systems so the company can manage its financial picture, comply with relevant laws and regulations, control costs, and so on.

It should also be noted that there is a key difference in the manner by which the top two boxes relate to each other as compared to the bottom two. This is shown in Figure Q1-2. On the bottom, the cost containment boxes represent the alignment of business and IT as two distinct entities.

And the methods to implement are different too

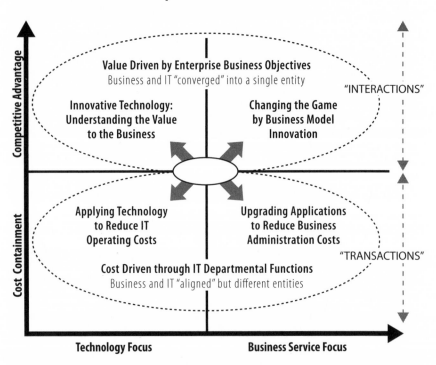

Figure Q1-2: The Dual Relationships of Technology to Business

However, for the top two boxes, those centered on creating value, it is important to view these as existing in a state of convergence where business and IT are a single entity.

Question 3: How Is the Long Tail Different from Other Business Models?

The Long Tail is a term coined by Chris Anderson, editor of *Wired Magazine*, who wrote a book of the same name that described a new kind of business model. Traditionally, the term "Long Tail" refers to a type of statistical distribution in which a small number of items in the distribution stretch out for a long period.

In business however, the Long Tail refers to a new kind of business model made possible by the Internet, the Web, and other advances in technology. As such, it means that, instead of companies selling a lot of a few products—the mass-market business model—it is possible to sell a little of a huge amount of products by using a pull-driven model. Think of it this way, rather than trying to only sell huge numbers of a few popular music recordings, the Long Tail is about selling a very wide range of recordings that recognize the diversity of musical tastes among customers. Each recording with its relatively small number of fans represents a niche market and when all of these niche markets are combined they form a very substantial level of sales.

By selling a little of a lot, you can end up with revenues that rival or exceed those that come from the mass-market model. In other words, selling to lots of specialized niche markets can be a bigger business than selling to the mass market. Further, the Long Tail can be done parallel to a company's mass-market sales as is being done in the story of Vorpal.

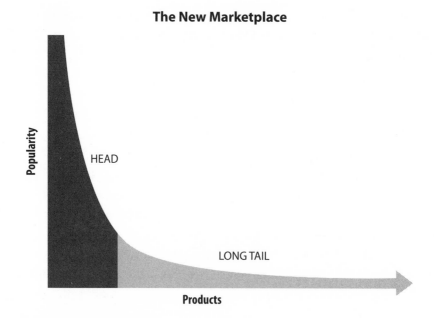

Figure Q1-3. The Long Tail

How the Long Tail Works

The principles of the Long Tail rely on three forces that Chris Anderson has identified:

- Democratizing the tools of production: The ability of more and more people to create content and products themselves without a huge capital investment
- Cutting the costs of consumption by democratizing distribution: The ability of the Internet to make it cheap to reach millions of people
- Connecting supply and demand: The ability of search, recommendations, social networking, and many other means to allow people to find content and products that interest them

It is important to note a few differences between the Long Tail model as described by Chris Anderson and the variation that Vorpal is pursuing. The Long Tail as described by Anderson involves a large amount of users finding what they want from an enormous collection of existing content—for example, all the books in print or the entire catalog of recorded music. Some of this content is produced by major publishers and some is created by much smaller entities and even individuals (consider the benefits of people self-publishing books and selling them on Amazon).

Vorpal's Long Tail works a bit differently. The company is using Web 2.0 technologies as collaboration tools to identify niches in which to sell products. Vorpal is then building products and assembling partners to satisfy the needs of those niches and to help market the products.

A critical component of this model is the use of APIs to allow web site owners to add a page to their site where visitors that share a common interest—for example being fans of a particular sports team—can find, customize, and order a product.[5]

As the company broadens out its product offerings and seeks a wider array of niches within which to market these products, it is:

- Differentiating its products on a much larger scale than it could in a mass-marketing model
- Placing its products in a number of different circumstances
- Segmenting the business into smaller niches in order to serve those niches and derive larger margins by providing higher value
- Using the Internet as a massive sales and marketing channel where customers are able to locate, evaluate and make choices, and purchase a far wider variety of products than is possible by only relying on traditional sales approaches

---

[5] This represents a web service where the API facilitates the interconnection of a portion of Vorpal's internal system with that of the website in order to remotely provide Vorpal's service.

In summary, most current models are about the volume of sales around a relatively small set of products that change rather slowly and an infrastructure created to support those products and the process. The Long Tail is a reversal of this and is made feasible by the technologies of the Web allowing enough customers to be found for a niche product.

It is a model where an idea for a product offering is created, prototypes are developed, the product is tested in the market via a number of means, a marketing strategy is developed, and then a product is launched into the market. As compared to a Long Tail process, the duration of product life is fairly long, the cost of offering a product is known, and profitability can be estimated. The duration of how long the product can be sold and create profit for the company is also relatively long.

This is distinct from Vorpal's Long Tail model, where experimentation happens as the product enters the market. Its lifecycle is short as the niche markets, though large in number, are relatively small in size. Therefore, product creation happens rapidly and the time during which the company can derive profits is short. It is a model of constant movement, of dynamic offerings and markets, and constant change requiring constant innovation.

A key challenge is establishing a business model that can support a much faster product lifecycle where multiple products may be in different lifecycle states simultaneously.

The Long Tail is about making decisions as to how you market the product based on its differentiated aspects.

It is in large part about creating new relationships between customers—who through interacting with the company's web-based network can really be defined as users within a company, and its strategic partners.

A real-world example of how new uses for the Web can be incorporated into a Long Tail offering, augmenting the user's experience, can be found in the new opportunities available to airlines to sell tickets. Essentially, rather than having a ticket price and seat location dictated to a traveler, users are now able to choose when they travel, where they want to sit on the plane, and how to negotiate what they are willing to pay for a particular seat.[6]

Question 4: What Are the Challenges of Pursuing a Long Tail Strategy?

One unacknowledged aspect of businesses like Amazon.com or Netflix is that those companies not only support the Long Tail model, but their infrastructure was also designed to support the mass market as well. Amazon and Netflix sell large amounts of a small number of very popular items (bestselling books and recently released DVDs of blockbuster hit movies) as well as selling a small amount of a large number of products. The infrastructure of both companies was built to scale to sell both large volumes of individual products and large numbers of a range of products.

Linking Back-end Core Business Processes with the Long Tail

The first and most important issue that Vorpal will have to negotiate if it is to regain control over costs is to recognize that by moving into multiple niche markets with multiple niche products the company has created a number of small businesses.

So, by essentially devolving into a number of small businesses, Vorpal is making too many quick and small decisions to keep the Long Tail running, which is resulting in inefficiency and increased costs. This can be seen when Cashtender says that costs for central services that support sales (such as indirect support costs) are much higher than predicted (these predictions were primarily based on the costs associated with the mass-market products).

---

[6] Consider how travelers will field offers from different web services such as Travelocity and Expedia as well as shop around among various airlines' websites.

The problem is that the mass-market model is rooted in creating large numbers of standard products at scale for very broadly defined markets without any customization. It is a relatively static model with relatively static products selling in a very conventional manner. It is a model built around a series of plateaus—product development, market testing, release, and then supporting the product for its lifecycle. In all, these plateaus are predictable, of a relatively long duration, and are planned. The Long Tail is less predictable, lifecycles are of shorter duration, and tends to defy a high degree of planning as opportunities are identified and acted upon very quickly. For Vorpal, it's not one popcorn popper model being created, tested, and marketed, but many, and all at the same time. And this is happening across a number of Vorpal's products.

When looking at the popcorn popper, the basic machine is the same, but depending on the niche market being targeted it will have different colors, decals, casings and whatever else would help differentiate it in that niche. Therefore, one could think of this dilemma as being that 20% of the change in the product becomes 80% of the organizational problem because all of those customization offerings must be supported by central services such as establishing vendor relationships, customer service, cost management, marketing, and so on.

This is why the company finds itself in the awkward position of having rising revenues, apparently large margins, and increased market presence, but with flat profits.

Vorpal has to find synergies between each product offering and niche market where it can standardize and begin to take advantage of operating the Long Tail more as a single business than a number of small ones. Vorpal needs to find a way to adjust to constant change across the business and innovate on its overall business model so that rather than doing small expensive things all over the place they are finding commonalities and synergistic opportunities.

However, so far Vorpal has only changed the front-end of the company without bringing the back-end up to pace.

Question 5: Where is the Long Tail growing?

One might think from the way that this idea is often presented that the Long Tail is only really about Internet businesses or businesses that are being created from scratch. The truth of the matter, as we will explore in this book, is that this model is far more than this somewhat limited perception. It is in fact a practical model that can be used by large established companies.

In fact, the Long Tail can also be applied as a very important element of globalization as companies such as Intel are traveling what could be described as the ultra Long Tail by broadening the global scope and presence of the company.

In the mid 1990s Andy Grove, currently a senior advisor to Intel's executive management, and previously CEO and chairman of the board, challenged Intel to achieve the goal of 1 billion connected users of the company's products. As the 20th century transitioned to the 21st, Intel was able to succeed at that goal with technologies focused in all major business and consumer areas.

The company has now set as its goal bringing in the next billion customers. However, despite strong profits and an extremely high market share the company's stock has actually dropped in value. Therefore, the company has come to the conclusion that using traditional methods to grow and improve the business will not necessarily generate the stockholder value one would expect.

To meet this challenge, John E. Davies, VP of the Intel World Ahead program, has championed a Long Tail model based on building ecosystems within developing economies and altering the manner by which the company works within these ecosystems. Rather than relying on a traditional model of creating manufacturing and partner ecosystems, the company is working on a model based on creating what could be described as community- or mesh-based ecosystems that are self-sustaining by forming more varied partnerships with governments, nongovernmental organizations, connectivity partners, banks, and so forth.

Ecosystems will be examined in greater detail in Chapter 10, but what this example demonstrates is that the Long Tail is going to also grow in these companies that are seeking their next billion or million or even 100,000 new users. And instead of it being a 20- or 30-year process it's going to be something that can happen much more quickly because people are becoming connected through the Internet and the Web.

However, finding the Long Tail is going to require that these companies work with a variety of partners in a new framework in order to engage that new set of users. Intel and other large companies are not going to abandon the strategies and ecosystems that have worked well to get them the first billion customers, but in order to get the second billion they—like Vorpal—are going to need to add a different approach.

Chapter 2 Questions and Analysis

Mass-Market Infrastructure—Meet the Internal Long Tail

Question 1: Has Business Model Innovation Become the Key to Sustainable Competitive Advantage?

One of the fundamental points being made in this book is that the business world and the technological landscape are in a state of continuous change. This may seem like a relatively trite thing to say, but the fact of the matter is that very powerful forces are working to transform markets and create new opportunities for companies in the position to take advantage of them.

When we talk about business model innovation we are describing a process to differentiate the company within the marketplace and find new and innovative ways to market and develop products. Business model innovation is about taking advantage of the Long Tail or similar effects and getting into new markets and doing new things by rethinking the company's business model.

It can then be said that the biggest risk to a company is not so much that they would do the wrong things, but that a company would continue to do what used to be the right things for too long. Corporate leaders must continue to seek out greater efficiencies and ways to control costs, but this should be done with one eye looking to new and innovative means and ways to add value to the company. Indeed, this is essentially the message of Clayton Christiansen's book *The Innovators Dilemma*. Staying too close to established ways of doing business and ignoring potentially disruptive trends can harm a company's prospects.

However, while they had built a model around the Long Tail that in many ways reflects the ideals of strategic agility, they built this structure on an infrastructure based on the more static mass-market environment—long periods of market and product stability before going through a process to change a product or change a market. In the previous chapter we described this as being a series of plateaus.

By contrast, the Long Tail requires adapting the infrastructure to be able to support a state of continuous change, which is something that Vorpal had so far not done. This means the company's internal systems and processes lack the strategic agility to integrate with the fundamental nature of the Long Tail.

Therefore, Vorpal's business model innovation must be incorporated in a new vision for its infrastructure. In other words, true agility from a strategic perspective involves not only having the new vision, but supporting it as well.

True strategic agility—the ability to listen to what's needed, to take strategic turns in a timely fashion, and to implement technology that adds value—is composed of three parts:

- **Resource Fluidity**—The ability to move resources around and to deploy them rapidly
- **Leadership Unity**—The ability to make collective decisions very quickly
- **Strategic Acuity**—The ability to see and frame opportunities in a fresh way

These elements, as they relate to strategic agility, are critical to a company's ability to adapt to an ever-changing world in order to sustain its competitive advantage in ever-changing markets. Business model innovation relies on all three.

Core Competencies

The key to getting the business model right is to understand what the underlying core competencies of the company are.

The most noted and best real-world example of what we mean by this is the contrast between how Toyota handled marketing two of its cars—the Scion and Lexus.

In the case of the Lexus, Toyota had decided it wanted to go up-market by extending its product line to include a luxury sedan. To do this they essentially built a parallel organization to handle the Lexus.

However, when they developed the Scion Toyota behaved in a very different manner. The intent with this offering was to engage in a somewhat unique market of younger more technologically savvy people. These are people who would want a relatively customized car and who would likely want to be able to do that online. The company realized that a Long Tail model would be effective for helping them compete in this market segment, and to help them manage the customization aspect of their plan they brought in an entire ecosystem of partners.

The Scion was built around a different model in how the company went to market and with whom it partnered to make the initiative successful.

To break this down a bit, Toyota didn't try and build a separate, vertically integrated parallel organization to handle the Scion. What they did was figure out what its core competencies and synergies are. For example, the company knows how to design really good cars and then manufacture them and the company has a dealer network to provide service and finance packages. All of these core competencies are related across all of the company's products—design, manufacturing, and sales.

So in a process of business model innovation, a company is looking at ways to offer differentiated and oftentimes personalized products and to do that it must identify its core competencies. These are processes that are in common to all or many of its products. Then the company will seek partners to support those activities that fall outside of its defined core competencies.

In order for Vorpal to fix the issues that are tearing the company apart and causing costs and inefficiencies to grow, it has to properly analyze what their core competencies are and determine how they relate to the business.

Enterprises tend to think of core competencies as the products themselves, rather than what are the shared core competencies across the business and how they can multiply the use of those competencies.

The Forces of Change

The need for continuous business model innovation is being driven by three primary forces.

Globalization

What we are really looking at when we talk about globalization is the continuing shift in terms of the entities a company interacts with (for example, who your partners are, your vendors, competitors, and so on) as well as how often and under what circumstances. For example, no longer is a competitor going to always exist within a known ecosystem or known location. Competitors could be from around the world and competing with you in new and sometimes nuanced ways.

Digital Literacy

People's understanding and relationship to technology has changed fundamentally. Technology is now a fact of life and digital literacy can be assumed, and it can also be assumed that people have the systems at home to be able to do things and behave differently than they have in the past. In short, they can go online and book a travel package themselves, seek out diverse relationships with various communities, find a wider array of answers to an ever-widening array of problems, and on and on.

The Evolution of IT

Technology is a driving force behind the first two points, but it's not the technology that one would understand as IT in a business context. IT is no longer the technology inside of a business used to keep track of administrative processes via proprietary applications. Rather, it is the Network of Everything. It is technology that is linking people together, it is open and involves sharing, and is providing new and innovative services for people to use.

Most enterprises can already recognize the impact of at least one or two of these challenges already. Usually when they investigate further they can find all three are in place and impacting their business.

Question 2: Why Do Traditional Models for IT Fail to Support Continuous Business Model Innovation?

Vorpal is not able to keep up with the dynamism of the Long Tail method because its back-end systems have yet to be transformed to support a state of strategic agility. As a result, the entire initiative to transform the business and find new markets is now at risk of failure.

So as Vorpal struggles to define its problem and then move forward to find a solution, one thing is clear: The new solution must exist alongside and build on the foundation of current systems. The company is not going to throw out its transactional systems such as ERP, CRM, SCM, and so on in favor of some Long Tail IT solution. Rather, they are going to adapt the systems they have and the processes around those systems to continue to support the mass market as well as Vorpal's niche strategy.

The Problem

The problem that IT departments have in making this transition to support new models can be explained by the two-by-two matrix diagram discussed in Chapter 1 Questions and Analysis.

The nature of IT at most companies is oriented toward delivery of stable, vendor-provided applications, not the dynamic assembly of solutions to respond to business. Too often, even when flexible architectures such as SOA are introduced, the capabilities stay in the domain of IT instead of becoming a tool for business transformation. Traditional IT is at a loss to support the kind of innovation taking place at Vorpal because it is not oriented to creating tools that those outside of the IT department can use to assemble solutions. Notions of control and stability become constraints. The company can only move as fast as the IT department lets it.

Vorpal has created this new sales method and layered it on top of the company's traditional sales support systems and processes without recognizing that IT has to go from following transactions to becoming a real-time partner with the business entities creating new products, exploiting new markets, and making these sales. It is about working as a mesh of people and resources, not a handful of predetermined connections—basically data-centric silos—set up by the IT department for the business.

Differentiate for Advantage, but Standardize for Efficiency.

The mass-market model is easy to understand as scale and standardization is a built-in aspect. However, when a company changes its business model by using technology to address Long Tail markets, the temptation is for everything to become different with consequences for cost and manageability. The challenge is to understand exactly what needs to be different in order to make the business offering successful and restrict the difference to this part alone.

Ideally, this should be focused on the in-the-market element and standardization should be the norm for all other elements.

In particular, the aim should be to standardize and reuse as many internal process elements as possible. This is a key role for Service Oriented Architecture as this permits horizontal shared business tasks to be reused in different ways to support many different Long Tail–style market offerings. This contrasts with a traditional enterprise application structure, which is inherently vertical and separates the various tasks and activities in order to ensure data integrity through procedures.

Many More Cooks in the IT Kitchen

Adding to the confusion and frustration of Vorpal's employees and managers is the fact that they have incorporated an entirely new layer of IT, which is the web services, into the company's business model. This new layer of IT has one very significant difference from the company's traditional IT systems, which is that it is not singularly controlled by Vorpal. Customers, partners, web site owners that add the service to their site, and others are also using these technologies. They're not closed and proprietary applications, but a broad range of open and adaptable technologies carried across the Web.

Web services are allowing a whole new set of users to access and affect the company's internal systems as these mashups are added to many, many web sites and the users of these web sites are selecting products and customizing them to their particular tastes. The company has some control over this environment, but it is not nearly the level of total control it has over its internal transactional IT environment.

This new set of users has taken some control away from the company. As they are placing orders and interacting with the network, they are drawing down on the company's resources in a way that Vorpal has never experienced, didn't understand prior to engaging in the Long Tail, and certainly had not planned for. And not only have they lost control, but the amount of resources required to keep the whole works running in this piecemeal, on-the-fly basis that Vorpal currently exists in is driving the company's budgets in directions it hadn't expected and in ways it is grappling to understand.

Vorpal doesn't have an adaptive data center, it doesn't have an adaptive infrastructure to achieve the strategic agility it needs because the company altered its front-end processes to differentiate and personalize and rapidly move into new markets without anticipating what it would do to the back-end sales support systems and processes.

Overall, what the company needs to understand and what it needs to develop as it moves forward is orchestration—the ability to orchestrate both processes and infrastructure to respond to the new business needs that are designed to continuously change. And as part of this the internal systems need to be able to monitor new events and trends in near real time to allow business managers such as Lovecraft and Cashtender to understand what is happening to the business and anticipate trends and needs.

Question 3: How Is Do-It-Yourself Shadow IT Enabling Users to Fill the Gap Between What IT Is Providing and What They Need to Compete in the New Marketplace?

The demand for do-it-yourself IT is being created every day, as people use what's available on the Web to live their lives. For example, consider the employee that uses Google at home to find information she needs on the Internet, while at work she is forced to rely on static IT assets and largely has to remember where information is located.[7]

At home she can seek answers to questions on the Web, which is a vast repository of knowledge and interactive ways to share it. At work she still must rely on static IT systems or asking a coworker or boss.

At home she can catch up on shows she may have missed using a number of resources such as YouTube or the web site of the broadcast station or any number of other resources. At work if she misses a meeting she will have to track down the meeting minutes, if any were taken, and hope they are complete.

---

[7] For an excellent explanation of the benefits of Web 2.0 go to: http://www.slideshare.net/TheShed/meet-charlotte

At home she can use Facebook, Flickr, Twitter, and other social networking sites to keep track of her friends and family. At work she is limited by physical proximity and perhaps only gets the opportunity to network while at a conference.

Further, at home as she explores these networking opportunities and finds communities of people interested in the things she is interested in she is expanding the people she can collaborate with and share knowledge with beyond the immediacy of her geographic location. She also makes use of blogs and wikis in combination with her social networking sites to broaden her reach to include thousands of people and many numbers of communities.

However, at work her interactions are controlled and limited to a handful of people.

Therefore, when considering the potential and empowerment she experiences at home, she likely would want to be able to make use of these tools and gain these advantages in her work life as well.

Transactional or Interactional

Traditional IT is based on designing applications that can record various types of transactions in a manner to ensure data integrity is achieved. The maintenance of data integrity is a major concern to any and all changes made to the integrated environment of enterprise IT. Any new form of technology is always considered against this background.

The new technologies of the mashup, Web 2.0 in all of its forms, are not based on this data-centric computing model. Instead, they are designed for person-to-person interactions. As such, they can in many cases be deployed as a completely separate entity requiring no connection or integration with existing traditional transactions of IT. In the previous book—*Mashup Corporations: The End of Business as Usual*—we described this phenomenon using the Diamond Model. In this model the transactional (the traditional IT environment) is on the bottom of the diamond and the newer interactional (Web 2.0) environment is on the top.

This model is used to explain in a relatively IT-centric way how the back-end IT environment relates to the front-end IT environment. The former is transactional and static while the latter is dynamic, interactional and the means by which products are personalized and differentiated. Further, in the last book the bridge that was built between these two IT modalities by Josh Lovecraft, Vorpal's CIO, is based on Service Oriented Architecture, SOA, as an intermediary between the two environments with open standards as the physical link, the interface between the two. The open standards are based on industry and business sector specific standards as well as actual de facto standards.

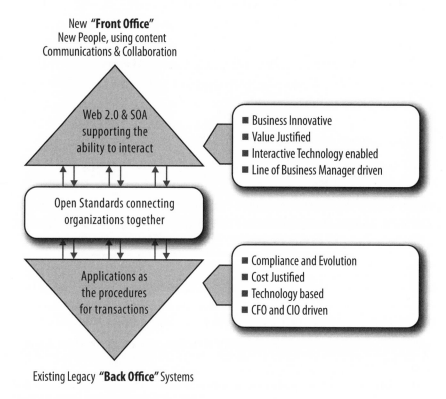

New **"Front Office"**
New People, using content
Communications & Collaboration

Web 2.0 & SOA
supporting the
ability to interact

- Business Innovative
- Value Justified
- Interactive Technology enabled
- Line of Business Manager driven

Open Standards connecting
organizations together

Applications as
the procedures
for transactions

- Compliance and Evolution
- Cost Justified
- Technology based
- CFO and CIO driven

Existing Legacy **"Back Office"** Systems

Figure Q2-1. The Diamond Model

As the story of Vorpal and its integration of a Long Tail sales method unfolds, the person most notably using these new technologies would be Hugo Wunderkind, Vorpal's director of online marketing.

He is using them to seek and understand new market and product opportunities for the company. Primarily, Wunderkind's use of these outward facing technologies as well as the technologies the company uses to provide its many web-based services have existed on the edge of the wagon wheel. They are used to enter markets, to personalize and differentiate the company's products, as well as to create competitive advantage.

However, in this chapter we have seen Wunderkind use these technologies in a manner quite a bit different from how he uses them as online marketing director. Rather than generating sales, Wunderkind is using these technologies to find information and develop an understanding and possible solution to an internal business problem. Traditional transactional systems such as ERP won't provide the information he needs, so he is looking in a new way for solutions. He is using new technologies to solve a problem he doesn't readily have answers to, problems that Vorpal's internal systems won't provide an answer for. Further, he can't go to his boss for the answer because his boss doesn't have it either.

The reason Hugo spends so much time on the Web is that he cannot do his job without it. If you go back about 20 years, 80% of the knowledge a person required to do their job was essentially in their head or their boss's head. Today, however, only 20% of the knowledge a person needs to do their job well is in their head. This means that people go and find the information they need to do their jobs and to optimize situations and opportunities. They have to use their judgment as to where they will find that information as well as make decisions as to how they would apply the information they find.

So back to the point: Wunderkind is now using this new technology that exists beyond his internal IT silo. He is using the mesh: blogs and wikis and social networking sites, not just as resources to sell things, but to seek external information and ideas in order to solve an internal issue. He is forced by the need for more information and ideas to use Shadow IT (IT that exists in the shadows of the big IT assets) in order to fill the gap in what the transactional back-end IT is providing.

In many ways, Shadow IT reflects the kinds of tools they use on their computers at home, and now they are using them at work as well.

We should be clear that we are not advocating for the unrestricted use of Shadow IT as there are risks and stresses that can be placed on the business. For Vorpal, as the business is being run by both the traditional IT and now the Shadow IT, the primary stress is related to additional costs to the company. In other companies, though, Shadow IT is defined as unofficial and secret application development. What we are describing in the above discussion is an enabling environment where IT can provide enough control for safety and the common good, but enough freedom to allow increasingly skilled users to decide how they want to work and what tools they will use.

Question 4: What Are the Characteristics of Innovative Companies?

Innovative companies in today's market follow a pattern. They are more open to working with others. They create internal pressure to change ahead of the market. They are focused more on leveraging technology. Based on research done for this book from a variety of sources, as well as our own experience in working with leading companies in a variety of industries, we have identified the following list of characteristics of innovative companies.

Business Model Innovation–Driven Transformation[8]

Simply put, rather than just seeking cost control and greater efficiencies, companies are exploring the costs and complexities of creating methods to add value to their products and services. They are doing this by embracing what would have once been thought of as on-the-fly experimentation, fast and highly responsive to-market strategies, and near real-time iteration on those experiments that worked.

---

[8] See: Bobby Cameron, "Next Up: The 21st Century CIO: Business Change Agent and Innovator—or Gone," published by Forrester Research Incorporated, December 6, 2007 at: http://www.forrester.com/Research/Document/Excerpt/0,7211,43784,00.html

Increased Use of a Wider Array of Technologies

These companies are spending less on siloed and proprietary applications and are instead embracing a host of new and emerging technologies that have so far been broadly defined as Web 2.0. They are also finding new and innovative uses for these technologies in order to drive business model innovation as a means to create value.

Broader Use of Strategic Partnerships

These companies are more readily able to delineate the core competencies they can use to support a differentiated product set. They are also creating strategic partnerships with companies that possess complementary core capacities in order to enter new markets and put forth differentiated and personalized product offerings.

As these companies are expanding their partner relationships they are also creating network platforms based on open standards in order to facilitate the integration of multiple partner systems into a unified network. As such, they are creating partner ecosystems based on a model of mutual value creation around their products.

Back Office Stability

As we have seen with Vorpal, the addition of a Long Tail sales model onto back-end systems and processes designed to support only mass-market sales creates quite a few issues that need to be worked out. Companies that have overcome these issues have altered their perception of these systems and processes from simply an order-to-pay model based on siloed and IT-centric applications to one where transactional systems and related processes are shared across the enterprise in a meaningful way.

Technology Adoption and Usage Is Being Driven by Non-IT Staff

As we have seen in our discussion of Shadow IT, employees are going to see the utility and empowerment gained by being able to match what they can do at home with what they can do at work. This means these people are going to want to add another IT layer onto the transactional applications in order to change the way they work so they can be better at what they do. These technologies include social networking sites; emergent and existent web services; communications tools such as cell phones, Instant Messaging, RSS feeds, and so forth; and ways to find and catalogue useful information such as tagging and Folksonomy. These people are also going to see the value of using these Web 2.0 technologies and strategies within the company by creating internal mashups, wikis, blogs and so on.

The companies that embrace the use of these technologies will see and work to mitigate the risks they may pose, but they will also recognize the value of allowing and empowering employees to innovate on how they work. The end result will be that these people can provide more value to the company than they ever could before.

IT Staff and Systems Are Far More Integrated into the Company

The IT department is no longer singularly concerned with the function and cost of running and maintaining the IT environment. Instead, technology and IT staff play an active role supporting interactions with customers and partners as well as working within the various disciplines of the business. As such, these people and systems will have reached a point of convergence with the business side of the company so that the gap between business and IT is dramatically less than at other companies. Business-side executives and managers will seem to display an advanced knowledge of IT, its strengths and limitations and how it is integrated to support business processes. In the reverse, IT executives and managers will display a heightened understanding and sense of business goals and the needs of the business as well as understanding their role to support these issues.

Customers as Drivers of Innovation

By using web-based services in a manner that promotes a more personalized degree of interaction with customers these companies are using information gleaned from these interactions to develop new products and product iterations and to create or improve the services they offer around these products. These companies are not simply developing an idea based on what they think a very large number of people might want to buy, but are allowing customers to tell them what they are interested in as well as allowing customers to customize products and services around the experience they are seeking. By doing this, these companies are recognizing and respecting the technical sophistication of their customers and are shifting their online presence from one that is singularly content based to one that is about communication, collaboration, and sharing, so that customers play a defining role in establishing what they are looking for and then are able to make a purchase.

Redefining the Use of Benchmarks

Recognizing that customers have a heightened expectation of the service and experience they are looking for from a company, there is a shift in how Long Tail companies will seek to benchmark their efforts. Rather than rely on industry accepted standards these companies will want to benchmark their performance against the goals and desires of the customer. The customer in turn, is assessing a company's performance based on what they are getting from those companies they perceive to be the best in online sales and services. Therefore, benchmarking is no longer industry-centric, but cuts across industries to develop comparisons based on entities that are perceived to be at the top of the game, such as Google and Amazon.[9]

---

[9] Jeneanne Rae, "Billion Dollar Innovation," published in *Business Week: Service Innovation,* December 7, 2007, at: http://www.businessweek.com/innovate/content/dec2007/id2007127_017956.htm.

Chapter 3 Questions and Analysis

Flowing Toward Synergy

Question 1: How Does the Design of Business Processes Change to Meet the Needs of Long Tail Business Models?

Prior to the previous chapter Jane Moneymaker and her team had been watching almost helplessly as the business appeared to be fracturing on a number of stress points due to the unique demands of the Long Tail. In part, they were in the process of learning that static back-end cost models on their own don't work with dynamic front-end go-to-market models without some help.

As they have sought to create a new and innovative business model Moneymaker and her team have come to realize that what is required is a model that expresses both its IT systems and business processes in a common manner. Basically, the company is in the process of learning how to break down its activities into granular tasks that can be readily reorganized, extended, edited, or reused as and when needed.

To achieve this, Vorpal is putting into practice the concept that a business task must become synonymous with a technology service. The real goal of Service Oriented Architecture is to be the layer that can be seen as a technology integration mechanism for business process redesign and flexibility from the other—interactional—direction. This has been described in a previous section with regard to the Diamond Model.

Primarily this model is a simple explanation of how to link these two different aspects in order to facilitate the fast moving front office activities such as Long Tail markets. Now, though, Vorpal has to take this model to a much more detailed governance model in order to give meaning to the concept of differentiate for advantage, standardize for efficiency. The company is going past merely needing to link disparate IT systems and is seeking to create a new model to explain the much tighter linkage of IT and business processes across a diverse enterprise as well as how to find commonality in order to promote a greater degree of efficiency and standardization even as differentiation and personalization are primary goals.

To start, we have separated out four layers of this new model, which are Personalize, Differentiate, Organize, and Comply.

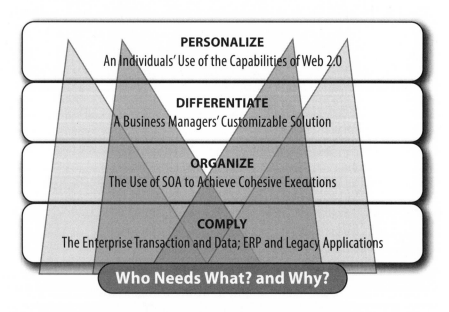

PERSONALIZE
An Individuals' Use of the Capabilities of Web 2.0

DIFFERENTIATE
A Business Managers' Customizable Solution

ORGANIZE
The Use of SOA to Achieve Cohesive Executions

COMPLY
The Enterprise Transaction and Data; ERP and Legacy Applications

Who Needs What? and Why?

Figure Q3-1. The Crown Model

Personalize—As we have explained, there is a shift taking place in the way that people are working, or at least, in the way they want to work. Web 2.0 is opening up myriad opportunities to empower employees in new and different ways; it is allowing people to innovate on how they work, making them far more productive than has been previously possible. Within this shift we have also described the use of Shadow IT and its implications for creating an unstable environment with numerous risks to the company.

Therefore, in order to minimize the risks associated with the use of Shadow IT and enjoy the many benefits of these interactive technologies, it is important to create a framework within which they may be used. In essence, it is the equivalent of allowing for a managed pool of tools from which people can select those that would work best for them.

Users in the Personalize layer may not only be within the enterprise, increasingly users in suppliers or customers will be found in this layer as well. They want to interact with other users and the differentiated offers in the next layer.

Differentiate—This layer is about empowering and creating a framework within which business managers are able to enter new markets and differentiate the product and service offerings and essentially exploit opportunities within the Long Tail. Simply put, this layer deals with the way a business manager organizes all of the aspects necessary to create a market and make a difference.

Primarily, the technologies used to support business tasks at this layer are going to be based on Web 2.0 and related interactional technologies in order to engage with the market and introduce a customizable set of products to consumers. These systems and processes are going to be defined by the ability to be rapidly built and deployed at a relatively low cost by these business managers. Above all the justification is built on the creation of value in the form of additional revenues, market share or margins and the differentiation is therefore the key to these gains.

The critical challenge here, though, is that these solutions must be able to connect in some way and at some time with internal transactional systems and processes in order to meet the necessary goals of back-end operations to support these sales, ensure compliance and security and so forth.

Organize—The organize layer is essentially where the highly distinct personalize and differentiated layers are connected to the back-end transactional systems. Though there may be a lot of movement above, all of that activity is still connected to the necessary back-end support systems and the company is able to gain back the efficiencies of operating as a business rather than fragmenting into numerous entities supporting individual niches. This is where standardization of common processes horizontally across the enterprise is affected. As an example, the product may be different, but the logistics for dispatch are the same and common.

The primary lever is SOA, which is used to achieve cohesive execution of the business processes and systems above and the link to exposed interfaces for transactional processes and systems below. The role of SOA is to act as the enterprise bridge between the interactions and business processes above and the transactional procedures and data below. As such, it can be likened in importance to the role that ERP played in creating a common data model for enterprises.

This is also the layer and Service Oriented Architecture, SOA, the lever where disparate external systems are able to interconnect via a process known as choreography, which refers to the defining of protocols and messages used to exchange information between groups of peers requiring a process or procedure to ensure a predictable outcome. As such, choreography is based on open standards and is defined by its ability to facilitate collaboration with multiple partners in support of a common business goal or task. This allows external partners to connect together to provide a seamless set of capabilities to underpin the market offerings sold through a single partner.

This is also where a company must begin to figure out how to really rethink what they should do to redesign business processes as a synergistic flow of services across the enterprise rather than current siloed procedures.

Comply—This final and bottom layer is the one that most people would be very familiar with because this is where the more traditional systems and processes sit—it is composed of the existing enterprise applications containing ERP, SCM, CRM, and other proprietary applications. These are the systems with their attendant processes that have been the core function of the IT department and are driven by the CFO and CIO around the issues of security, cost, and compliance.

As such, the compliance layer needs to operate in a standardized and predictable manner in order to operate efficiently and fulfill its role to notice, record, and aid the management of transactions.

This governance model must also answer the challenge for better understanding of what is happening in the business spread across its greatly increased numbers and types of market activities. All of which will frequently change. An existing model with general and administration costs allocated on a yearly basis for the enterprise will fail to cope, which is an issue that Vorpal found out in this chapter.

Prior to this chapter Vorpal had a more traditional P&L structure that was located toward the back-end of the organization essentially where Cashtender sits. However, this system wasn't agile enough to be able to keep up with the dynamism and speed of the Long Tail, which was causing Cashtender and Lovecraft to lose visibility with regard to how these new markets and products affected core support services. In the previous chapter Cashtender said he knew that costs are rising for the company, but they were beyond what had been allocated to each product and were for things such as suppliers or the call center.

So what Cashtender and Lovecraft have come to realize is that instead of having larger centrally located P&Ls they needed to design a system of smaller P&Ls handled by the product managers as they engage in each deal in the Differentiate layer. Basically, they would create mini P&Ls around each product or market so they can more directly attribute costs to sales and understand how these smaller sales affect back-end support systems—they will understand the implications of each small and very variable offering within the Long Tail by making sure the product manager running the offerings is in charge of making sure the right costs are covered and allocated.

In much the same way as a previous generation of managers learned to use spreadsheets on PCs, this generation of managers is using enterprise mashups to create many different views of the dynamic and active business.

Because this information is also accessible to the individual product managers they will have a better sense of what is working and how they could improve upon what isn't as they continue to drive new products and markets. Individual business elements can create various forms of content on their own activities while mashups can be used to place any of this content into any combination to obtain either overall or focused views.

Question 2: How Does the Structure of IT Change to Support the Crown Model?

In the past, IT has been all about supporting applications and relatively stable processes centered on cost controls and savings for the back office of the business, which we have described previously as being transactional systems located in the hub of our wagon wheel model.

However, as the drivers of change continue to press companies to transform their business models to include Internet and web supported initiatives similar to the Long Tail, IT is no longer simply IT. It is now a complex intermingling of a number of technologies that can be broadly separated into those that are cost based and those centered on supporting the business' efforts to create value.

An À La Carte Menu of Software

By adopting a Service Oriented Architecture, companies will also be opening up the range of software provisioning options available to them. Decisions can be based on the two criteria inherent in the transactional and interactional technologies, which are cost and value respectively. Decisions can also incorporate the utility, individual needs, and idiosyncrasies of each functional area and their respective technology needs.

For example, as we have noted, the technology and strategies around that technology used by Wunderkind in the Personalize layer are going to be significantly different from those in the Comply layer. This is also true for the Differentiate and Organize layers.

Therefore, CIOs and CTOs must adapt to the idea that they will have to be far more flexible in the way that software is supplied and supported. As such, there are five recognizable and different ways to provision software as is demonstrated by the chart below:

	VALUE PROPOSITION	WHAT IS PROVIDED?	WHERE PROVIDED?	NATURE OF RELATIONSHIP	TYPE OF EXPENDITURE	EXPENDITURE ELEMENTS	AGILITY
SAAS	Designed as a utility for web delivery with all elements provided by the SaaS operator	Hosted set of services	Delivered on site via the web using a standard browser as a client	Client buys a service on a utility basis with no expectation of individual service elements	"Pay as you use"; no long-term commitment; often no minimum notice period	Initial service deployment charge with ongoing user-based subscription charge	Designed as a highly configurable application
ASP	Service provider of 3rd-party remote-access software generally via Web from a hosted facility	A hosted application	Delivered to user via local client software from a remote-hosted environment	Client rents or leases use of 3rd-party software running at the ASP's remote-hosting site	"Pay as you use"; generally with no long-term commitment but with a minimum notice period	Subscription for license use plus charging for number of users and amount of use	Customized deployment but limited application flexibility
MANAGED SERVICE	External service provider that continuously manages & supports software for which it is contracted	Customized services	Delivered on site but could be provided by on/off site resources	Client generally buys in 3rd-party software (may be internally developed) and separately contracts with an external service provider	Periodic payments against a multi-year agreement	Software license and upgrades; maintenance; hardware; managed service fees	Customized solution
BPO	External service responsible for specific business functions like HR or financials & linked technical functions	A customized service	Internal/external resources on/off site, specific to supporting the process	Client contracts with external service provider on basis of everything required to ensure business functionality is maintained	Long-term fixed contract with periodic payments on a fixed cost over 3 or more years	In addition to fixed cost and payment, can be shared risk-reward to improve performance or reduce costs	Generally fully customizable
TRADITIONAL	Software vendor product that bundles required functionality into a package	A product	On premise software; deployment as part of client IT estate	Customer or vendor with high degree of "lock-in" and commitment from the customer	Capital intensive investment with annual license cost and upgrade investments	Software license; implementation; integration; maintenance; hardware; training; support	Limit with the package

Figure Q3-2: Menu of Software Provisioning Options

IT will still have the traditional systems and methods of provisioning them as is indicated in Figure Q3-2, but they will also have all of these other options that could be applied depending on the situation and who will be using them.

For example, Wunderkind and other members of the sales and marketing team may prefer a Software as a Service (SaaS) option, but their activities are going to have to be captured and recorded in an automated way. This may mean that software is provided via ASP (Application Service Provider). The Comply layer could maintain its traditional vendor relationships or it could shift to some other method. For example, are billing or payroll core competencies of Vorpal's? If not, then why not eliminate the responsibilities and cost of ownership of these systems by using a solution provided by a BPO (Business Processing Organization).

In all, these decisions can be driven by cost, value, function, and so forth. moving IT from seeking ownership of solutions to perform well recognized functions for the back office to one where there are multiple methods and sources to choose from, and that can be combined in a number of ways depending on who is driving its use. Agility will finally begin to look like a realizable proposition.

Changing Relationships

Now that IT is a driver both for cost and value, altering its role within the enterprise, its relationships throughout the company will also be changed. The most obvious and important role will be that between the CIO and the CEO as is expressed in the previous chapter by the way in which Josh Lovecraft and Moneymaker interact and her reliance on his skills and expertise to better understand how technology can support the business. Basically, Lovecraft and Moneymaker have defined their relationship as a strategic partnership.

However, in the real world there are a number of challenges as these two titles alter the nature of their relationship. Not the least of which is the divide created by a lack of understanding on the CIO's part with regard to strategic business issues. CEOs commonly lack understanding of the business impact that IT can have for the company. Therefore, communication and increasing the scope of what each title has knowledge of is necessary.

This is a worthwhile endeavor, as transitioning this relationship as well as the role of IT will have a number of strategic benefits:

- IT can become a strategic center supporting value creation as well as being a center for cost control
- IT will play a role increasing productivity as well as transforming business processes for customers, suppliers, and employees
- Web 2.0 under the guidance of IT will better enhance opportunities for communication and collaboration across the enterprise
- And IT's value will extend across the enterprise as it never has before

The CIO's role will not be the only one affected. The CTO will play a larger part in the development, acquisition, and operation of new technology products and services in what is a much more diverse IT environment that includes transactional and interactional systems as well as the integration of partner systems on shared platforms.

And the CIO, CTO, and IT staff will spend more time with business managers across all functions, helping to fine tune and develop solutions that best meet and support business needs. Not only will this work to ensure that IT systems and technologies are as standardized and cost effective as possible, this new role will also now include understanding and implementing the art of the possible in terms of new business-creating technologies rather than being limited to just the current state of IT.

These people will support experimentation, innovation, create mashups, enable entire ecosystems of partners, and more. They will be more than tech geeks, as these people will also have an understanding of marketing, HR, finance, customer service, product differentiation, compliance, and every other functional unit of the enterprise in order to better understand how technology can extend and support those capabilities. Also, they will be working with increasingly technically savvy users and managers who will demand more from them.

Summing Up

Supporting the Crown Model and the new opportunities created by the Internet, the Web, and related technologies requires a rethinking of the technologies that constitute IT, as well as the relationship with and role of IT with the rest of the enterprise.

No longer is IT's role encapsulated in maintaining and supporting back-office systems. Rather, it is expanding to include a wide range and ever-growing number of new technologies in order to support value creation. And with this change has come the need to reevaluate the relationship a business has with technology as well as the people that support that technology.

Question 3: How Can SOA Be Used as a Tool for Business Transformation?

When we look at the transformation that Vorpal has undergone we can see that it is a fairly dramatic one. And underscoring this change has been the use of the concepts and technologies associated with Service Oriented Architecture to enable the company to build an adaptable business model that will allow it to engage in the Long Tail.

As such, Vorpal has taken the current technology-driven perception of SOA as primarily an integrator of disparate technologies to one where it can be viewed as an architected approach to business change. They have in fact laid out a course for building out a next generation of architecture that transcends current IT-centric notions of what an architecture is about by changing it to an architecture for business by creating converging links between business processes, technology (transactional and interactional), and the network.

What this means is that the company is creating an architecture based around the interactive roles of these three elements. All three are important to the smooth functioning of the company—front-end and back-end as well as the Organize layer of the Crown Model—and they must fit together in a prescribed manner in order to create a functioning whole.

This architecture model also means that Vorpal is recognizing that the role of the network is more than just an efficient infrastructure for transporting data. Rather, it is a platform for the delivery of a rich portfolio of services, data, voice, and video across the enterprise as well as to partners and customers. It is the one thing that touches everything to enable the delivery of new services to the marketplace. In this they are recognizing the fundamental relationship between the Internet and the Web in creating this combined capability. It is similar to the realization that client/server technology was the capability to support a new generation of business tools around ERP.

And perhaps the best part of this transformation is that it incorporates the back office, transactional IT systems that it already had, rather than requiring the company to purchase and integrate a new set of costly and time consuming solutions to match its new to-market model.

However, as we have seen, this was not easily accomplished as the company did what most companies would do, which is to look for the revenue in the new markets first before doing the necessary work of business model innovation. So what they quite literally did was place highly adaptive technologies—Web 2.0, mashups, web services, and so forth—onto an IT infrastructure that was anything but able to cope. This infrastructure is designed for the relatively slow changing and fixed enterprise application environment. The result is that the transactional IT systems where stability and integrity is prized got in the way of the company's ability to manage the interactive, dynamic markets and offers of the Long Tail sales.

This was evident in Chapter 2, but what is now equally as evident is that here in Chapter 3 the company is using the concepts of SOA to better understand how to build an adaptive infrastructure to match the technologies that enable the Long Tail. Rather than a series of siloed applications, the company's IT infrastructure and related processes are being turned into services at the Connection level in SOA that are better able to serve the goals of the business; especially when those goals are in a constant state of change such as in the Long Tail where speed to market and agility are critical differentiators.

In many ways one could think of this in terms of the Internet, which is architected in a manner that facilitates a massive amount of function and innovation with an underlying infrastructure that is adaptable to whatever is placed on it. Routers and servers could care less if an IP packet is transmitting video, an email, a web page, or anything else because the infrastructure is tuned out to those kinds of specifics. There is no Internet for video, or for email, or for any other function and application. It is an end-to-end solution that passes information in a standard and open format to where it needs to go. Let the end users sort out how the applications run and the nature of the data.

SOA accomplishes much the same thing in that no matter the software being used or the use it is being put to, data and function are able to be transported across the enterprise, or to customers, or partners, or other web services, and so on. For Vorpal, SOA doesn't care whether they are selling popcorn poppers or waffle makers, because what it is doing is providing a scalable, reusable, secure, reliable, and robust end-to-end means to support whatever the business need is.

Chapter 4 Questions and Analysis

Moneymaker and Facebook

Question 1: What is Mesh Collaboration and How Does It Differ from Previous Generations of Collaboration?

In the previous chapter, Jane begins to recognize the value of a new sort of collaboration. Of course, the idea of working together is a concept as old as human labor itself. The key here is the new *form*—mesh collaboration.

Simply put, the mesh is an open, unpredictable, emergent form of collaboration created by Web 2.0. Mesh collaboration exploits all the capabilities of this brave new Web—such as blogs, social networking, wikis, RSS feeds, and tagging—to harness the collective power of more people and more information.

The folks at Vorpal have begun to appreciate a new set of competencies that initially sound more like games than business tools. They're learning how to plug into a network and start up a massively powerful engine for creating business relationships. They're engaging in mesh collaboration—and this requires a fundamental paradigm shift.

Matrix Working

First let's examine the concept of mesh collaboration and how it differs from the current form of working called matrix working that arose from the capabilities that PC networking technologies introduced. Matrix working was itself an innovation. By changing the structure of work by freeing people from direct hierarchical management and centralized systems of departmental mini or mainframe applications. The advent of the PC created a series of clients that could each collect and consolidate data from many different servers, and allowed the individual to do their own work in their own way, subject only to the structure of the application. Together with personalized applications, such as word processing, this enabled individuals to handle their specialized tasks for a variety of different people and processes—the so-called ability to work in a matrix of people and applications. Further enabled by email and other information sharing mechanisms, communication has increasingly flowed across the enterprise, not just up and down.

However, one of the key aspects of matrix working is that the scope of the matrix is limited and contained to only the applications and people that are known in the various systems and directory structures. Matrix working is essentially a tool for improving working practices and efficiency both internally and between people who already know each other and share the same applications.

At heart, it's still a very traditional data-centric or transaction-oriented environment where relationships between people and systems are "managed." The relationships can be described as predetermined, defined, and limited to a prescribed body of known information. It's fundamentally a computer-centric view. Workers perform specific, specialized tasks within an environment that's deliberately isolated from users outside the enterprise with a few exceptions such as email and Internet access.

The closed matrix follows a model of interaction that can be summed up as "write and send." The tools, unless designed to promote collaboration for a selected community—word processing documents, emails, spreadsheets, and presentations—are limited in their potential for collaboration. In fact, most personal productivity suites assume that individuals will not be working together to create a document. Instead, they labor individually and, eventually, merge their respective efforts. This model has not changed since the original computer mainframes in the 1960s. In fact, it's not that much different from the age of paper. In this environment, collaboration often means pulling up your chair next to your colleague so you can look at the same screen. We call matrix working "weak collaboration," as it is based on a model where collaboration was added as an afterthought. The limitations are most clearly seen in the blitz of emails as individuals struggle to find answers to their issues. As business change and events happen faster and faster, the increased email volume is becoming close to unbearable for many people.

Infinite Collaboration

Web 2.0 opens up a better future as it was designed from the start to support and enable people to work together collaboratively in any combination of predetermined or ad hoc relationships as a situation demands.

The Internet has created a "Network of Everything," a multi-dimensional, overlapping grid of connections of technology, people, information, language, thought, and culture that stretches well beyond the firewalls of the enterprise. This affect is known technically as a Mesh Network. Armed with the mechanisms of Web 2.0, users are empowered for a new way of working, which we refer to as "strong collaboration," that is both dynamic and far more powerful than matrix working. Strong collaboration is an open, proactive form of problem solving that uses modern collaboration tools to cast ideas onto the network so the natural human forces of curiosity, competition, and social connection draws together the right combination of people, resources, and content to attack each particular issue.

Today's workers resist the idea that their technological reach should be restricted. They have different expectations of personal privacy, which can cause problems for enterprises when they bring this behavior to work. In their personal lives they've grown used to exploring the infinite mesh of Web 2.0 and use tools like smartphones, that can play music and retrieve emails as well as enable calls, and social networking. Not surprisingly, they expect these capabilities in their professional lives as well. Like Hugo, they grab the best tools at their disposal—no matter whether or not they're sanctioned by company IT. Frequently, their direct managers will appreciate the quality and effectiveness of their work and encourage the use of such tools in their department.

Hugo uses Instant Messaging, Facebook, Wikipedia, marketing blogs, and an IP phone to create relationships, learn, and generate sales leads. Jane realizes that Hugo has tapped into something powerful so why can't the company borrow some of these lessons? Hugo in fact accesses the expertise in people's brains that has yet to be, or, if it is external to the company, will never be captured. He is also able to access and use traditional internal content and knowledge management databases.

This opens up an infinite number of possible connections with people and content. It also opens up exposure to new risks that must be carefully managed. Social networking sites like Facebook and MySpace, and others that use the Open Social standard help us find like-minded people—no matter where they are. A programmer in the Silicon Valley can discover that he's working on the same problem as others in Europe and India. In business, the role of social networking is more than finding and recording connections; it's finding the mesh of people, ideas, data, content, and other things that are useful. These clusters can collaborate and create synergy. They become nodes in the mesh. The more connections they make, the stronger they become.

People use blogs to demonstrate their topics of expertise, others use blogs to find a person who continually communicates on and around the topics that interest them. The blogger will usually provide links to other blogs and content, this becoming akin to their guide or mentor on a selected topic. Blogs often help to signpost the existence of communities with the same interests and are compiled and built with tagging to allow community members to find what and who they need to know. Shared working environments like wikis help them cooperate to complete a task.

The next generation of technology is all about moving toward "people-centric" environments where people are placed at the center of activities. They rest on the simple idea that technologies should enable collaboration between people, not limit it. In addition to people and mesh connectivity, it should allow them to choose the services they want and use them according to their separate or joint needs for tools. The old model was essentially transactional; the new one is interactive. For example, new office suites such as Google Apps involve multiple people in creating content in a single document that everyone can edit. Collaboration is an integral part of the process from the beginning.

In a sense, this is the same change as took place with word processing in the late 1980s to early 1990s, when the function was provided from a central mini-computer application. As more and more people started to work in the PC network environment they needed to find word processing solutions that were based on a PC. People are today looking for a new style of word processing that fits the environment they are now working in—the Web 2.0 and Mesh Working.

These changes can dramatically alter how we do business. Say a company needs to write a new user manual for a software release. In the past, a few members of the team wrote a draft that was emailed back and forth through various parts of the company. Everybody suggested revisions in "track changes" mode. Too often, somebody used the wrong version with the unfortunate result of two separate revisions that had to be reconciled. It was an example of weak collaboration.

Now imagine the same team engaging in strong collaboration. For the next software release, the company uses Web 2.0 and works on a single version of a document. The document is available online and everybody can edit the same version simultaneously. Delay and confusion are minimized.

For specialized sections the team can add external collaborators thus expanding the expertise to embrace external resources as well as internal colleagues.

Weak collaboration is data-centric and relies on a "push" model to send content specific people. By contrast, strong collaboration is based upon a "pull" model and takes advantage of tools like RSS feeds, social networking, blogs, and communities of interest that feed information to people interested in that particular subject. You define your interest and relevant information and contacts flow toward you.

Why does this matter? Twenty years ago, most of the knowledge we needed to do our jobs was kept in our heads; now only a small fraction of the required knowledge lies in our existing mental database. No, we haven't dulled our intellects. Rather, the amount of available information that could affect our work has risen dramatically thanks to forces like the tech revolution, globalization, and the Long Tail. We need to be open to new and unknown connections with people and content to exploit the mesh, to capture as much of it as possible and turn our labor into something greater than the sum of its parts.

Question 2: What Are the Mechanisms of Web 2.0 and How Do They Support Mesh Collaboration?

How to attain the collaboration described above? Look to find your local version of Hugo Wunderkind. S/He lives in a world of the infinite mesh: Instant Messaging, Facebook, Wikipedia, blogs, IP phone, and multiple screens. It's no coincidence that they are so effective at their jobs. Web 2.0 provides powerful tools for mesh collaboration and provides access to a world of people and ideas that make workers like Wunderkind smarter and more productive.

The New Web

Many people toss around the term "Web 2.0" without a clear idea of what it means. Admittedly, it is an amorphous, ever-evolving concept that defies precise definition. This lack of fixed definition is deliberate as the whole point of Web 2.0 is that it continually adapts and changes around the way people want to use it. Still, this movement exhibits a few fundamental traits that make it distinct from the earlier generation of the Web.

What is Web 2.0? Some people focus on the mechanisms of blogs, wikis, social networking, tagging, RSS, and other feeds as a definition. But these are just tools. The bigger news is their transforming effect on the people who use them. According to O'Reilly media, the company that invented the name Web 2.0, the essence of the term can be captured in eight core patterns:

- Harnessing Collective Intelligence: Web 2.0 creates an "architecture of participation" that uses network effects and algorithms to produce software that improves as more people use it.
- Data Is the Next "Intel Inside": Web 2.0 relies on unique data sources that are hard to recreate. It becomes the "Intel Inside" for this era in which data has become as important as function.
- Innovation in Assembly: These platforms foster innovation. The remixing of data and services creates new opportunities and markets.
- Rich User Experiences: These platforms combine the best of desktop and online software to create rich user experiences that surpass traditional web pages.
- Software Above the Level of a Single Device: Software spans Internet-connected devices and builds on the growing pervasiveness of online experience.

- Perpetual Beta: These technologies move away from old models of software development in favor of online, continuously updated, Software as a Service (SaaS) models.
- Leveraging the Long Tail: These technologies can profitably tap into niche markets through the low-cost economics and broad reach enabled by the Internet.
- Lightweight Models and Cost-Effective Scalability: These lightweight business- and software-development models help to build products and businesses quickly and cost effectively.

These technologies do more than entertain and inform; they actively draw people into the conversation. There's an implicit ethos of participation. The service improves as more people use it. It acts as a broker that connects people to each other and harnesses the collective intelligence of users.

Tapping into the infinite mesh of users is the key to success in the era of Web 2.0. What's the best way to do that? Let's examine the tools of Web 2.0.

The Tools

Web 2.0 provides A few key building blocks for collaboration. Social networking, Blogs, wikis, RSS and tags all provide vehicles for "strong' collaboration."

Blogs

A blog is a signpost of sorts. It tells the global community about who you are, what you do, what you know, and who you know. It's useful for finding people and being found. People read these blogs, subscribe to them, write responses, and share items of mutual interest. They find each other by seeing who made comments. They provide URLs to other sites. They provide a locus for an online community united by common interests.

The term blog is a contraction of "web log." The main purpose of blogs is to communicate to broad audiences. They are a "one-to-many" medium somewhat like broadcasting. These informal musings can be surprisingly powerful tools for business. Many companies find that a good and highly interactive blog can attract more unique users—first time visitors—than the traditional content downloads on their Web 1.0 site.

Social Networking

Social networking has been widely perceived as a way for people—and especially young ones—to mingle online. This perception is certainly valid but it obscures the potential business value. Like a blog, social networking establishes connections between people to create a framework structure for a community. These people have access to a variety of tools in the form of mini applications or services that they can choose to use to manage their activities within and between the members of the community. Social networking creates value through providing a central feed that tells you what the people you have selected to be friends with are doing. Once you find one like-minded person, you can connect to them, map out a web of other people with similar interests, and be constantly aware of their activities.

These networks are invaluable tools inside and outside the enterprise. Within the company, managers can gain valuable insights into how their employees are interacting and using various technologies. Outside the enterprise, it can help locate potential business partners, customers, suppliers, employees, and people with expertise. We'll explore this phenomenon in more depth later.

Wikis

Wikis sprang from the mind of Ward Cunningham in the mid-1990s as he sought a better way to communicate and create shareable content. The wiki is simply a web page that anyone can edit. This simple mechanism has become a profoundly powerful platform for collaboration. Wikis are constantly expanding repositories of knowledge. Better yet, they don't require the creators to master HTML. Only a few markup commands, or formatting tags, are needed to organize the material. Users are free to add new material, edit, and even erase entire passages.

Wikis have found much use by teams of researchers, software developers, technical support reps, and others who want to capture and share knowledge.

Wikis often follow a few common patterns:

- Content-based wikis enable communities of people to jointly create and refine content that's of interest to them. The prime example of this pattern is Wikipedia.
- Process-focused wikis help to track the progress of a project—the construction of a building, for instance, or new software.
- Communities of interest employ wikis to share information about a particular subject such as a business opportunity.
- Ease-of-use wikis take advantage of the simplicity of wikis to allow people to build web sites.

RSS

RSS refers to "RDF Site Summary," "Rich Site Summary" or, more colloquially, "Really Simple Syndication." These are web feeds that alert users to "news" of interest such as updates to blog entries, web sites, headlines, or podcasts. These automated feeds enable people to keep up with their favorite web sites without checking them manually. An RSS feed contains either a summary of content from an associated web site or the full text. Content can be read using software called an "RSS reader," "feed reader," or an "aggregator." Essentially, this is like ordering a menu of content to be delivered to you.

The business value is obvious: users are notified whenever critical information is published. Externally it can be used much the same way as an example in the freight forwarding industry for providing general notifications of changes or specific notification of events.

Tagging—People-Oriented Data Taxonomies

A tag is a keyword that is assigned to a piece of information such as a picture, article, or video clip. This subjective description enables classification of the content based on these keywords. Unlike conventional data classification taxonomies assigned by IT management, tagging is an informal process that allows users to evaluate information and decide what they would call it in a manner that is meaningful to human reuse.

The same content may have multiple tags from any number of people, depending on their interests. All of these tags can be in use at the same time, offering a degree of flexibility and syndication that goes beyond conventional data management, but is very in tune with the way people refer to any object in the real world: for example, car, auto, automobile, voiture, and so forth.

Imagine a user perusing a blog on Service Oriented Architecture. The list of associated tags might include services, architecture, standards, etc. A reader could select the tag on "standards" and immediately find an index of all the content that has been tagged as such by other users. More importantly, the content found would usually have other tags such as Object Management Group, OMG, and this would enable various strings to be followed to build a complete picture or just to focus on a selected aspect. This people-oriented method of managing content is called "Folksonomy," to distinguish it from the conventional "Taxonomy" approach.

Tagging provides a missing piece to other Enterprise 2.0 applications: it organizes information to support ad-hoc, people-oriented interactions. These demand increasing amounts of information, often from external sources. It thus fosters a very different form of collaboration.

Communications

Other new technologies enable real-time collaboration. Web conferencing allows collaborators to have live virtual meetings via their computer screens. Teleconferencing allows entire teams to have face-to-face meetings with other teams thousands of miles away. Instant Messaging and text messaging keeps them in touch around the clock no matter where they are. Services such as Twitter allow people to stay hyper-connected with updates about their whereabouts and doings. Telepresence is a virtual presence experience that uses advanced visual, audio, and interactive technologies to create an "in person" meeting over the converged IP network.

Summing Up

One of the most powerful aspects of Web 2.0 technologies is their ability to harness so-called "network effects." As more and more people contribute knowledge and add structure, their collective contributions make the knowledge more useful to everyone involved. The challenge is to decide where and how to harness these effects in your business. Capgemini has identified seven specific clusters of new technologies that can be defined in such a manner that it is possible to test the statements directly on your business managers.

- **You Experience:** New generation of user interface technologies and Internet-based collaboration platforms. An individualized experience for the user to connect freely to the outside world to act, interact, collaborate, co-create, learn, and share knowledge. A new generation of technology with a myriad of features that change buying and communication habits.
- **From Transaction to Interaction:** Organizations and individuals in a steady, continuous rhythm of learning, creating, and collaborating. Creating new value through business innovation with markets, players and consumers constantly shifting position. Global "open" markets where information on what is for sale, and by whom, vastly increases the competition from the level experienced in existing localized "closed" markets.
- **Process "on the fly":** Processes assembled "on the fly" by orchestrating the building blocks of underlying services.

Organizations will need to change their processes in near real time to quickly reflect and accommodate changes in the business ecosystem. The underlying information systems that support and enable these processes must consist of fine-grained, configurable services that can freely be composed and orchestrated into new solutions.

- **Thriving on Data:** Increasingly, the secret to success is how to read, and react, to the succession of events that occur. Events are opportunities to make money by optimizing a given situation; or to lose money, by being unable to identify and manage a problem. The call for more "interaction" is the basis for rapidly assembling information, opinions, and then making a decision. It also involves many more people within the organization, as they will all be operational consumers *and* suppliers of intelligence.

- **Sector as a Service:** Helping organizations focus on the differentiation by providing standard and non-differentiating business services "on tap." This is achieved through little-customized implementations of standard software or through the generation of systems out of reusable industry reference models. Delivering the business services through a SaaS (Software as a Service) approach is just one further step toward supplying integrated business services—including processes—as an in-sourced or out-sourced utility.

- **Invisible Infostructure:** Using virtualization and grid technologies to deliver infrastructural services—including all facilities to exchange and process (inter) company information—as a commoditized, preferably almost invisible utility. Eventually, even core business services will merge into it, creating a true "business infrastructure." An invisible infostructure captures and supplies information as if it were via the ether.

- **Open Standards Fundament:** Enables boundaryless information flow between all players in the business ecosystem. Open standards do not only pertain to "horizontal" requirements for data exchange formats, authentication, and security, but also pertain more and more to "vertical" requirements that address the business tasks and rules of a specific sector. Furthermore, globalization and regulatory compliance demand more standardization of architectural and development methodologies and of professional certification.

Question 3: How Is the Increasing Sophistication and Power of Consumer IT Creating Demand for Better Collaboration in the Workplace?

Hugo Wunderkind represents a familiar figure in the modern enterprise. He's a young person steeped in consumer technology and thus feels hamstrung by the confines of corporate computing, which he doesn't recognize as relevant to, or even part of his world.

This is a very real dilemma for modern businesses: the revolution in consumer tech has produced a new generation of "Digital Natives." These people instinctively turn to the infinite mesh whenever they want to communicate or learn (these "Digital Natives" are described in more detail in another question below). They rely on devices to automate every aspect of their lives. Their iPod doubles as a running stopwatch. They use their smartphone to check the weather or find recipes. Their parents used dictionaries, phone books, and phones. They use Google, Facebook, and Instant Messaging. Technology keeps them connected around the clock—and this trend is driving major changes in the workplace.

Complex problems require strong collaboration. Merely talking to people by phone or email isn't enough; workers demand more advanced methods of keeping track of each other's actions simultaneously. Consumer technology provides this capability in our personal lives and is forcing the enterprise to follow suit.

Consumer Tech

The consumer revolution has forged a dramatic shift in the way we live. Obviously, the biggest change has been the explosive growth of the Web and communications devices. Now the Web is the "go to" destination for virtually every aspect of our lives—socialization, communication, shopping, news, research, and so on. The modern person is supported throughout the day by communications devices like Blackberries, Treos, laptops, and cell phones. We spend most of our waking lives in touch and online. This change has created whole new markets and is the basis for Long Tail markets, as with these tools individuals become more and more discriminating in finding exactly what they want to buy.

This revolution, however, has created a fundamental disconnect between our personal and professional lives. People are employees of Enterprise 1.0 by day and citizens of Web 2.0 at night. This is a recipe for frustration.

This dilemma is captured by a web slide show titled "Meet Charlotte" about a fictional knowledge worker.

- At home, Charlotte uses Google to filter the Internet. At work, she has to remember where everything is because their enterprise systems lack searchability.
- At home, if she misses a favorite TV or radio show she can catch up with TiVo or a podcast. At work, missing a meeting obliges her to search a document repository for minutes—if someone bothered to take them.
- At home she keeps up with dozens of friends via Facebook. At work, she has to wait until the annual industry conference to catch up on networking.
- At home, she can see what friends are up to via YouTube and Flickr. At work, she might not even know what the person in the next cubicle does all day.

- At home, she visits blogs and chat rooms to keep abreast of hobbies and personal interests and might have a network of hundreds of people. At work, her network might be limited to handful of business contacts.

In short, the company firewall, whether a real and deliberate barrier preventing actual access or a physiological one creating a "them and us" mentality, represents a great divide in capabilities. These workers know the power of technology in their personal lives. In their professional lives, where they spend the majority of their waking hours, they're confined by the enterprise.

The Vision

Now imagine the prototypical Enterprise 2.0 worker. In an ideal world, this worker should feel his professional tools are on par—or better—than his consumer ones.

This vision is spelled out in another web slideshow titled "Meet Charlie,"[10] which is summarized as follows: A few years ago, he relied on desktop tools like Microsoft Outlook, Explorer, Excel spreadsheets, and Word documents. Now he and his workmates use Google mail, documents and spreadsheets, and BaseCamp—all via Firefox browser. They rely on web-based "social software" that takes a "bottom up" approach.

These people have been unchained from the enterprise, literally and figuratively. They can work from remote locations and assemble "virtual teams" of the best talent no matter where they might be located. This person might not even have met his boss in person. They both blog about their doings and subscribe to each other via an RSS feed. They use BaseCamp and assign projects and manage them online. These systems are so easy to learn that they don't require days of orientation; everybody can just sign up and get to work. They collaborate on wikis. They tag bookmarks on the Intranet and everybody

---

[10] This slide presentation can be found at: http://www.slideshare.net/slgavin/meet-charlie-what-is-enterprise20

else can see them. They provide updates with blogs, podcasts, and RSS feeds so everybody can keep tabs on what teammates are up to. By using video, they have meaningful face-to-face meetings from miles away and easily swap and comment on the same document, because they all can access it at the same time. They can find out how they would prefer to be contacted and when via presence-based services. All members of the team have LinkedIn profiles and use the social networking to find business contacts.

These people no longer see the yawning chasm between their technological capabilities in their home and work lives. In fact, the two have become intermeshed with each other. There are profound implications in this in terms of further removing geographic working limitations or reducing travel and encouraging home working for Green reasons.

In ensuing chapters, we'll learn more about how to move closer to this vision.

Question 4: What Is Enterprise 2.0 and How Is Mesh Collaboration Different in the Enterprise?

Enterprise 2.0 is the application of Web 2.0 technologies and practices inside a company. Its value isn't attained by simply buying a bunch of new technological tools. It also requires a fundamental shift in attitudes and working habits.

Mesh-style strong collaboration, one of the most important byproducts of Enterprise 2.0, faces unique challenges. It must integrate an array of existing technologies and weave "silo" applications into the new network. It must balance the freeness of the new Web 2.0 with respect for existing data integrity, security, confidentiality, and compliance. In addition to the technical challenges it also faces "human" ones. It requires cultural change in the enterprise, including openness, a new spirit of teamwork, and a move away from hierarchy. Managers must strike a delicate balance between leadership and getting out of the way.

The closed environment of the enterprise also offers some initial advantages, particularly a sense of teamwork and trust. This familiarity will ease the transition and allow established teams to find the benefits of Enterprise 2.0 for themselves while working with existing colleagues.

Web 2.0 Leading to Enterprise 2.0

What is Enterprise 2.0? Simply put, it's the arrival of Web 2.0 in the working environment. Dr. Andrew P. McAfee, Associate Professor at Harvard Business School, popularized the term in a 2006 paper in the *MIT Sloan Management Review,* titled "Enterprise 2.0: The Dawn of Emergent Collaboration." McAfee argued that this trend would "usher in a new era by making both the practices of knowledge work and its outputs more visible."

Enterprise 2.0 technologies create so-called network effects. In other words, they create synergy between users so their combined efforts are greater than the sum of their individual endeavors. The more people contribute, the more valuable the resource becomes and the more people want to participate. Dr. McAfee has summed up these contributions with the acronym, SLATES:

Search—facilities that help users to find content

Links—encouraging users to make connections between different pieces of content

Authoring—ability to elicit input from users

Tags—accepting users' annotations concerning the meaning and topic of content items

Extensions—inferring interest and taste from past behavior

Signals—the ability to notify users of new content

Still, Enterprise 2.0 is more complex than it appears. It's not simply a wholesale importation of wikis, blogs, and social networking into the enterprise. Those who have tried this without paying attention to the working environment as well have generally been disappointed with the results. It is an attitude change in the values and management style of how a business works.

There have been earlier attempts to improve various aspects of operating effectiveness, but all of these improvements have been internal, IT-centric approaches providing "fixed" additions, rather than the people-centric approaches of Web 2.0 supporting both an internal and external environment, which allow constant adaptation and change as internal users and external customers, suppliers, partners, etc. learn how they want to use the capabilities.

Now a new generation of Enterprise 2.0 technologies are earning a place in the workplace and offering useful "dashboards" on the enterprise systems. The new arrivals include mashups, widgets, social networking, RSS feeds, AJAX-based user interfaces, and the like. Some analysts foresee a new generation of much lighter web-oriented ERP extensions that will truly allow Enterprise 2.0 to take off.

However, for all of the desire to adopt these new practices one key question has to be addressed: how will these structured systems for information be reconciled with the freer form of working and collaboration?

The Bull's-Eye of Social Networking

The following graphic demonstrates the different types of relationships that people are able to form as a result of collaborative working.

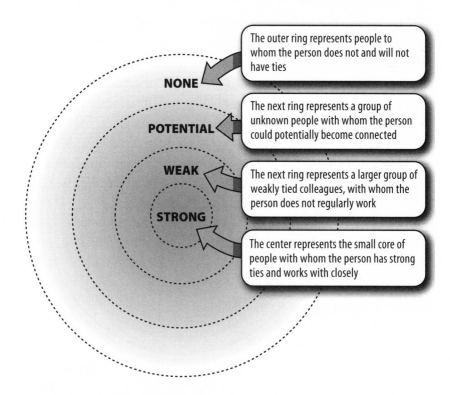

Figure Q4-1: The Bull's-Eye of Networking

In the zone closest to the center are the people with whom this worker has particularly strong ties. McAfee describes them as long-term colleagues and work partners.

The next circle contains those who are "weakly tied" to the worker—people who she knows more casually such as former colleagues.

The third circle of people represents those who could potentially be valuable collaborators, but remain unknown to the subject. These people may be inside or outside the organization—perhaps a fellow programmer in another part of your company who's grappling with the same software problem, or a manager in another company who's found a solution to a problem that vexes both of you.

In the outermost ring of the bull's-eye are people with whom the worker has nothing in common, even if she were fully aware of them.

Web 2.0 technologies can be useful in each ring, but some are more appropriate to a particular ring. At the core, within the network of strong ties, a wiki helps you get your work done better with less redundancy. The team can work on documents without emailing them back and forth.

At the second level, McAfee sees social-networking software, such as Enterprise Facebook, as the most appropriate forum.

In the third circle, the corporate blog offers the best method of developing potential ties. If members of work teams are encouraged to blog and the company has appropriate search capability, people can find items of mutual interest.

At the outermost circle, McAfee sees prediction markets—a technique that aggregates the choices of large numbers of people to produce an answer to a question—playing a role.

Companies must pick the right tool for each particular circle. They must ask themselves a few basic questions: What are we trying to do? Are we trying to help strongly tied people collaborate better? Or create new connections between strangers? Only then will they effectively match each particular network with the appropriate technology.

Summing Up

But social networking is only the beginning. For business, the key is to turn the mesh of connections into the mesh of things that are useful to you. Tools like Facebook may help to establish these connections initially. But they might not necessarily be the best mechanisms for working together once these connections are formed.

The goal is to select from a range of technologies those that help capitalize on the connections formed by social networking.

Chapter 5 Questions and Analysis

Scaling Strong Collaboration

Question 1: How Can a Culture of Emergent Collaboration Be Encouraged?

Many global forces are at work driving a change in how we can collaborate. We have laptops, mobile devices, web-based applications, wireless networks, internet video conferencing, collaborative software, and VPN network security. But technology itself is not enough; cultural change is required as well. This is a story that is similar to when the PC first appeared and how it led to a similar need to change the working environment. This included backing off of the heavily managed hierarchical structure in favor of the increased self-management of matrix working. It's not so different to relax certain restrictions still further. Why even call them restrictions? Because current IT systems and data integrity demands them and may well still require them, but only for the internal back-office enterprise functions.

The shift from matrix working in the back office to mesh collaboration in the front office represents a fundamental shift in our ways of working. History shows that paradigm shifts are disruptive events. In fact, changing habits about anything—diet, exercise, relationships, you name it—is very hard and requires conscious effort.

Yet change we must. Collaboration is the wave of the future. According to Gartner Dataquest, the average worker in 1985 spent about 70% of his time working alone and about 30% collaborating with a group. By 2010, the average worker will spend only about 20% of his time laboring solo and 80% with the group.

How do we nurture this culture of emergent collaboration? This requires a variety of measures ranging from specific inducements to subtle encouragement. Sometimes it means just getting out of the way and letting people figure it out themselves.

Tips

Here are some general principles that will help encourage collaboration:

- Let go. Giving up control runs counter to the values that have governed IT for years. That said, many companies are finding that letting go of control brings far more beneficial effects than negative ones.
- Let people find roles. Mesh networking requires a different view of roles and responsibilities. Professor Ann Majchrzak of the University of Southern California has identified 12 roles played by people in these networks. Some are shapers, others connectors, and some gadflies. People will naturally step into these roles; in fact, they often assume these roles in conversation. The trick is to convince them to articulate these functions in the collaborative environment. Who will be your company's Hugo for the next market?
- Keep a limited amount of hierarchy. Contrary to popular belief, there are few open source movements that have done away with hierarchy. Even Linux and Wikipedia have strict hierarchy about submitting and evaluating contributions. Just as web chat rooms have monitors to keep the discussion civil and on task, Web 2.0 tools need oversight. You should add enough supervision to keep the discussion moving and productive.

- Get people out of their silos. It's not just enterprise applications that fall prey to siloism. This condition also describes humans who become so habituated to their jobs that they can't see beyond their own walls. They become the personification of thinking inside the box. Sometimes these people need prodding to collaborate. Vorpal made the right move when its code of conduct urged people to participate in blogs, wikis, and social networking sites. Without such nudging, many people won't budge.
- Provide simple tools. End users don't want to be software developers. They need tools that are easy to use and deploy. Collaboration means they should be talking about a business problem, not a problem with the platform.
- Build networks of expertise. Assemble teams with diverse backgrounds. Breakthroughs often come from approaching an old problem with a new frame of analysis. Think of teams like movie crews that round up lots of specialists like directors, actors, gaffers, camera operators, makeup artists, stuntmen, and so on. For the next picture, they may assemble a different crew. This circulates expertise to different corners of the organization and gets people to think outside of their silos.
- Create a culture that rewards innovation. Innovation rarely follows a safe or predictable path. Instead, it results from risk taking and experimentation—and sometimes these experiments fail. Intel calls these "noble failures."
- Listen to the wisdom of crowds. As the old business adage says, the best source of advice is the customer. We can extend this idea to users and the open source community. Sometimes perfect ideas come from perfect strangers. We saw that in Chapter 4: Vorpal's managers made good use of ideas from people they met through mesh collaboration.

- Treat people like adults. Mesh collaboration requires an open management style, not autocratic one. The whole spirit of Web 2.0 is openness. It implies an implicit trust. Modern knowledge workers want respect. Enterprise 2.0 is a frame of mind as much as a technology. Onerous restrictions destroy the whole purpose.
- Don't be a perfectionist. Sometimes good enough is good enough. Not everything has to be hardened. Maybe it's okay for some stuff to stay on the spreadsheet or not be scalable.
- Lead the way. Although mesh collaboration is largely a "bottom up" approach, it does require leadership from the top. Ideally, this should come from senior management or even the corporate board. Cultural change is hard and managers must set an example. Vorpal's new guidelines specifically instructed managers to make use of the new collaborative tools. Executives must reassure employees that posting on the wiki and chat rooms aren't the corporate equivalent of the underground resistance. Nor do they have to fear being penalized if they voice unorthodox ideas. Once managers get people using these tools, they should know when to get out of the way.
- Build it and they will come. Businesses must provide venues for collaboration. You can assemble a fantasy team, but if you don't provide a field, they won't have a place to play. All the good intentions won't matter if you don't provide an appropriate platform.
- Be open to experimentation. It may be messy, but the end result will be better. You don't come up with good rules by burying your head in the sand. Sometimes people succeed, sometimes they fail, but the important thing is they tried and learned something in the process. Enterprise 2.0 tools can help capture that learning, pinpoint root causes, and prevent repeating mistakes. It thus creates a culture of high performance.

- Get away from blame culture. How do you create a culture that allows 1,000 flowers to bloom? Don't punish people for ideas that don't work out. Blame culture just inhibits people from taking risks.
- Let users innovate. An enterprise shouldn't care about how the knowledge sharing looks. So let users integrate data in mashups or whatever else they want. Let them have their wikis. The enterprise should facilitate innovation and, when appropriate, harden and scale successful ideas.

Question 2: How Will the Role of IT Change to Support Collaboration?

The glass walls that surprisingly still either physically or mentally cordon many computer rooms symbolize a major problem at the heart of the enterprise. Until now, IT has operated what Kevin Parker of Serena calls a "glass house." When users need information, they ask and let IT figure out how to provide the answer. IT holds up the answer to the figurative glass wall. Users can't go into the room and help themselves. It's a cautious arrangement, and with good reason—if the data is corrupted or if the system crashes, the whole organization can be brought to a standstill.

This system is no longer sufficient. Businesses like Vorpal are looking for a new generation of front office interactions, they need them right away, and they may not want to change them again within months. Traditional back office solutions are not designed for this and IT as a department is not used to working this way.

Thus the challenge: how to reconcile IT systems built around proprietary applications with the new generation of Enterprise 2.0 technology built around sharing and standardized communications? One can think of this as a dichotomy between the worlds of designed IT, where the technology staff is the creative force, and the world of emergent IT, where the user drives innovation. IT departments are accustomed to the world of designed IT, where they are in charge.

A transition must take place to encourage and support emergent IT, not as a replacement for designed IT but as a supplement to it that enables users to solve problems for themselves.

Mind Shift: Service Provider

IT must become a provider of services that create value for the business. Of course, this is easier said than done. Think of the world of emergent IT as a chemistry lab. In this analogy, the lab operators represent IT and the experimenters represent the users. IT provides the ingredients to users who are qualified to check them out. These users would be allowed to experiment and create their own concoctions as they see fit. In turn, these users would be expected to follow basic safety procedures and rules governing the use of these materials. IT's job is to provide the basic tools and help when asked—and, of course, to make sure nothing blows up.

This opens the door to the benefits of user-driven innovation, a topic discussed in greater detail below. It also makes the job of IT easier. IT can't build 500 mashup solutions for the myriad of different business units in a large corporation, but it can provide the framework and connectivity to the systems of record and let the users built their own. Even if it could provide the number of people required, it would defeat the purpose of using mashups as a mechanism to personalize and support continuous dynamic change. These are not meant to be built or maintained like typical IT projects.

The IT department shifts into a role of support, matchmaking, brokering, even evangelizing. But in the domain of emergent front office IT, it's no longer a role of central control, except in unusual circumstances or when the applications created need to be hardened. In emergent front office IT, the IT staff looks for patterns in what users have created. Positive patterns are propagated. Negative ones are quashed.

To enable emergent IT, tools must be provided and services must be created to provide gateways to systems of record. Providing the right tools and services makes it easy for users to construct mashups, widgets, and the like in a safe and understandable manner. These generally have little if anything to do with transactional IT systems, but are ad hoc, often temporary, groups of services. Often IT doesn't need to get involved at all because these ad hoc solutions will have only limited use. The easy analogy is to think of users with spreadsheets, and consider why they should all use the same application to facilitate enterprise-wide use and why the provisioning of certain templates can be of great value to the users or their managers.

Intermediaries and Simulations

While the world of emergent IT has clearly taken hold, there are certain people and problems for which it will never work. Users wouldn't have a clue about how to create a large-scale complex application, which is clearly in the domain of designed IT. Moreover, many people just don't want to create technology for themselves. Intermediaries and simulations can help overcome these hurdles.

An intermediary is essentially a translator, someone who is dedicated to improving the communication between users and the technologists who build solutions. The role of the Business Process Expert, popularized by SAP, is one example. Business Process Experts have deep knowledge of business practices and processes and also have a sophisticated understanding of the tools used to create solutions. Armed with these skills, Business Process Experts are able to rapidly gather requirements from users and communicate them to the technology staff. The role has proven to create better requirements, which increase the voice of the user in the processes and accelerate development.

Simulations also can help involve the user. Instead of building a solution, the IT staff creates a working simulator that shows what the proposed solution would do. Consultant Corey Glickman uses this method for rapid development. This allows designers to create a solution in a safe environment and get feedback from users without raising objections from IT. Users can provide input and interact with the solution but don't have to build it themselves.

This approach also brings in the collaborative efficiency of "design thinking" where everybody brings something different to the table. Stakeholders can try different ideas and see what works before spending a penny on code.

A Common Language

Businesses need a common language. This language must be inclusive enough to meet the needs of users and service providers. It should be simple enough to be understandable for non-IT types on the business side, but also detailed enough for the techies to create a solution. If definitions are consistent, these solutions can be reused as "services" within SOA, thus avoiding reproduction and providing efficiencies.

How should IT perform this new role? In the book *Lost In Translation: A handbook for information systems in the 21st century,* Nigel Green and Carl Bate suggest an approach based on five common principles: Value, Policies, Events, Content, and Trust (VPEC-T).

- Values—Focus on understanding the values and desired outcomes of both the individual and the business as well as the values of the individuals and businesses you interact with. Values can be thought of as constraining beliefs (ethics), as well as identifying outcomes (goals).
- Policies—Focus on the broad range of mandates and agreements including internal policies, legal requirements, commercial contracts, and other issues that will govern and constrain what and how things are achieved.
- Events—Focus on the "real world" proceedings that stimulate business activity, sometimes in a predefined sequence and sometimes not, that act as the trigger for actions.
- Content—Focus on the documents, conversations, and messages that are produced and used by all aspects of business activity and construct the dialogues by which plans, actions, and previous references, are used to determine decisions.

- Trust—Focus on fostering a trusted relationship between all parties engaged in a system of value based upon Trust = Intimacy + Credibility / Risk. Trust values change with time and circumstances and are determined by the authenticity developed by the value of disclosures.

This approach focuses on key elements of the business interaction that are often lost in translation in conventional development methods. Unlike old models, this approach does not put precedence on the process or technology. The goal is to build a solution based on actual behavior and goals of users.

Keeping Oversight

Much of the traditional internal IT structure will remain, as will aspects of matrix working. But the emphasis will shift.

IT still will need to play an oversight role. For example, if a mashup works splendidly, IT should take note, reuse some elements elsewhere or harden the application. On the other hand, if the mashup is written so poorly that it overtaxes the system, IT should step in and shut it down.

In the future, the governance model will focus less on the choice of hardware and software and the current "one size fits all" approach. Instead, it will cover two main areas: standards and behavior. We'll explore this in more detail below.

Finally, IT should make peace with imperfection. In the competitive environment, a workable solution now often is better than a perfect one that arrives too late. Maybe it's okay for some stuff to not be scalable. Maybe it's okay if some stuff never went through months of testing. Kevin Parker of Serena sums up this ethos by saying, "Good enough is good enough."

Summing Up

In the end, IT may gain more control than it loses. By providing tools to users, it can gain more visibility into Shadow IT. Instead of being an impediment, IT will be an agent for empowerment and innovation. As Kevin Parker says, "IT gets to be the heroes."

Question 3: How Will Users Be Empowered to Do For Themselves?

Pushing do-it-yourself capabilities to the edge of the organization is the Enterprise 2.0 version of the saying "Give a man a fish and he will eat for a day. Teach a man to fish and he will eat for the rest of his life." People are empowered to help themselves and do their jobs better. Who knows better how to address a problem than the person who encounters it every day?

The earlier generation of IT was the dictatorship. But, as history has shown, central planning doesn't produce innovation or efficiency. Now the enterprise is moving toward more of a democracy where people are allowed to devise new solutions.

Users must think of themselves as doers, people who have the initiative to devise better business solutions.

User-Driven Innovation

A sustainable program of innovation is perhaps the only source of lasting advantage in the modern business environment.

Now corporations are waking up to the realization that internal and external users of technology can be valuable sources of innovation that can supplement the traditional research and development process. This process is termed "user-driven innovation." The pioneering researcher in this field is Dr. Eric von Hippel of MIT. He has spent more than 30 years researching user-driven innovation and is the author of the books *Sources of Innovation* and *Democratizing Innovation*. User-driven innovation empowers people with do-it-yourself capability so they can solve their own problems.

User-driven innovation offers many benefits: users can customize solutions to the way they do their jobs. They don't have to settle for clumsy solutions devised by tech people who fail to grasp the business requirements of the front office. It widens the pool of potential innovators. It creates better tools to capture the synergy of mesh collaboration.

Advances such as Web 2.0, Enterprise 2.0, improvements in the service grid, and consumer technology have accelerated the trend toward user-driven innovation. Another factor is the growing "tech savviness" of the public. More and more people are literate in web apps and Web 2.0—hence the growth of Shadow IT—and have the wherewithal to devise solutions themselves. Choice of the tools is becoming a matter of individual preference.

Internal Users

Pushing innovation to the edge empowers the business side to do their jobs more effectively. These people want the ability to do "innovation without permission."

As discussed previously, the traditional version of IT doesn't allow them to solve problems fast enough. Such a centralized approach often takes weeks or months. By the time an application created via traditional methods is ready, the business opportunity might have vanished or a competitor might have gotten a head start.

Businesses want the ability to jump without waiting for IT. In this emerging vision users (or possibly a new class of business analysts such as business process experts) rather than programmers would configure applications. This might include syndication, mashups, and "drag and drop" reuse of application functionality. This vision emphasizes Software as a Service, takes advantage of the rich capabilities of Web 2.0 to give a "web-like" feel to enterprise applications, and allows for user personalization.

Some platforms make this task easier. Jotspot (recently acquired by Google) provides a simple way to design collaborative web applications. Nsite (acquired by Business Objects that was in turn acquired by SAP) enables custom applications from a browser without programming.

Often IT doesn't need to get involved. Users often seek very practical solutions. How do we combine data from disparate systems? How do we meld information from two separate portals? Luis Derechin of Jackbe argues that mashups aren't strictly user-driven innovation but user-driven integration. The ability to customize these quick solutions enables business teams to exploit the potential of the Long Tail. Small, or rather lots of small niches, become the new big.

Empowering users also overcomes a nagging problem known as "stickiness." Information about user requirements is difficult to transfer because much is lost in translation. Imagine going to a restaurant and ordering a dish that must be cooked in a particular manner. You can easily do this in your native tongue, but in an unfamiliar language your order will fail to capture the subtleties of what you really want.

So it is with technology. The user has all of his or her solutions encoded in a private terminology—their native language. Forcing them to speak in IT lingo runs the risk of losing something in translation. This is the stickiness problem. Users generally have a more accurate model of their needs while manufacturers have a better model of potential solutions. If users can devise solutions themselves, less is lost.

Yet this vision of user-driven innovation faces barriers. Programmers often resist because it reduces their own value. It requires a new class of employees on the business side who are able to both understand and configure platforms. It requires a new software development process in which design, configuration, and integration are done by analysts or, when necessary, farmed out to a pool of developers. User-driven innovation also requires a shift in the role of the software professional to become more focused on domain understanding and business innovation.

This is the very challenge that this whole book, and the shift to Enterprise 2.0 in fact, set out to address. It is no more or less than a transformation, hence the notion of business model innovation and the focus on training a new generation of MBAs to lead this charge—similar to when they led the last wave of transformation by introducing PCs and spreadsheets.

The Outside World

Of course, the number of innovators within the enterprise pales in comparison to the potential outside the firewall in the infinite mesh. Bill Joy, one of the founders of Sun Microsystems, once said, "There are always more smart people outside your company than within it."

Innovation often comes from outside the organization, sometimes from places you never expected. Mesh collaboration taps the wisdom of these people—no matter where they are.

So-called "crowdsourcing" can provide a goldmine of ideas. It recruits users as a virtual R&D force. It thus addresses a problem faced by many companies: R&D budgets increase faster than sales and new sources of ideas are needed.

One example is the organization InnoCentive. Founded by pharmaceutical company Eli Lilly in 2001, the group invites companies to post unsolved challenges and tap the problem-solving skills of an open source community of ad hoc experts.

Companies like Boeing, DuPont, and Procter & Gamble now post scientific problems on InnoCentive's web site for anyone to crack. The companies pay solvers $10,000 to $100,000 per solution. InnoCentive claims that more than 30% of the problems posted on the site have been solved.

Colgate-Palmolive needed a way to inject fluoride powder into a toothpaste tube without dispersing it into the surrounding air. This challenge had stumped in-house researchers. The company posted the problem on InnoCentive—and it was solved by a freelance inventor working above an auto-body shop in Ontario, Canada who won $25,000 for a solution he figured out before he'd even finished reading the problem.

There are many such stories. A University of Dallas undergrad came up with a chemical for art restoration. A North Carolina patent lawyer devised a novel way to mix large batches of chemical compounds.

MIT researchers surveyed 166 problems posted on InnoCentive and found the strength of the network arose from its intellectual diversity. The odds of success actually increased if the solver had no formal expertise in that field. This bolsters the concept of "the strength of weak ties." The most efficient networks are those that link to the broadest range of information, knowledge, and experience.

Mesh collaboration is the net that catches these ideas.

Summing Up

Simply put, empowering users makes the organization more responsive and innovative. They'll be better equipped to take advantage of emerging opportunities and have appropriate tools to do so. By viewing users as a source of ideas, the enterprise will also become more receptive to ideas from outside—and, in the world of the infinite mesh, more and more wisdom and wealth will result.

Question 4: How Can You Secure Proprietary Information and Maintain Privacy and Security?

Leaping into the mesh can be terrifying for those entrusted with securing the enterprise. Vorpal's venture into Enterprise 2.0 and mesh collaboration raises immediate concerns about security. Not surprisingly, much of this concern comes from its CIO and its CFO, as this is a key part of their current roles. Unquestionably, this new approach brings risk—as the management of Vorpal understands all too well.

As the previous section discussed, computing is moving from dictatorship to democracy. Notice that there is no mention of anarchy. Governance and security are essential preconditions for the success of Enterprise 2.0 and mesh collaboration. Trust is vital for social collaboration. Without trust, the tools simply won't work. Managers won't rely on them. The perception of anarchy is one of the biggest PR problems that make managers wary of this new world.

Vorpal illustrates two basic approaches. In some areas, specific, written guidelines are appropriate for absolute forbidden areas like illegal activity or releasing personal information. In other areas, a collaborative approach is more effective. If people are treated like adults, they're more likely to behave responsibly. This collaborative monitoring also helps keep up with the constantly changing nature of the mesh world; it's almost guaranteed that unforeseen issues will arise.

What sort of oversight is required for this new environment? How will the enterprise ensure compliance with regulations such as Sarbanes Oxley? How will it ensure that its activities withstand the scrutiny of audit? New governance and security procedures are needed both for technology and human behavior.

People

Obviously, the new world of mesh collaboration requires new computing solutions, as we'll discuss below. But security and governance should not focus only on hardware and software; increasingly it will emphasize the way people use this technology. It will come to be an extension of the existing behavior codes of HR, just as it did at Vorpal.

In some cases extra security measures may be appropriate. As we saw in the last chapter, Vorpal management considered scanning technology to search messages as they passed the firewall to ensure no proprietary information was leaked. But it's significant that Vorpal's managers placed more emphasis on social controls.

The best way to control security is through behavioral mechanisms, not top down edicts. After all, this whole book is about moving away from centralization, right? Knowledge workers demand to be treated like adults and stand to gain the most from collaboration when they're not shackled to rigid ways of operating. They want to be educated, not policed. They want to be trusted to control their own behavior and, more often than not, they will live up to expectations. As the staff at Vorpal observed, people began to behave differently once they realized that the company kept logs of emails and instant messages. They regulated their own behavior mostly by their very role as knowledge workers, instinctively placing a high value on knowledge.

There will be more freedom, but it will come with checks and balances. In some cases, this may mean higher levels of auditing and more severe punishment when somebody is caught misusing data.

Fortunately, the collaborative nature of this new environment serves as its own control. Peer pressure becomes an ally in influencing behavior. People want to be recognized for their contributions—and they don't want to be tarnished as someone who violated security, damaged the brand, or "let down the team."

Any behavioral guidelines are only that—guidelines. The dynamic nature of this area almost guarantees there will unanticipated issues. Thus the first point on Vorpal's code of conduct: when in doubt, ask a supervisor.

Technology

Mesh collaboration poses new technical challenges for security. The old model largely consisted of constructing a secure perimeter around the organization. This approach is adequate for an organization that wants to remain closed to the outside world except for email. Unfortunately, such organizations are becoming extinct.

- Business is demanding more connectivity outside the enterprise
- Consumer trends are moving toward an IP address on every electronic device, with those devices having ever lower cost with more business functionality built in
- Business relationships increasingly require connectivity
- Social Networking sites with associated adware and malware threaten enterprise penetration
- The Internet is everywhere

The network perimeter no longer matches the borders of business. Businesses want to directly interconnect systems with partners in business-to-business (B2B) relationships. They rely on distributed and shared applications across these relationships. An increasing number of applications use web-based technology that bypasses firewall security. More and more, traditional perimeter controls are unable to fend off malware, or software designed to infiltrate or damage a computer system via web- and email-based techniques. And we haven't even mentioned the rising expectations for business-to-consumer (B2C) connectivity and interactivity.

What to do? Many security professionals now envision a future of "de-perimeterization." One example of this movement is the Jericho Forum, an international group of industry professionals that seeks to define IT security solutions for the networked world of the future. They recognize that the new role of technology in business will make current security mechanisms inadequate. Appropriately, the group takes its name from the Biblical story of Jericho where the walls tumbled down. It provides a number of basic principles and practices for security in the new interactive collaborative world of Mesh Working.

Jericho Forum Commandments

Fundamentals

1. The scope and level of protection should be specific and appropriate to the asset at risk
   o Business demands that security enables business agility and is cost effective
   o Whereas boundary firewalls may continue to provide basic network protection, individual systems and data will need to be capable of protecting themselves
   o In general, it's easier to protect an asset the closer the protection is provided
2. Security mechanisms must be pervasive, simple, scalable, and easy to manage
   o Unnecessary complexity is a threat to good security
   o Coherent security principles that span all tiers of the architecture are required
   o Security mechanisms must scale, from small objects to large objects
   o To be both simple and scalable, interoperable security "building blocks" need to be capable of being combined to provide the required security mechanisms

3. Assume context at your peril
    o Security solutions designed for one environment may not be transferable to another. Thus it is important to understand the limitations of any security solution
    o Problems, limitations, and issues can come from a variety of sources, including geographic, legal, technical, and acceptability of risk

Surviving in a Hostile World

4. Devices and applications must communicate using open, secure protocols
    o Security through obscurity is a flawed assumption—secure protocols demand open peer review to provide robust assessment and thus wide acceptance and use
    o The security requirements of confidentiality, integrity, and availability (reliability) should be assessed and built into protocols as appropriate, not added-on
    o Encrypted encapsulation should only be used when appropriate and does not solve everything
5. All devices must be capable of maintaining their security policy on an untrusted network
    o A "security policy" defines the rules with regard to the protection of the asset
    o Rules must be complete with respect to an arbitrary context
    o Any implementation must be capable of surviving on the raw Internet; it should not break on any input

The Need for Trust

6. All people, processes, and technology must have declared and transparent levels of trust for any transaction to take place
    o Trust in this context is establishing understanding between contracting parties to conduct a transaction and the obligations this assigns to each party involved

- Trust models must encompass people/organizations and devices/infrastructure
- Trust level may vary by location, transaction type, user role, and transactional risk

7. Mutual trust assurance levels must be determinable
   - Devices and users must be capable of appropriate levels of (mutual) authentication for accessing systems and data
   - Authentication and authorization frameworks must support the trust model

Identity, Management, and Federation

8. Authentication, authorization, and accountability must interoperate/exchange outside of your locus/area of control
   - People/systems must be able to manage permissions of resources and rights of users they don't control
   - There must be capability of trusting an organization, which can authenticate individuals or groups, thus eliminating the need to create separate identities
   - In principle, only one instance of person/system/identity may exist, but privacy necessitates the support for multiple instances, or one instance with multiple facets
   - Systems must be able to pass on security credentials/assertions
   - Multiple loci (areas) of control must be supported

Access to Data

9. Access to data should be controlled by security attributes of the data itself
   - Attributes can be held within the data (DRM/metadata) or could be in a separate system
   - Access/security could be implemented by encryption
   - Some data may have "public, nonconfidential" attributes
   - Access and access rights have a temporal component

10. Data privacy (and security of any asset of sufficiently high value) requires a segregation of duties/privileges
    ○ Permissions, keys, and privileges must ultimately fall under independent control, or there will always be a weakest link at the top of the chain of trust
    ○ Administrator access must also be subject to these controls
11. By default, data must be appropriately secured when stored, in transit, and in use
    ○ Removing the default must be a conscious act
    ○ High security should not be enforced for everything; "appropriate" implies varying levels with potentially some data not secured at all

Summing up

Like democracy, mesh collaboration places great faith in human potential. Both require certain controls to ensure that this potential is fulfilled. Security, compliance, and governance will remain vital concerns for the enterprise. This task will become more complex in a more global, fast-moving, and collaborative world.

Question 5: How Do You Set Metrics for This Level of Collaboration?

Toward the end of the discussion in Chapter 5, we see the executives of Vorpal pose an important question: how do we measure the results of mesh collaboration? As managers, they have been taught that you cannot manage what you cannot measure. But how can mesh collaboration be measured?

Actually, they are focusing on the wrong question. It's not how well or whether people collaborate that is the issue, but rather how well the traditional aspects of business perform with the additional benefit of strong collaboration.

Alas, benchmarking is not as simple as it used to be. In the old days, setting metrics was a relatively straightforward matter. Your markets, competitors, and collaborators were relatively predictable. But the mesh world changes all that. Now there are more changes more often, more variables through Long Tail niches and the cast of potential players and playing fields is infinitely larger. The mesh is the background to increasing these factors, so not surprisingly it must play a role in providing the answers. Benchmarking for mesh collaboration is so much more dynamic and harder to measure that it deserves both a new method and a new name: mashmarking.

Mesh Metrics

Benchmarking is a management process in which organizations evaluate themselves in relation to best practices within their own sector. Consulting companies such as McKinsey, Boston Consulting Group, Baines, and Capgemini have carved out a consulting industry by producing sector market overviews, benchmarking clients, and advising those that want to improve performance.

But is comparison to one's own industry enough in the mesh world?

No.

The business world has changed. Competition is more intense, customers demand more individualized products and services, product/service lifecycles have shortened, and new entrants can rapidly move into a market on a massive scale. Comparison to your peers has become less important. Hans van Grieken, VP for business innovation for Capgemini Netherlands, is one of the leading thinkers in this area and he sums it up this way: If you're not on par, you're dead anyway (or at least for sale).

It's time to develop a new set of metrics.

Thus Capgemini has come up with a unique concept, the mashmark. The mashmark is an indicator of innovative power. As defined by van Grieken, a mashmark should give a company the ability to scan the environment for anomalies that might signal new business opportunities and new coalitions inside and outside its normal business sectors. A mashmark indicates the level at which an organization is able to integrate with the outside world and quickly arrive at new insights based on continually changing events. It also would capture the ability of an organization to enter collaborative ventures with partners and customers, even in totally new sectors.

Van Grieken urges businesses to consider these questions:

- Does your company have an organized outside-in radar screen that detects anomalies outside and inside your market segment?
- Does your company have an ecosystem of business partners available to team outside your vertical market?
- Does your company have "rules of engagement" to deal with issues of intellectual property when interacting with potential mashup partners?
- Does your company have an IT architecture that allows you to easily and securely interact with potential mashup partners (SOA, de-perimeterization/Jericho principles/risk appetite, Web 2.0)?
- Does your company have the collaborative tools in place for border crossing to support these business processes?
- Does your company have the "open innovative culture" that is vital to make this work in a sustainable fashion?

Similarly, businesses must reexamine their internal metrics. Vorpal's experience shows how traditional models don't provide a good picture in the mesh environment. Revenues looked great, but the overall financial picture looked bleak. Obviously, they needed a better form of analysis.

As we saw earlier in the book, the old metrics don't work in this new environment. The margins might look fine because they don't cover the General Sales and Administrative expenses. But, as we've seen, it's no longer a fixed business. Businesses must find ways of breaking up the cost model that was previously based on a fixed GSA budget allocated for the year ahead around an equally fixed business mix of markets and sales.

This goes far beyond spreadsheets and moves toward why mashups are required. Once again there are strong parallels to the shift to the PC and widespread adoption of the spreadsheet as a management tool. Now it's time to use mashups.

Summing Up

A new world requires new tools. The increasing pace of business adds greater credence to the warning above: if you're not on par, you're dead or on the selling block. Companies need new metrics to calculate their position and seize opportunities in the mesh world.

The Supplier Revelation

Question 1: How Has Globalization Changed the Competitive Landscape?

The world has changed. The Power Plus CEO may not realize it, but his playing field has grown infinitely larger and more competitive. Power Plus is in danger of becoming yet another victim of globalization.

Global competitors are making cheaper products and claiming a growing share of the market. Costman is about to lose his longtime supplier—to the same Korean company that has been taking his business.

The Power Plus CEO mistakes this as a simple matter of wringing savings from the existing process by squeezing his suppliers. This is a losing proposition. If this is simply a matter of cutting costs, there's no way he's going to keep up with competitors in low-wage countries. Globalization requires companies to adapt or die.

The World Is Flat

International boundaries and oceans are shrinking as barriers to business. According to Forrester Research, global exports nearly tripled from $3.45 trillion in 1990 to $9.12 trillion in 2004, fueled by the growth of emerging nations like China and India.

The playing field has been leveled. In *The World is Flat*, author Tom Friedman ascribes globalization to a "triple convergence" of new players, new playing fields, and new processes for collaboration.

A quick recap:

The fall of the Soviet bloc, along with the opening of communist regimes like China, expanded the global force of free labor. Harvard economist Richard Friedman calculated that the economic world increased from 2.5 billion people in 1985 to 6 billion in 2000.

Computers became cheaper and more dispersed and took on new forms such as intelligent products, components, and packaging. This revolutionized global supply chains allowing them to stretch into an ever more intricate root system that spanned the globe. Technology allowed companies to collaborate horizontally among suppliers, retailers, and customers. Armed with cutting edge IT infrastructure, Wal-Mart became the best supply-chain management company in human history. This meant that a greater proportion of supplies and services could be outsourced to whoever did it best, fastest, and cheapest—often overseas.

The dotcom bubble was sometimes derided as a fool's paradise, but one of the significant achievements was a massive investment and build-out of infrastructure such as broadband and undersea cables. Suddenly masses of people around the globe came online. A knowledge worker could plug in anywhere in the world as long as he or she had a reliable Internet connection. A contractor in India could communicate with a company in Europe or North America as easily as one down the street.

Intellectual capital could be delivered from anywhere. Technologies like Unified Communications, desktop videoconferencing units and TelePresence allow companies to find and employ talent no matter where they are located. Accounting firms in India prepare taxes for U.S. citizens and call centers in India take calls on computer problems. Even the voice on the other end of the speaker at some drive-through McDonalds has been outsourced to locations thousands of miles away.

There was an explosion of ever-more powerful software, such as Internet browsers, email, and search engines and the ability for business applications to talk to each other using common XML standards. Web sites like Google and Yahoo! gave users the capability to find information with a few keystrokes. A kid in Slovenia has the same access to web-based information as a CEO in the top floor of a skyscraper on Wall Street. Now, notes Netscape founder Marc Andreessen, a teenager in Romania, Bangalore, or Vietnam has all the tools of the first-world knowledge worker.

Workflow software allowed the service industry to create a virtual assembly line of knowledge workers. Like Henry Ford's famous assembly line, it allowed specialization, but the key difference was that these specialties didn't have to be located in the same factory, country, or even continent. The earlier era has been characterized by individual innovation; the new one was marked by collaborative innovation.

The World Economic Forum held in Davos, Switzerland in February 2008 took as its theme the impact that collaboration will have on innovation. In the report following the event appeared the following statement: "User-centric technologies, crowd-sourcing, shared working practices; next generation collaboration tools such as these may be in their infancy, but they will change the business of business forever."

All this has lead to a trend known as "disaggregation." Simply put, it refers to the dispersal of functions that used to be centralized in one location. Companies can now send a greater portion of their work overseas and reap economic benefits that these low-cost economies offer.

Players

Emerging nations provide vast reservoirs of new talent. China and India now account for 2.4 billion consumers. They also host a growing pool of talented engineers, scientists, and professionals willing to provide cost-competitive R&D and IT services.

Of course, globalization also means that these countries will have greater access to U.S. and European markets—and compete directly with companies like Power Plus. In China, for example, export of goods and services represent 35% of GDP.

Goldman Sachs predicts that the middle class in the four nations known as BRIC (Brazil, Russia, India, and China) will quadruple in the next decade and contribute nearly 70% of global growth by 2040. Goldman Sachs also predicts that the GDP of BRIC nations will surpass the G6 by about 2040. Around that time, China's GDP will pass that of the U.S. Says Friedman: "Either you get flat or you'll be flattened by China."

Or India. Or Russia. Or Brazil. Or Malaysia, Ireland, Mexico or—in the case of Power Plus—Korea.

How Not to Get Flattened

What does this global world mean for our children? Says Friedman: "There is only one message: you have to constantly upgrade your skills."

The same advice applies to business. Friedman offers a few bits of advice to corporations:

- When the world goes flat—and you are feeling flattened— reach for a shovel and dig inside yourself. Don't try to build walls
- And the small shall act big
- And the big shall act small
- The best companies are the best collaborators
- In a flat world, the best companies stay healthy by getting regular chest X-rays and then selling the results to their clients
- Develop the systems you need…then sell them to others. Commercialize your own internal innovations
- The best companies outsource to win, not to shrink. They outsource to innovate faster and more cheaply in order to grow larger, gain market share, and hire more and different specialists—not to save money by firing more people
- Outsourcing isn't just for realists. It's also for idealists

Cisco Systems has followed some of this approach while evolving into a truly globalized company by setting up its Globalization Centre in Bangalore, India. The company has long had sales offices in the country but it took the movement of senior executives to the region to harness the true opportunity that exists to realize Cisco's globalization vision. In late 2007, Cisco officially opened its Globalization East campus in Bangalore to add to its existing R&D Centre in the city. The new facility provides an environment for closer collaboration with partners in spotlighting solutions for customers in emerging markets such as India, China, the Middle East, Africa, Asia and Latin America. The Cisco Bangalore facility also houses the largest campus datacenter outside the U.S. and provides a focal point for demonstrating next-generation virtualization technologies and service oriented architectures that support customers' global environments. The new Globalization Centre East offers a collaborative work environment to help Cisco attract and retain top talent as well as a focal point to drive partnerships with some of India's largest and most successful technology companies and outsourcers.

Overall, Cisco has committed extensive venture investment initiative in India to drive growth with high-potential Indian companies as part of its overall $1.1 billion investment plan for India. And all this is far away from the view that India offers opportunity for cost arbitrage; rather it's about pinpointing cutting-edge innovation, and harnessing a highly skilled workforce who will be constituents of the company's future success.

Cisco is also looking at alternate ways to grow and maintain a truly global workforce—to discover talent regardless of location while also reducing travel expenses—by investing $20 million in Cisco Unified Communications collaborative technologies. This investment includes 116 TelePresence units worldwide that provide "higher than hi-definition" video screens that allow face-to-face life-like interactions. These collaborative mechanisms allow knowledge workers to be virtually everywhere and reduce the need for travel. As an example, consider the case of Cisco Services Europe.

In 2007, the 190-person team enacted a change that stunned many managers—they largely abolished the conventional face-to-face meeting. At the time, the services business in Europe was booming, but travel costs were escalating and travel in the post-9/11 world was time consuming and frustrating for employees looking to improve work-life-balance.

As leader of the team, Nick Earle decided it was time for radical change. People were asked to think carefully about how they collaborated and encouraged to use an array of new media-rich options rather than rely on face-to-face interactions.

But just making the technologies available wasn't enough to change longstanding habits. After all, desktop videoconferencing units had been available but under-used for several years. Earle created five councils to drive change management and a change in the culture. The team classified meetings into three different categories. Important gatherings, such as quarterly board gatherings, would still be held in person, due to the high degree of personal interaction needed. Routine meetings and training sessions would rely on Cisco Unified Communications, phones, desktop videoconferencing units, and TelePresence. Finally, one-on-one meetings used Cisco MeetingPlace technology to collaborate and share materials.

These efforts paid off. In the next quarter, travel & expense expenditures fell by 14%. An overall annual reduction of 20% is forecast for 2008. Travel no longer took such a personal toll and better work life balance increases productivity. In only the first six months, Earle calculated a 20% gain in his personal potential productivity from reclaiming hours that otherwise would be lost to travel. He expects a 57% reduction in his carbon footprint for air travel in 2008. In one day, Earle spoke via video to an audience of 250 employees spread out in 21 European countries, held a series of smaller meetings via a TelePresence 1000 terminal in his office, and participated in a meeting of the worldwide Cisco Services Executive Board—all from Cisco's London office. Most importantly, breakfast with his family is no longer an unusual occurrence and he recently attended his youngest daughter's school play for the first time in several years.

This is just one team and one person, but Cisco is looking at change on a worldwide scale to improve work-life balance for their employees, harness talent on a global scale, and reduce carbon emissions via travel reductions. Cisco employees flew about 1 billion miles in FY 2006, creating a total carbon footprint of 730,000 tons. Through this effort, the company has plans to reduce air travel by 20% and save more than $100 million and hopes to reduce emissions by up to 10%.

Globalization and Its Discontents

Yet these long supply lines are vulnerable.

The 9/11 terrorist attacks exposed the soft underbelly of global trading networks as manufacturers like Toyota and Dell were nearly forced to shut down U.S. factories because cargo planes carrying their foreign-made parts were grounded. Similarly, a pandemic of avian flu could close seaports and airports for months.

It doesn't take a global crisis to slow down these intricate supply lines. The case of Boeing's 787 Dreamliner provides one recent example where tighter collaboration could have saved several months of time-to-market efficiencies.

The Dreamliner is Boeing's first major design since the mid-1990s. It will be the world's first large commercial airplane made mostly of carbon-fiber composites, which are noncorrosive, lighter, and more durable aluminum. It also represented a new approach to production. In the past, Boeing controlled design and production and relied on suppliers for parts built to Boeing's exacting specifications. For the Dreamliner, Boeing acted as the architect and farmed out much of the production.

The 787 took outsourcing to new heights: The wings come from Mitsubishi Japan, wing tips from KAL-ASD in Korea, the moveable trailing edge from Boeing Australia, forward fuselage from Spirit US, Forward fuselage II from Mitsubishi in Japan, center fuselage from Alenia in Italy, aft fuselage from Vought in the U.S., passenger entry doors from Latecoere in France, cargo doors from Saab Sweden, and so on. Cargo jets flew whole segments of the new Dreamliners to Washington state for assembly.

The company soon learned painful lessons about the downside of outsourcing. Suppliers outsourced work to smaller companies. These subcontractors overloaded themselves with work from multiple 787 suppliers. Some partners were unable to build parts to Boeing's specifications. Boeing learned that it did not provide adequate performance goals for its suppliers. The company simply lost control of its own production.

The snafus caused a series of delays and raised serious questions about Boeing's decision to restructure itself as a "systems integrator." The Dreamliner's inaugural flight would be delayed up to three months, pushing delivery of the first plane into early 2009. Pat Shanahan, Boeing's general manager of the 787 program, was quoted as saying, "We underestimated how long it would take to complete someone else's work…We thought we could modify that production system and accommodate the traveled work from our suppliers, and we were wrong." It's clear that simply disaggregating isn't enough. A new model for collaborative working is needed.

Summing Up

The world has changed. Businesses are less apt to stick with partners for the sake of loyalty or geography. Customers look for lower prices, no matter if the goods are produced locally or on a distant continent. Costman, like the plaques in his office, is a vestige of the previous millennium. Competitors from halfway around the world are virtually at his doorstep.

Question 2: How Are Business Models Changing in Response to Global Competition?

Adaptability is the key to survival. Alas, Power Plus remains stuck in the old way of doing things. Tilo Costman is operating under a business model and mentality more appropriate to the 1980s and 1990s.

His world is largely vertical: top-down management, vertical process alignment, and an authoritarian style that leave little room for innovation. New partnerships? New markets? He fails to recognize potential new sources of revenue. Instead, he wants to cannibalize his own business relationships. This strategy is doomed to failure.

Costman didn't get the memo: it's time to adapt or go out of business. A new world requires new business models. Navi Radjou of Forrester Research calls these "Globally Adaptive Organizations." This new breed of corporation is characterized by flexibility, efficiency, altruism, and openness. Such organizations are highly collaborative, create shared value between partners, and are diverse and structured for rapid response.

Globalism poses a new set of geopolitical and sociocultural risks. Forrester Research believes that globalization will not follow the "hockey stick" growth curve envisioned by some optimistic forecasts; instead, it will take a more discontinuous course of ups and downs. In other words, traveling through the flat world may be a bumpy ride.

Market opportunities will appear and vanish overnight. Threats will arise just as spontaneously. In order to survive in this chaotic environment, firms must adapt business models that evolve as quickly as the world around them.

The New Model

This turbulent world requires agility. Unfortunately, many multinational corporations remain stuck in 20th-century mindsets. Some are "hub-and-spoke" models marked by a command-and-control structure and inflexibility on the front line. Others have tried to empower local units by creating decentralized silos that lack knowledge sharing and collaborative problem solving.

One of the companies that has pioneered successful business models for a globalized, or "flat world" is Infosys. Starting in Bangalore, India in 1981, with just $250 of funding, the company has grown into an established global solutions provider with offices in 23 countries, over 80,000 employees, and revenues in excess of $3 billion. The company specializes in helping its customers "win in the flat world."

The world is being flattened by the forces of globalization, changing demographics, and ubiquitous access to technology. Consequently, the Flat World offers a level playing field for start-ups and established companies alike.

To compete in this rapidly evolving business environment, Infosys believes that companies need to speed up, slim down, and become more nimble. In short, to "Think Flat" they must shift their operational priorities along four dimensions:

- **Think China price.** The only way to compete with China and the emerging markets is to have the same cost model. Achieve a competitive cost structure to differentiate your offerings and enter new markets. This is Tilo Costman's dilemma in a nutshell—he's competing with the Korean price, not with James Hughes' negotiation strategy.
- **Think faster innovation.** Innovate faster to retain customers. Cocreate with customers and partners, and undertake cutting-edge research in global R&D centers. Jane Moneymaker has done the consumer and partner component of this very successfully with Vorpal but clearly this has not been the strategy at Power Plus.
- **Think money from information.** Harvest information to create profit—use information across the globe, improve efficiency and identify new revenue opportunities. This is extremely relevant for Power Plus. Costman has data, but not information, and he certainly does not have a strategy to make profit from information. He's stuck in the world where the definition of a solution is the product and all his products hit the marketing bull's-eye—after all they conform to the specification in the datasheet perfectly. What's wrong with that?
- **Think winning in the turns.** Plan a strategy to navigate an industry downturn. Respond fast when the industry cycle turns. Costman's industry is changing. He's no longer facing just standard competitors from North America and Europe. The game has turned a sharp corner and new, more

nimble competitors from Asia have found a way to overtake him. This is typically when companies fail—when market conditions change and they are slow to react. It seems that Sun Szu was right after all when he said, "Beware, your strength will become your weakness." Costman is not responding fast. He's responding by denying the new rules of the game.

Summing Up

At the risk of repeating ourselves, it's time to change the game.

The challenge for managers such as Costman is that they don't know the game has changed, so they keep playing by the rules that have served them so well so far. This is why revolutions are always triggered by the colonels, because the generals have reached the top by doing things the old way, so why should they change? Are the middle managers in your company seeing the world more clearly than your top executives?

Chapter 7 Questions and Analysis

Moneymaker Tells Her Story to the Executive Team

Question 1: How Have Open Models For Innovation and Open Business Models Created New Ways to Respond to Competition?

Vorpal has realized the value of openness. Moneymaker and her team have opened themselves up to new partners, new ideas, and new sources of revenue. They think in terms of mutual value creation and collaboration.

In contrast, Power Plus doesn't. Costman views his vendors almost as competitors in a zero sum game. This adversarial relationship with suppliers is a race to the bottom. His paradigm is closed—and pretty soon his business may be too.

Open For Business

Innovation is becoming an increasingly open process. Companies are becoming more specialized and the division of labor is occurring on a grander scale. Open business models allow companies to capture and create value. They allow companies to focus on core competencies and develop profitable partnerships.

More and more companies are shifting to open models. Qualcomm no longer makes its own cell phones and base stations. Now the company makes only chips, sells licenses to its technologies, and lets other companies take care of manufacturing.

Genzyme, a biotechnology company, buys ideas from outsiders and refines them in house. The company has turned these external ideas into novel therapies, such as cures for previously untreatable diseases. It has also built an impressive financial record in a notoriously tough industry.

Procter & Gamble has rejuvenated itself through its "Connect and Develop" program. It employs a network of scouts to keep an eye out for new ideas, acquires products from other companies, and brings them to market as P&G brands. This method has produced successes like the Crest SpinBrush, Olay Regenerist, and Swiffer Dusters. P&G even has a policy that any internal idea that remains undeveloped for three years will be offered to outside firms, even direct competitors.

Under the Connect and Develop initiative, the company has set a goal of receiving half of its ideas from the outside. At the start of that initiative, P&G had roughly 8,200 people working on innovations, 7,500 inside the company. Now the R&D force has more than doubled with more than half coming from suppliers and partners.

Changing Models

R&D is no longer the strategic asset it used to be. The closed model of innovation could be summed up as: If you want something done right, do it yourself. Companies controlled the entire cycle of innovation: ideas, development, manufacturing, marketing, distribution, and service. They guarded their intellectual property from competitors and reinvested profits in more R&D.

This model began to lose its grip around the turn of the millennium and companies are finding it increasingly difficult to justify investments in innovation.

Henry William Chesbrough, author of *Open Innovation and Open Business Models,* is one of the foremost authorities in this field. He identifies two factors that drive this trend: higher costs and shorter lifecycles.

R&D costs are consuming an increasing portion of corporate budgets. In 2006, Intel Corp. announced plans to build two new semiconductor fabrication facilities in Arizona and Israel at a cost of more than $3 billion apiece. Twenty years ago, such a facility would have would have cost about 1% of that. In the pharmaceutical industry, the cost of developing a successful product now exceeds $800 million, up more than ten-fold from just a decade earlier.

Even for the small percentage of ideas that are commercialized, shorter lifecycles bring decreased revenues. The computer industry provides a good example. In the early 1980s, hard drives would typically remain on the market four to six years until replaced by a new model. By the 1990s, the lifecycle had shrunk to six to nine months.

Meanwhile, it has become easier for new players to enter the market. Knowledge workers are more mobile and more numerous. The venture capital industry provides new sources of funding for ideas outside the R&D labs of the big companies. Startups can raise additional cash through public offerings or partner with larger companies to take their ideas to market.

Until recently, the cost of R&D represented a formidable barrier to entry to many markets. Now, however, the giants are facing competition from upstarts.

"Such factors have wreaked havoc with the virtuous cycle that sustained closed innovation," writes Chesbrough. "Now, when breakthroughs occur, the scientists and engineers who made them have an outside option that they previously lacked. If a company that funded a discovery doesn't pursue it in a timely fashion, the people involved could pursue it on their own—in a startup financed by venture capital."

Open Season

In times of stability, knowledge is guarded because it holds lasting value. But in times of change, stocks of knowledge become less valuable and more quickly obsolete; information flow becomes more vital. Ideas must be used before they grow stale. Collaboration often offers the quickest way to mobilize expertise and bring an idea quickly to market.

In open innovation, ideas flow both ways. Companies no longer guard their intellectual property. Instead, they seek to profit by partnering with other companies for mutual gain. These alliances can lead firms to new markets and new revenue streams through licensing fees, joint ventures, and spin-offs.

Ideas of limited or no use within the company can find new life when shared with partners. Every company has unique expertise, assets, resources, and market position. An idea that is a bust for one company may be a boom in another. "Companies look at opportunities differently," writes Chesbrough. "They will quickly recognize ideas that fit the pattern that has proven successful for them in the past, but they will struggle with concepts that require an unfamiliar configuration of assets, resources, and positions."

Innovation often happens when somebody with a new perspective looks at an old problem. A similar phenomenon can occur when a new company steps in. The Xerox Palo Alto Research Center developed Ethernet and the graphical user interface (GUI) but did not consider them promising ideas for the company, which specialized in copiers and printers. Later, they were commercialized by other companies with great success.

Innovation invariably produces more ideas than successes. But the existing system, brokered by patent attorneys and intellectual property lawyers, is inefficient and lets too many ideas die a slow death on the shelves. One way to quantify this waste is to look at a company's patent utilization rate—the number of patents that the firm uses in its business divided by the total number of patents that it owns. In an informal survey, Chesbrough estimates that 75% of 95% of patented technologies lie dormant.

High R&D costs and uncertain payoff keeps companies from pursuing all but the most promising ideas. Open innovation creates a marketplace where unused ideas can find more fertile ground. IBM donated 500 of its software patents to the open source community in hopes that the intellectual commons would cultivate ideas that failed to sprout within.

New Models

Reaping the benefits of open innovation requires reforming the organization itself. Companies must revisit their basic business models. In most organizations, nobody but the CEO bears responsibility for the business model and most managers simply take it for granted. As Chesbrough notes, changing it is a radical step and requires leadership from the top. Oftentimes, companies don't do so until forced by crisis.

"It takes courage and vision to try out new ideas during a time of financial difficulty," writes Chesbrough. "Yet absent such experiments, companies could easily fall into a cycle of slowing revenues, leading to head count and expense reductions, which trigger further business declines, resulting in still more cuts."

A new model can revive a failing company. Such was the case with IBM. The company has revamped its approach to intellectual property. It has shifted from a defensive approach of guarding IP to an offensive one of licensing it to outside parties and, as a result, has enjoyed significant new revenues. One such example is IBM's semiconductor copper-on-insulator process technology, which provides higher-speed circuitry with greater manufacturing reliability. In the past, IBM would have guarded this technology, but under the new mindset it has widely licensed it to companies such as Intel, Motorola (now Freescale Semiconductor of Austin, Texas), and Texas Instruments. IBM also has embraced the open source movement and Linux.

Many firms are wary of turning loose unproven ideas that may damage their brands. But some have figured out ways of sending up trial balloons such as spin-offs, investing in startups, or launching "white box" brands that have no obvious connection to the parent company. These strategies allow companies to explore without risking the reputation of the brand.

As firms scale up an experimental model, it must be adjusted to handle significant volume. Models that work with a small number of highly trained people can easily break down when expanded to a larger group. If certain processes cannot be automated or standardized, the company may suffer a loss of quality.

Important stakeholders must "buy in" to the new model before it rolls out to the entire organization. A new model usually diverts resources from somewhere else and may spark resistance from people whose budgets and jobs have been affected.

Open innovation poses other drawbacks. A company must surrender control of the process and intellectual property, but advocates argue that these problems increasingly are outweighed by the upsides. Internal R&D still must play a role. Ideas often must be refined in-house. Despite these caveats, open innovation and open business models offer increasingly attractive options for generating and profiting from these ideas.

Contrasting Principles of Closed and Open Innovation

Closed Innovation Principles

- The smart people in our field work for us
- To profit from R&D, we must discover, develop, and ship it ourselves
- If we discover it ourselves, we will get it to market first
- If we are the first to commercialize an innovation, we will win
- If we create the most and best ideas in the industry, we will win
- We should control our intellectual property (IP) so that our competitors don't profit from our ideas

Open Innovation Principles

- Not all of the smart people work for us so we must find and tap into the knowledge and expertise of bright individuals outside our company
- External R&D can create significant value; internal R&D is needed to claim some portion of that value
- We don't have to originate the research in order to profit from it
- Building a better business model is better than getting to market first
- If we make the best use of internal and external ideas, we will win
- We should profit from other's use of our IP, and we should buy other's IP whenever it advances our own business model

Question 2: How Can the Generation Gap Be Closed at the Management Level?

In Chapter 6 we saw a scenario that occurs in many corporations. Subordinate managers have ideas that don't quite register with Costman. It's not only his business model that is closed—his ears and imagination are too. Even people outside the company can see signs that Power Plus is in trouble.

Older managers like Costman are digital immigrants—people promoted rapidly in a business world that is very different from the one they find themselves in today. It's not that they need to know all about the latest IT products and capabilities; those are just the tools after all. What they need to know is that these new tools enable new business models, which will definitely change their world for better or worse. Clearly they know that there are younger, more IT savvy employees underneath them, but they feel that it is an admittance of failure to reach out for help. Senior managers know what to do and see it as part of their job description to lead by directing the organization to implement their plans and their methods. What would it look like to the organization if they had to ask younger staff for help?

These conflicts can afflict even the most successful and tech-savvy companies—including Microsoft. In the 1990s the company earned the lion's share of its profits from operating systems and client-centric applications. Younger employees filled Bill Gates' inbox with warnings that the company was neglecting the Web. Microsoft's share price stagnated as new technology-driven business models emerged, particularly from Netscape radically deciding to give their Internet browser away for free to get a rapid, massive user base from which they could then upsell applications. This model was initially unthinkable for Gates who had founded a company that made all of its money from selling software licenses and for whom the Internet was interesting, but not a threat. After months of warnings, which went unheeded, Gates responded with a now famous memo declaring that the Internet would henceforth be at the center of everything the company did. Microsoft adapted and thrived, but only just.

How Can the Generation Gap Be Closed at the Management Level?

The answer lies in the wider definition of leadership in the mesh world. If executives don't understand the mesh world and how it changes their role, there's less chance that they or their organizations will survive in it.

The generation gap often means that ideas will filter up, but how can top managers learn to listen? One way is to view their younger employees as sentinels. These digital natives understand technology almost instinctively and older generations would be wise to pay attention. This doesn't mean simply inviting them into management meetings. For example, former GE head Jack Welch had his top 1,000 managers mentored by younger GE employees who better grasped the new technologies.

These young employees can be agents for positive change—but only if heeded. If ignored, they may take their ideas elsewhere. Managers should retain a healthy sense of humility about the limits of their own knowledge. If nothing else, they should fear the consequences of their own lack of understanding.

Healthy Fear

In the book *Only the Paranoid Survive,* former Intel chairman and CEO Andrew Grove describes how fear can play a healthy role in motivating us to keep abreast of technological changes that pulse ever faster. Business is about creating change for other companies. Competition and technology are all about constant flux. The ability to detect shifts in the wind is essential, and mid-managers, especially those in contact with the outside world like sales, often are better at it than upper management.

Unfortunately, the CEO is often insulated by layers of management and sits in the middle of what Grove describes as a "fortified palace." Grove recalls being rebuffed when he warned the CEO of another company about problems with its software. The man simply hadn't heard what was going on outside his company. Grove's IT manager responded, "Well, that guy is always the last to know."

Managers must avoid complacency and remain vigilant about what is going on outside the company. That means keeping abreast of technological change and listening to those on the front lines, no matter whether the news is good or bad. When it comes to forming strategy in today's technology-enabled world, a technologist or engineer may bring as much to the table as a senior executive, albeit in a different form. Grove says his company worked very hard to "break down the walls between those who hold knowledge power and those who hold organization power."

"We can't stop these changes," writes Grove. "We can't hide from them. Instead, we must focus on getting ready for them."

Collaborative technologies are a key enabler here. Results from many companies that have implemented unified communications systems involving tools such as IP voice, instant messaging, desktop video, and high-end telepresence systems show that one of the key benefits that these tools provided was the extent to which they leveled the playing field for employees at all levels. The more people who collaborate, the more the smart ideas bubble up to the top, leading to a decrease in focus on management hierarchy and an increase in focus on radical business propositions—regardless of the seniority of the presenter.

Never Too Old to Learn

Like Costman, Jabberwocky CEO Charles Dodgson doesn't understand the mechanism for Vorpal's success and initially assumes it's a result of tightening the ship rather than generating new value.

Dodgson is no technophobe—he has an up-to-date computer and relies on his PDA to send and receive messages. But he hadn't grasped the potential of the mesh until the margins started increasing.

Dodgson doesn't understand all this Web 2.0 stuff but, to his credit, he relies on a younger assistant who does. He also knows a crisis when he sees it and recognizes that his enterprise better catch up with the times. He's wise and humble enough to learn some new tricks from his younger subordinates. This didn't cost him anything. All he had to do was to identify the source of innovation, reach out, and sit back and listen. Other managers would do well to heed his example.

Chapter 8 Questions and Analysis

Moneymaker Finds Out
How Bad It Is

Question 1: How Have the Challenges of Creating a Strategy Been Transformed in the Modern Marketplace?

As Moneymaker observes, companies don't fail because they do the wrong thing. Instead, they fail because they continue to do what used to be the right thing for too long. They find a successful formula and stick with it even though the world around them continues evolving. They become slaves to the conventional wisdom of the past.

So it is at Power Plus. They can't see change from the inside. As it turns out, they have the raw ingredients and ideas for success at their fingertips, but they're so used to the old way of doing things that they've become blind to their own potential.

Something is missing. They build the best machines in the world and boast a great track record of reliability and service but just can't beat the prices of their competitors overseas simply because their cost base is so different. As Strauss laments, they're the best at what they do, but they just can't figure out how to make that work anymore when there is extensive choice and the product has become a commodity.

This is a common challenge, one that eludes managers stuck in old ways of thinking. The new marketplace demands a different kind of strategy.

Old Habits

Success can make you deaf. One classic pitfall is that companies institutionalize the strengths that made them great in the first place. Claudia Funke, Director of the Munich office of McKinsey & Co., calls these "orthodoxies." These beliefs and habits become part of the DNA of the organization, so ingrained that leaders are not even conscious of them.

Business model transformation requires the company to abandon these established ways of doing business. It forces managers to confront, and even renounce, their orthodoxies.

Business model transformation is much more complex and difficult than changing a product. Many companies mistakenly view technology as the magic ingredient of transformation. Although technology is an essential ingredient, it is only part of the overall picture. Rather, business model transformation is a fundamental change in many basic elements such as market model, pricing scheme, deployment of resources, partnerships, teams, and so on.

Another common mistake is to assume old functions still apply to the new game. For example, traditional risk management or financial measurement systems don't necessarily work in the new model.

Being Unorthodox

How to change? The first step is to identify our own orthodoxies. This requires introspection and open dialog in top and middle management.

Then the company must go through what Funke calls "targeted interventions." For example, if a company is accustomed to working in silos, a massive effort is needed to create cross-functional teams. The company might have to appoint new managers responsible for facilitating this new collaboration. Business units might make weekly reports to the CEO and top management team instead of monthly ones. They might stop using their old advertising agencies, turning instead to new media agencies.

The company needs to become an engine of innovation. This means creating organizational structures, incentives, and open collaborative forms of working practices and tools to sustain the transformation. Some companies spin off new business units. Ideally, these are bona fide independent organizations that can separate themselves from the old culture and grow according to the new rules. Other companies change the entire organization, a monumental task. IBM and Nokia are two examples of big companies that have done this successfully; both bear little resemblance to what they were 10 or 20 years ago. Oftentimes, these transformations come in response to crisis.

Power Plus has reached such a crossroads. They've been innovative when it comes to matters like production. But, as Moneymaker quickly ascertains, they've stopped short when it comes to innovating the business model. The company, and especially its CEO, is chained to its own orthodoxies.

Adaptive businesses continue to reinvent themselves. General Electric didn't survive by continuing to make light bulbs. Nokia started off in paper products, including toilet paper; one of the first products of the forerunner of IBM was a cheese grater; and Dave Packard of HP experimented with automatic lettuce picking machines when he started out.

As Moneymaker is starting to see, there is untapped potential for revenue and competitive advantage right under their noses. They have the tools and expertise to transform their business and create added value. They've spent years perfecting how to run their generators efficiently. They can take the skills they've mastered in running their own business and sell them as services. But it takes an outsider—someone not steeped in the orthodoxies—to see the possibilities.

Power Plus will embark on a makeover as radical as the one that Vorpal went through. Soon its employees will recognize that they have the ability not only to sell products, but also comprehensive energy management systems that are so efficient that they pay for themselves.

With that kind of package, those less-expensive Korean motors and generators begin to look like very cheap substitutes indeed.

Question 2: What Are the Roles That Need to Be Played in Order to Execute a Program of Business Transformation?

Business model innovation requires companies to rethink the roles played by their employees.

One of the best ways to succeed in the mesh world is to use value-based services to seek new markets. There are many benefits, not the least of which is that executed properly these services allow enterprises to generate additional revenues while at the same time relieving pressures on the margins of existing markets. If Tilo Costman transformed his business and allowed his people to execute on this strategy, his company wouldn't be forced to squeeze itself and its partners to the point of strangulation.

Unfortunately, finding these opportunities requires a combination of knowledge that lies outside the existing competencies of most enterprises. Traditional business and IT practices simply have not prepared most managers to play the required parts.

Role Models

How does a business assemble the cast for business model transformation? The company must ask itself two questions: who are the decision makers? And what is the basis for their decisions? This brings us back to the quadrant discussed in Chapter 1.

The bottom half of the quadrant represents the traditional approach of cost containment. In this view, IT managers view technology as a means to reduce operating expenses. On the business side, managers view applications as a means to reduce administrative costs. This world has predictable roles and metrics: it's always clear who does what and what is supposed to be measured. Business and IT remain largely separate entities and follow a transactional model. The "transference point" moves from business to IT, or from bottom right to bottom left. IT aligns itself to the requirements of business.

The bottom half of this model has obvious shortcomings. It may be efficient at doing business as usual, but business isn't so predictable in the mesh world. To the contrary, the world of business becomes less "business as usual" every day. The bottom half lacks agility and doesn't fully appreciate business value. Tilo Costman represents this mindset: when presented with an innovative idea, he fixates on how it will inflate his payroll and training budget and fails to see how it might generate new revenue.

The top half represents a different mindset. It seeks competitive advantage by emphasizing value. Technology, represented by the top left quadrant, focuses on understanding the needs of the business side and enabling it through technological innovation. IT must adapt to a new mission of using technology to serve new markets. The business side, the top right, takes a value-driven approach— the "changing the game" we described earlier.

In the top half, business and technology converge into a single entity driven by business objectives and built jointly around business and technology. They follow an interactional model. These technologies allow the business to do things it couldn't do before and create new markets and new sources of revenue. The "transference point" has reversed direction and now technology is driving the transformation.

The CEO sits in the middle of this quadrant. Ideally, the business manager would like to move toward the top right. After all, this is the route to model transformation and achieving all the important goals such as revenues, market share, and increased margins.

This requires "strategic agility." This means not only quickness, but also the ability to shift directions. It's not only the full-speed-ahead of a sprinter; it's also the agility of a soccer player who can pivot, sprint, and change course instantly, depending on what's happening on the field at any given moment. Strategic agility requires several key attributes. Resources must be fluid and people must be capable of rapid redeployment. Second, leadership must be open and unified. The third element is strategic acuity, or the sharp vision to scan the horizon and spot opportunities.

Vorpal already has made this transformation. Hugo personifies the top left. He takes advantage of Web 2.0 and other technologies to make contact with more people and sell more products. He also drives changes to the business side, the top right box, to execute on those sales.

Clearly, Power Plus is still locked in the basement of our quadrant. Costman is still playing the old game in the paradigm of cost reduction. It's a top down, authoritarian hierarchy. The workers on the floor are way ahead of the CEO and ready to step into the roles symbolized by the top half, but their ideas have been locked out. This lack of agility leaves the company flat-footed and ham-fisted: it simply hasn't given itself the tools to be innovative and generate new value.

With Jane's help, Power Plus can revive itself through business model transformation. The company puts IT to work on behalf of the front office. Eventually, it combines expertise and the tech innovation to fill a market niche of end-to-end energy systems. The employees of Power Plus have the expertise and passion to excel at these jobs. All they needed was the roles they could step into.

Summing Up

Companies must have people who play these four parts represented by the boxes of the quadrant. Businesses must ask themselves, who should act these parts? Of course, this requires a change in the business model. These changes often threaten existing business operations, managers, and their budgets. These roles must be clearly defined or else tensions will develop within operational areas of the business, no one will be able to address the issues and make decisions. In the next section, we'll learn how to tailor these roles to specific types of innovation.

Question 3: How Can Innovation Be Supported from Within?

Power Plus doesn't support innovation from within. Moneymaker and Hugo's tour shows that employees have lots of ideas but nobody is seizing upon them. Costman simply doesn't see his employees as sources of innovation.

How can innovation be supported from within? As we'll see below, innovation is a bit of inspiration and a lot of perspiration. Companies must create the conditions to encourage creative thinking, capture the results, and refine them for the market. The structures for encouraging such creative thinking are perhaps the most valuable innovations of all.

Managing Innovation

People often erroneously conceive of innovation as random bursts of thought that happen to strike undisciplined, artistic types. The reality is far different—and more manageable. In the 1985 article "The Discipline of Innovation" in the *Harvard Business Review,* management guru Peter Drucker said that innovation rarely comes in a flash of inspiration. More often, it's a long grind that combines several basic ingredients: expertise, ingenuity, focus, and—as much as anything—diligence. "Above all," he wrote, "innovation is work rather than genius."

During his 30 years of research, Drucker said he encountered few entrepreneurs who had so-called "entrepreneurial personalities." Instead, the successful ones had a common commitment to the systematic practice of innovation. They shared "a conscious, purposeful search for innovation opportunities, which are found only in a few situations."

Drucker identified seven sources of innovation:

1. **The Unexpected**—An unexpected success, an unexpected failure, or an unexpected outside event can be a symptom of

a unique opportunity. In the early 1930s, IBM developed the first modern accounting machine for banks. But the timing was all wrong: after the 1929 crash and Great Depression, banks were in no mood to invest in new equipment. So IBM shifted its market to libraries and sold hundreds of machines.

2. **The Incongruity**—A discrepancy between reality and what everyone assumes it to be, or between what is and what ought to be, can create an innovative opportunity. For the first half of the 20th century, the shipping industry worked hard to make ships faster and more fuel efficient. Even as they made great progress toward these goals, the business worsened. By 1950 or so, the ocean freight industry was dying. They had solved the wrong problem. The real costs actually came not from time at sea but idle time in port. Once managers understood this, they developed new innovations such as the roll-on and roll-off ship and the container ship. These solutions simply extended existing technology for railroads and trucking to ocean freighters. Once again, shipping turned into a growth industry.

3. **Innovation Based on Process Need**—When a weak link is evident in a process, people often work around it instead of fixing it. Thus there is an opportunity to provide the "missing link." The modern newspaper industry had its origin in two innovations developed in the late 1800s. Linotype made it possible to produce newspapers quickly and in large volume; modern advertising generated profit to distribute news practically free of charge.

4. **Changes in Industry or Market Structure**—The opportunity for an innovative product, service, or business approach occurs when the underlying foundation of the industry or market shifts. "New opportunities rarely fit the way the industry has always approached the market, defined it, or organized to serve it," says Drucker. "Innovators therefore have a good chance of being left alone for a long time."

5. **Demographics**—Changes in the population's size, age structure, composition, employment, level of education, and income can create innovative opportunities.

6. **Changes in Perception, Mood, and Meaning**—Innovative opportunities can develop when a society's general assumptions, attitudes, and beliefs change.

7. **New Knowledge**—Advances in scientific and nonscientific knowledge can create new products and new markets. Knowledge innovations are particularly challenging for entrepreneurial companies. They are the slowest (it often takes decades for new knowledge to turn into usable technology), most unpredictable, and have the highest casualty rates. For example, the computer integrated several strands of knowledge that had been available since 1918: binary arithmetic, the model of a calculating machine, punch cards, the audion tube, an electronic switch, symbolic logic, and concepts of programming and feedback that came out of abortive attempts to develop antiaircraft guns during World War. Yet it took four decades to combine these elements into a workable machine. Not until 1946 did the first operational digital computer appear.

Although difficult, knowledge-based innovation can be managed, according to Drucker. It requires an understanding of the different sources of innovation, analysis of how to best meet the opportunity and rigorous study of how it will work in the real world. "Successful innovators use both the right and left sides of their brains," he writes. "They work out analytically what the innovation has to be to satisfy an opportunity. Then they go out and look at potential users to study their expectations, their values, and their needs."

Typically, innovations are not blockbuster ideas. More often, they are small improvements that make people say "That's so simple! Why didn't I think of that?" Successful innovation aims to reset the direction of technology or industry; if it does not become a leader, it's not innovative enough.

Innovators are most productive if they stick to specific areas of expertise. As Drucker notes, Thomas Edison, for all his inventions, worked only in electricity. Innovators should aim for narrowly defined applications that fill a specific need. Finally, there's no substitute for hard work and a systemic, step-by-step approach. As Drucker concludes, "the very foundation of entrepreneurship is the practice of systematic innovation."

Innovative Innovators

A number of entrepreneurial companies have devised unique systems to cultivate new ideas. A few examples:

- Google has a well-known "20% rule" that allows employees to spend one day per week on projects outside their job description. Employees have great latitude: they can pursue new ideas or improve an existing product. Employees can dedicate one day per week to these pursuits or bank it to spend in the future. This program has spawned Google News, Google Suggest, AdSense for Content, and Orkut. The rule recognizes that managers have a limited ability to generate new ideas from the top down and that people are most productive when working on things they are passionate about.

- Cisco has launched an internal Idea Zone (I-Zone for short), a wiki that allows employees to contribute new business ideas. The program worked so well that the company decided to try a similar tactic outside the company in the Cisco I-Prize. People are invited to submit ideas for new business opportunities with the possibility of a $250,000 signing bonus and $10 million investment if Cisco pursues the idea. Cisco expects that in the future it will have several new businesses that will have come directly from ideas submitted to I-Zone. Several are in the incubation phase now and four new business units have already been launched as a result.

Cisco is also using wikis and social networking technologies to power several efforts that encompass several teams including Cisco's Green efforts, the company's Sarbanes-Oxley compliance initiatives as well as a Communications Center of Excellence, a multi-team effort to redefine communications and innovation within the company based on Web 2.0 concepts.

- SAP and Oracle are using "prediction markets" to turn collective intelligence into quantifiable information. Prediction markets aggregate the responses of many people to predict the likelihood of certain outcomes. These tools are helping a growing number of companies to tap into the "wisdom of crowds." Google uses marketplaces to predict timing for launching products. Hewlett-Packard uses them for forecasting sales. Eli Lilly does so to forecast new drug applications.

Combining Models: People and Technology

Now let's put some of these ideas together. Drucker's seven sources of innovation can be plotted onto the quadrant we discussed in Chapter 7. Where is the force of change in your business or industry? The answer will determine what roles should be assigned and played by your employees and partners.

Now that we've addressed the human side of the solution, let's turn to the technological one.

Once you've identified the source of change, the next question is: what technology clusters will address it? Capgemini has identified seven technology clusters:

- **You Experience:** A new generation of user interface technologies and internet-based collaboration platforms create individualized experience for the user. They can freely connect to the outside world to buy, interact, collaborate, cocreate, and share knowledge.

- **From Transaction to Interaction:** Organizations and individuals engage in a steady, continuous rhythm of learning, creating, and collaborating. They create new value through business innovation with markets, players, and consumers constantly shifting position. Global "open" markets vastly increase the competition compared with existing localized "closed" markets.

- **Processes "On the Fly":** Processes can be assembled "on the fly" using building blocks of services. Organizations will need to change their processes in real time to accommodate changes in the business ecosystem. The underlying information systems that support these processes must consist of fine-grained, configurable services that can freely be composed and orchestrated into new solutions.

- **Thriving on Data:** Increasingly, the secret to success is how to read, and react, to a succession of events. These are opportunities to make money by optimizing the situation—or lose money by being unable to identify and manage a problem. Businesses need more "interaction" for rapidly assembling information and making decisions. They also must take input from many more people within the organization because all are operational consumers and suppliers of intelligence.

- **Business Services "On Tap":** Organizations should focus on differentiation and provide standard and non-differentiating business services "on tap." This is achieved through little-customized implementations of standard software or through the generation of systems out of re-usable industry reference models. Delivering business services through a SaaS (Software as a Service) approach is just one further step toward supplying integrated business services—including processes—as an in-sourced or out-sourced utility.

- **Invisible Infostructure:** This approach uses virtualization and grid technologies to deliver infrastructural services—including all facilities to exchange and process (inter) company information—as a commoditized, preferably almost invisible, utility. Eventually, even core business services will merge into it, creating a true business infrastructure. An invisible infostructure captures and supplies information.
- **Open Standards Foundation:** This enables boundaryless information flow between all players in the business ecosystem. Open standards do not only pertain to "horizontal" requirements for data exchange formats, authentication, and security, but increasingly to "vertical" requirements that address the business tasks and rules of a specific sector. Furthermore, globalization and regulatory compliance demand more standardization of architectural and development methodologies and of professional certification.

Summing Up

The employees at Power Plus have been powered down. But, once given the opportunity to voice and pursue ideas, the company's future could begin to brighten.

What needs to change? They need to develop a system to capture and direct the innovative ideas of their own employees and customers. Such systems can take many forms, depending on the circumstances. A solution that works for Power Plus might not work for Google. One that works for Vorpal might not fly at 3M.

Innovation arises in many circumstances—and each one requires a unique mix of people and technology. By understanding the models described above, managers will gain a better grasp of how to deploy their resources most effectively and turn ideas into business. Essentially, they will have unleashed the power of innovation through collective inspiration.

Chapter 9 Questions and Analysis

Moneymaker Finds a Solution

Question 1: What Are Smart Services and How Are They Implemented?

The big story behind Power Plus' transition into Energy Plus is that it represents the switch from an old-line manufacturer to a smart services enabled company. What Moneymaker is proposing is not just a change to the business model of Power Plus. She is proposing a new business model that is executed by an ecosystem of companies, including the company that makes the controllers on the generators, and those that provide other critical parts. Energy Plus is at the center, as an orchestrator and enabler of this new model. The bet that Moneymaker is making is that the value and efficiencies created by the ecosystem are rewarded with more revenue with higher margins from its customers, revenue that will be harvested by Energy Plus and all the participating companies. For this to work, the ecosystem has to deliver the business results better than the ecosystem customers could do by themselves. The mechanism by which this is allowed to happen is Smart Services.

The critical pieces that enable companies to offer smart services are the extent to which they have already added technology to their products that could support this move, or are already a traditional-service business that can see how to extend their role in the business-value chain by aggregating other services to improve the value of the offering. In the case of Power Plus the generator controllers are the high-tech products and are "network-aware" devices that share information about the Power Plus products and collect information about other devices on the network. Many businesses are in the same position as Power Plus—they have not considered the capabilities that they have built into their products from a different point of view, nor have they considered how this could be used to change their business model.

The second key enabler of smart services is the ability to thrive on data, which is more—much more—than merely collecting data. It's not just about collecting data, and then mining it: it's about real-time, event-driven interpretation and proactive use, in this case by empowering service technicians to monitor, evaluate, and imme-diately take action on what is happening at a customer site. Data mining techniques can also be used to track patterns, find ways to increase efficiency, and find mistakes in configuration or indicators of impending equipment failure.

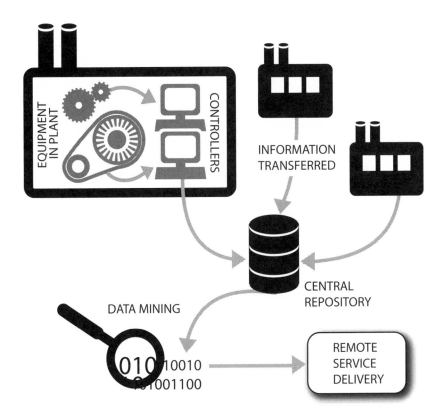

Figure Q9-1: Model of Smart Services

Because Energy Plus will be the clearinghouse for the devices' information, it now has an edge over competitors that make cheaper equipment. Smart services create intelligence about the business value delivered by all of a customer's energy-producing equipment. This intelligence can be used to optimize performance of existing equipment, proactively find problems, improve maintenance strategies, recommend new designs or products, and better deliver other value-added services. Energy Plus will deliver some of these new services itself, but other participants in the ecosystem will deliver others. The other participants in the value chain around Energy Plus will be drawn to the ecosystem because of the unique information Energy Plus possesses. The smart services run by Energy Plus allow these companies to build new services they perhaps couldn't have before. In one move, Energy Plus has captured unique end-user loyalty—by solving the business problem, not just by providing components—and has also created sustainable competitive advantage. The more knowledge Energy Plus gains about its customers, the more value they can deliver, which should lead to more revenue from smart services.

How is this done in the real world?

The Technology is Already There

The reason a lot of pie-in-the-sky technology projects don't take off is because they often come with a huge price tag and a risky dive into a new or heavy-duty build of technology that is also time-consuming and resource-sapping. But smart services are based on technology that's already embedded into nearly every device you can think of.

Virtually every product that uses electricity is in the process of becoming a "smart" device with Intel reporting that sales of chips to "consumer" devices massively exceeds sales to the IT industry. Each has an incredible amount of information to offer about its current status, use history, and performance. Manufacturers of heavy industrial and sophisticated medical devices have made a concerted effort to shift the burden of margin contribution in the direction of services, and as such, they more actively participate in the post-purchase lives of their products.

Consider GE's power turbine business. The electronics embedded in its turbines, sending signals about temperature, wear and tear, and capacity back to headquarters, mean that a technician or engineer can be proactively deployed to the site before a failure even occurs. That is the valuable kind of service that customers will pay for—in GE's case, five to six times as much as a comparable traditional call-us-if-it-breaks technical support contract.

The same company also provides free installation of its hospital MRI machines—which, because of their expense, are traditionally leased—and simply bundles maintenance into the overall contract. In order to do this profitably, and get the pricing level just right in order to be competitive, GE depends on the high quality of reportage that emanates from its machines, which makes a business plan look something like an actuarial chart. It comes down to estimating as closely as possible how long something is going to last, then stepping in at the exact right moment with a suggestion about how to move forward. Network-aware devices help companies do exactly that.

HP takes this idea one step further on a much simpler, commoditized device. It's well known that printer manufacturers make most of their money on the cartridges, which must be replenished. HP's smart printers now automatically order a new print cartridge when the old one is about to run out. This has given HP an edge over its lower-cost clones, which offer cartridges, but not embedded intelligence.

You don't have to be a manufacturer of costly, technically sophisticated devices to benefit from smart services. Nor is the value of smart services limited to maintenance, because almost anything you learn about your product has the potential to enhance its profitability.

Think of everything a customer does that intertwines with a product's lifecycle. They have to determine the requirements for and justify the purchase of the product, find a supplier, finance the purchase, install the product, maintain it, train others to use it, upgrade it, and dispose of its waste and of the product itself. In each of these activities, there is an opportunity for the customer to have a relationship with the producer, which can be enhanced if the product volunteers information that allows the producer to proactively become involved at each step of the lifecycle.

Integrating Existing Smart Networks

Smart services are not limited to individual consumer or commercial devices. They can be applied to entire buildings, networks of buildings, even entire cities.

An incredible amount of electronics has been installed in buildings. Thermostats, garage door openers, smoke alarms, telecommunications, and control systems for heating, ventilation, and air conditioning (HVAC), to name a few. Although all of these systems individually serve their purpose well, they are isolated from each other. It's common for a building's computing network, telephone, security, and climate-control systems to be made by different companies and operate on different information protocols. Cisco's architecture for Connected Real Estate shows how a diverse collection of systems communicating over the IP network can function in synch with each other, which can increase efficiency in the way buildings are operated, managed, and secured.

Communication with physical security systems, VOIP telecommunications, video surveillance, access control, visitor management, and fire safety all takes place on an IP network. Converged IP technology can also fold in HVAC, lighting, transportation (elevators and escalators), and energy management (such as turning lights off when not used).

Converging on IP saves physical space in a building and consolidates communications more efficiently. But it does far more than that. Through IP architecture and the use of open communication standards, buildings gain enhanced value because their various constituent systems can now be aware of each other, and can carry on many activities that would have required redundant supervision by isolated groups of people.

For example, a physical security system may be able to detect whether there is motion in a room, check the time of day, and use that intelligence to direct the building's automation system to turn off the lights and turn down the air conditioning. Or, a fire alarm goes off after business hours, notifying not only the fire department, but also the building security manager on his PDA, or via an instant message to the facilities manager, who is working on his computer at home. Information is integrated, and available to whoever needs it, on whatever device is needed, whenever it is needed.

For the same reason, the presence of microchips and an IP network afford a great opportunity for Moneymaker and Energy Plus to create smart services.

Energy Plus will invest the time and effort to become the coordinator of this information—the center of a smart services ecosystem—therefore, it now has an enviable opportunity for making an offer to take responsibility for delivering more business value. Going beyond a service-level agreement covering equipment, as its skill and the power of its ecosystem grows, Energy Plus will offer a Business Level Agreement for delivering the outcome the components are intended to create: reliable and efficient delivery of energy and emergency power. Like Cisco, which started with its expertise in IP switching equipment, and moved that expertise forward into a new smart service that helps customers create converged IP networks for their buildings, Energy Plus will leverage the components of energy management and take responsibility for finding partners that will make the smart services concept work.

Question 2: How Does the Central Repository of Data Used in Smart Service Delivery Create Value?

The main tenet of the transformation of Power Plus into Energy Plus revolves around its proprietary ability to capture information about the performance of its own devices, as well as the devices of its competitors, and learn from that information.

Energy Plus is able to do this because it had already established a central data repository that is collecting this information from the devices in use at each customer location. Over time, that repository will become even more valuable, because it is collecting specific information about each customer that will allow Energy Plus to offer tailored maintenance, support, and consulting services, keeping the company one step ahead of the competition. Eventually, Energy Plus will have better information about the performance of its competitors' products than its competitors do, increasing its hold on customers and extending its reach beyond its traditional sales base of physical assets, into the realm of professional services. Much of this is a conventional use of data, what's new is how to use this data in combination with other data and, most of all, in response to events.

For the business to thrive, the ability to be more intelligent and optimize every situation is key to the strategy. Energy Plus will store traditional types of information in its repository:

- Master data that will describe the equipment in place at each customer
- Operational data that will describe how the equipment is operating

To succeed in getting the most out of this central data repository, Energy Plus must become deft at creating, managing, and learning from both kinds of data. The challenge for Energy Plus is not to create a system for master data management or an operational data warehouse. Expert partners can and should be brought in to implement the solution. The tough part is not the plumbing. The tough part—the valuable part—is understanding what the data means and putting it to good use.

Question 3: What Business Models Are Enabled by Smart Services?

So far we have focused on "smart" in the context of services—remote diagnostics and remediation enabled by the electronic connection to the end user. However, the availability of detailed end-user configuration data at the device level or network level, as a result of an intelligent device that transmits data back to the vendor, opens up the opportunity to transform several areas of a company's operations in a way that becomes personalized, or customer specific, and significantly transformed. In short it's not just services that can be smart.

The Smart Selling Process

The traditional sales process is triggered either when the prospect responds to a marketing offer delivered through direct mail and tele-marketing, or when they themselves decide that they need to purchase something and go out to tender. In both cases the sales process relies on the prospect comparing an offer against the budget and value requirements they have already decided upon internally. With smart services it is possible to use software to compare the installed base of customer equipment against the current vendor product catalogues and make a customer-specific proposal to replace older equipment with newer models wrapped into a finance offer, such as a lease.

This is proactive as opposed to reactive selling. As such, a company may alter the telemarketing script from the classic cold call, hard sell, to a personalized customer interaction, which can go as follows: "Hello Mr. Smith, this is Mandy from Power Plus. We've noticed from our databases that you have 25 of our generators installed in your factory and four of them are older models that we have recently replaced by newer, more efficient ones. We've also done an analysis of your power usage and your total maintenance costs and we believe you can reduce your monthly support fees by 5%, while at the same time improving the efficiency of your electricity production by 8%. We've prepared an individual finance sales proposal for you showing how you can do that for the same monthly fee you are paying today. Additionally, we can see that you also have four generators from another manufacturer on your energy grid. We could also roll those into the same proposal with the same benefits. Would you like to discuss this with one of our energy technicians via a web-based video conference? He's available to talk right now and he has all of the information."

There are three key differences between traditional selling and smart selling. First, the smart selling company is now creating a new budget, not selling against an existing budget. Second, each smart sales proposal has a customer specific ROI attached, making it easier to justify internally. Third, smart sales proposals are proactive and so by definition are submitted without any competitive bid. Not a bad set of advantages to have in the sales process for any company.

The Smart Marketing Process

It's long been the case that traditional marketing is one of the most difficult areas of a company's expenditures to examine and determine its effectiveness.

Smart marketing by contrast is laser focused because it works by analyzing the data from the installed base of intelligent devices; matching that data with current marketing offers; and then ensuring that only those for whom the offer is relevant ever see it. So for example, say your company invents the "Whizzo 2008," which has been specifically designed to replace the "Whizzo 2005" model that you know you have sold 2 million of over the last three years. Unless you know exactly where each 2005 model is—and if you sell through channels you almost certainly don't—then all you can do is mail everybody on your customer list. With smart marketing you simply email every customer who has a "Whizzo 2005" and achieve a 100% hit rate each and every time.

The Smart Design Process

The new product design process in most companies is driven by significant end-user research and on-site customer testing before the product manager and manufacturing team make the critical decisions on the product specification. However, once the product ships it is very rare if the company truly knows which features are used and which ones are not. The end result is often thousands, if not tens of thousands of different ways in which each product can be configured by the end user. There's no clearer example of this problem than the thick user guide, which is found in the box of most consumer electronics devices and which few people ever read.

Whereas this abundance of features plays well when marketing the values of user choice and flexibility, it causes a significant amount of extra work and cost in the design, build, and testing process. Companies not only load up their products with too many features, but they typically have to test every combination of every feature with each new release of the product or software associated with the product. The reality is that the Pareto rule is alive and well here in that 80% of customers only use 20% of the features. In fact, research shows that often 50% or more of the features in most devices are never used by more than 1% of customers. After all, how many of the features on your mobile phone or your handheld device do you use?

Because companies don't have the data on what is or isn't being used in the real world, they take the only course of action they can and test 100% of all the combinations, while at the same time loading up the newer models with as many bells and whistles as they can.

In this case an intelligent device capability gives obvious benefits. The marketing department gets exact data on not only which products are being used, but also the next level of detail down to which specific features or combination of features are being used. Testing and new product creation can now be done on just the features that are being used by real users and not the educated guess of product managers. Over time, product lifecycles shorten, products become more relevant and simpler to use, and manufacturing and component costs are reduced.

This smart design process is not a future vision. For example, Cisco is embedding a "Smart Call Home" capability in many of the devices it ships, which, if enabled by the end user when installed, will transmit this type of data back to Cisco. With tens of millions of routers and switches installed worldwide the potential to create future products that are simpler and designed around real customer usage patterns is very real and being implemented today.

Question 4: What Are Value Networks and How Are They Related to Smart Services?

When Moneymaker first introduces the concept of smart services and business model transformation to the board, they are basically terrified. How can the IT staff, trained to support only the sales, operations, and accounting around electric generators, develop Web 2.0 capabilities, build a data warehouse, and transform itself from supporting Power Plus, a maker of things, into a support network for Energy Plus, a provider of integrated products and services?

"Don't worry," Moneymaker says. "You don't have to go it alone." There are hundreds of companies out there in the world who have the expertise to make Moneymaker's vision a reality. But the relationship with these companies would not work if it were unidirectional or hierarchical. This network of companies, using Web 2.0 technology, can connect with Energy Plus and form mutually supportive relationships that benefit all parties in the web of connections. This concept of shared empowerment is dependent upon understanding business relationships as a value network, and it is a key to the successful deployment of smart services.

Definitions:

According to the Information Technology Infrastructure Library, value networks are webs of relationships that generate economic, social, or environmental value through complex dynamic exchanges of both tangible and intangible goods, services, and benefits. In the context of smart services, value networks encompass mutually dependent relationships between customers and service providers, with business outcomes at the core.

It's important to think of this web as a nonlinear entity, because that allows the business practitioner to create nonlinear processes. The world that Energy Plus is leaving behind is monolithic, unidirectional, and linear. The world it's entering is collaborative, connected, and nonlinear.

Value networks respect the fact that knowledge is contained in two formats: explicit and tacit. Explicit knowledge includes what would be called "hard data," or "information," such as sales and accounting figures. This type of knowledge has been relatively straightforward to capture in electronic form for later incorporation into processes.

Tacit knowledge includes more esoteric information that is contained mostly in individuals' minds, and it includes relationship-management tactics (such as knowing that on Mondays, it's a bad idea to call a sales prospect until after lunch) and other difficult-to-document activities that collectively constitute "good practice." But just because these intangible exchanges are difficult to document does not mean that it should not be attempted. Good practice may make the difference between a good business relationship and a failed one.

Business relationships also consist of two kinds of interaction between parties. One is "tangible flow:" A vendor performs a service or provides a customer with a product, and the customer pays the vendor. It comprises goods, services, and revenue. In short, it is the traditional value chain.

The other is "intangible flow," which consists of qualities that are more difficult to put a price tag on. These include sense of community, collaborative design, image, brand recognition, product development feedback, customer loyalty, and references.

The ideal value network is a framework that incorporates an optimal balance of good process and good practice, intangible and tangible flows into a single ecosystem. To get there, we can employ Value Network Analysis (VNA), a process perfected by the Information Technology Infrastructure Library, ITIL, and the Value Networks Consortium. This would reward companies like Energy Plus, which have heretofore been locked into traditional Business Process Modeling (BPM). VNA is a great first step toward putting smart services to work for your company.

The technique uses the methods of a traditional BPM approach, but adds unique features for identifying intangible flows. The VNA map consists of participants, whose ovals (see Figure Q9-2) represent human decision makers at the individual or group level. The arrows represent flows—the solid lines are tangible flows, the dotted lines intangible flows. Labels on the arrows are deliverables that move from one participant to the next.

Tangible flows are characterized by contracted activities ("I do this, you pay me"), while intangible flows are not formally contracted, but are essential to achieving a smooth operation.

Figure Q9-2: VNA Map—Basic Components

Question 5: How Do Smart Services Help Create an Ecosystem?

Power Plus has a valuable stable of assets—its generators with intelligent controllers embedded. These controllers are programmable and connected to an IP network, allowing people to interact with them in a number of ways; chief among them remote control and data collection.

The technology that allows this interactivity and Power Plus' unique ability to understand its devices and how its customers use them, together provide the tools to transform the company into Energy Plus, a smart services–enabled energy management company.

The momentum behind Energy Plus' drive into smart services is Moneymaker and Wonderkind's unique capability to recognize the potential for creating an ecosystem—an interdependent network of service providers, partners, and customers that together create valuable services. In some ways, the ability to see, remotely administer, collect, interpret, and present information about an asset—in this case the generator—is more important than the asset itself. The person or company that brings all the assets together under business logic owns the value of those assets, because the company now has an ability to reach out to customers far afield from its original base, through partners who will reinterpret and use Energy Plus' core data-collection capability to offer new services. These services will have a regenerative effect on Energy Plus, which is now the center of an ecosystem.

Key to this is that all of the ecosystem partners will be creating their own value-added services based upon Energy Plus' core intellectual property. Therefore, Energy Plus becomes strategic to every one of the partners, which follows along the lines of an Intel Inside model. As such, this is very different from the confrontational vendor/supplier battle around price that Tilo Costman found himself in. In effect, what Energy Plus would create becomes an ecosystem of shared value powered by Energy Plus' core capabilities.

The Value of an Ecosystem

It's not an exaggeration to say that the value of an ecosystem can be summed up in one phrase: "It's all about the aggregation."

Business models used to be defined around assets. Companies would buy or sell assets or define elements of business around the assets they owned. A consumer formerly purchased a mobile phone (an asset) and then tried to find a service contract. Now, the service is purchased and the phone is thrown in for free.

Businesses are moving away from buying assets and managing them, to negotiating for and aggregating control of information about assets. The electrical power industry is moving in this direction. At present, the business is still largely vertically integrated, with most of its resources dedicated to managing assets, including transmission lines, generators, and meters. But as utilities deregulate, companies have the option to shed those assets and instead take over only certain aspects of power delivery, or to create managed services on top of power generation and transmission, which may be provided by several different companies under contract to the aggregator.

Rather than selling a product to a customer and competing on cost, which is a "race to the bottom" scenario, now companies are looking to create value out of a process over which they can gain substantial control of the information. Now companies can make a profit from products whose physical fulfillment may not be under their direct ownership or control.

They don't do it alone. They use an ecosystem of interdependent partners working together, and drawing revenue off the core company's ability to assemble information.

The value of an ecosystem is not in the assets themselves. The value is in creating smart services around those assets. The value is in giving your employees the time and space to think about competitively advantageous business logic. That could involve outsourcing the lower-value aspects of your business to someone who competes on cost and volume, or it could involve acquiring, or writing a contract with, boutique consulting firms that already have an advanced methodology for collecting the information you need to build smart services. Both of these companies, the outsourcer and the boutique, are now part of your ecosystem.

The value is in the "black box" of intellectual property—your business model—that holds the ecosystem together. Your competitors can see you are doing something different, but they don't understand how you are doing it. And your ecosystem partners aren't talking. Before anyone else thought of it, you had the advantage of allowing them privileged access to your information, for a price, upon which they have now built additional services that can be offered to the customer. And, the more information you accumulate, the easier it is to create customized products for your customer, whether your business is mortgages, autos, or electronics. Eventually, your competitors won't be copying your product catalog, because you won't offer one. Each of your customers now has a unique product, built out of multiple recombinant elements, perhaps provided in part by your ecosystem partners and controlled by SLAs.

Chapter 10 Questions and Analysis

Fighting to Change IT

Question 1: How Does the Role of IT Change to Support a Smart Services Ecosystem?

In this chapter, Moneymaker serves up an ultimatum to the doubters. She tells the IT department it's time to change and grow, or seek new employment. Why have things become so tense?

The IT department heads balk at the idea that, in a few months' time, Energy Plus will be on its way to becoming an end-to-end energy management services company, rather than just a manufacturer of generators.

This is a shock to many, but not all IT people. They have spent their entire careers building systems to support vertical business processes almost always focused on tightly coupled integration and data integrity. They have learned to speak in a common language with business around general ledgers and ERP processes, and to work together on technology elements like databases and firewalls to prevent malicious attacks and employees wasting company time. They are unsure of having a new business model foisted upon them, along with a call for using technologies with which they are not familiar—at least not in a corporate IT context.

They balk at implementing a Web 2.0 model of loose coupling and collaboration because they fear the impact on the well-regulated systems that they have in place and new demands that they don't know about, such as remote monitoring. Further, they often want the time to learn about these new things in a traditional manner. Also, Moneymaker has redefined the definition of their customer and their value-add. They no longer have to provide IT services to internal users; they have created a platform for the entire ecosystem of Energy Plus channel partners. This new way cuts at the command-and-control, internally focused model under which they have been operating up to this point.

In short, IT must convert itself from a locked-down manager of internal functions to an entrepreneurial, interconnected aggregator of technology, partners, and services, if the company is to survive.

Seven Ways IT Must Change

In order to support a smart services ecosystem, we suggest seven ways corporate IT must change.

1. IT must begin to accept the role of other players in the newly extended partner network and realize that it cannot, and should not attempt to build an ecosystem single-handedly. The economic benefit of an ecosystem is that the burden of creating its value does not rest on a single player. Interdependent partners, each working from an identified position of strength (core competency) contribute technical know-how to, and reap the revenue from, the ecosystem. The IT department of the aggregator, the center of the ecosystem, must develop a sense of trust and accept that other partners, outside the firewalls, are going to be playing a strong role in supporting the new business model.

2. IT must learn to relinquish its control-all mentality and learn to think collaboratively. It must learn how to play the role of conductor, rather than trying to play each instrument simultaneously. The mindset must change from "the People's Republic of IT" to a technology-based business.

3. IT must move from supporting the operations and sales of manufactured products to playing a role in a front-end, business-aligned group that creates dynamic offerings of value for the customer and for ecosystem partners. This means it turns from the current necessity of being a centralized organization into a flexible, proactive, and entrepreneurial organization. IT focuses on business objectives, not "science projects" or building castles.

4. IT must actively involve itself in looking for customer behavior around and use of assets, rather than simply building, deploying, and maintaining them—which it still must also do, unless it specifically contracts some of this work out to a third party. Those patterns that pop up frequently are candidates for automation, leaving "breathing room" for higher-value transactions (such as consulting) to take place.

5. IT must realize its ongoing value will be in creating and maintaining business logic that constantly optimizes those assets and enables business processes. This is where the "black-box IP" is located, and that's what gives the company the competitive edge. Although IT's role is changing, it's certainly not becoming less significant. It's only becoming less rigid, more innovative, and more collaborative.

6. IT must think of itself as enabling the basis for business and interactions and transcend the normal boundaries of corporate IT with its focus on procedures and transactions. That means thinking about the overall quality of the end-user experience at the beginning of any design process, as opposed to focusing on technological metrics like throughput and processing speeds. One simple way to set down this path psychologically is to reorganize titles and roles to be more business focused. At BT (British Telecom), the title of CIO no longer exists. Each former CIO is now a managing director, because the company considers them fundamentally to be managing directors of businesses. The head of technology design at BT is called a CEO, demonstrating that technology is so pervasive that it

represents disciplines far beyond the boundaries of IT. The old IT built and maintained technology, often in an isolated silo. The new IT combined with the new technologies represents products, people, and processes. The new IT enables processes and products for people through its support in the use of technology and existing IT systems.

7. IT must make objective decisions about which services it will support directly, and what is best left to partners. IT will be of greatest value to the company, and IT employees will feel they are providing the most value, if it focuses its energy on market-differentiating and revenue-generating services. Any service or technology asset that represents a cost center or is commoditized (someone else could do it just as well) is a candidate for some form of outsourcing, and that means Business Process Outsourcing (BPO) as an option as much as Technology Operation Outsourcing. The role of corporate in technology-based business increasingly passes from directly managing every piece of technology in an organization to managing only mission-critical IT, orchestrating the work of partners, and developing new business-focused solutions that differentiate the company in its chosen market.

Question 2: What Skills Must IT Departments Develop in Order to Support a Smart Services Ecosystem?

It's understandable that Elaine Lamfort is uncomfortable with Moneymaker's radical vision for Power Plus. It requires a sea change in how the IT department operates, as illustrated in Question 1. That change also means that IT personnel will have to address their skill sets and rethink how they approach project management, organization, and their use of vendor products. Here's how it can be done.

Architectural Design Skills

A traditional IT department supports the business with a combination of vendor products and internally developed applications. Much of the work of the traditional IT department revolves around integrating vendor and proprietary applications. The emergence of open standards in recent years has made this job much easier, but at the same time, business logic has become ever more complicated. Nonetheless, the focus has been on internal business processes. That means traditional IT is really good at squeezing vendor products for maximum performance, and squeezing vendors themselves for a good price.

The emphasis is on creating a stable, low-cost framework for operating applications. The focus is on managing components, and not so much on business outcomes.

Ecosystem IT

In ecosystem IT, however, the skill set must be augmented so that personnel are thinking about an information structure that provides value and improves the way everyone works, at a higher level of abstraction than is required for designing a framework for components as described above. In an ecosystem IT, the goal goes beyond creating a client-server network that simply "hums along" and doesn't crash. Personnel are actually designing new forms of doing business, and using technology to create new ways of working. That means switching your *modus operandi* from buying a set of assets to support each vertical process, to thinking about a small group of assets as an almost infinitely configurable number of products.

Vendor management skills must also be improved. There are likely to be many more vendors in your universe as an ecosystem creator, and, just as the business you support no longer follows a "sell at high volume and squeeze the suppliers" model, your IT policy can no longer follow a "squeeze the vendor and good enough is good" philosophy. Some vendors, such as outsourcers, will be satisfied by a bilateral SLA that allows them to offer you volume discounts. But your vendors are now your ecosystem partners, and many are going to be looking for a way to participate in the new revenue streams you are creating. In exchange for this role, vendors are more likely to be willing to perform some of the customization work your IT personnel once had to perform themselves.

Sit on the Business Side

The process of designing ecosystems may reveal inefficiencies and disconnects in a traditionally organized IT outfit. A restructuring of the IT organization may be necessary. Although "old-timers" will find this proposition jarring, today's business and technical schools are training CIOs to take on roles that more closely resemble those held by COOs in the past. (And in some cases, their titles are changing to reflect the smart services ecosystem—see Question 1).

Because an ecosystem breaks with many time-honored conceptions of how businesses are organized, the business side of a company is forced to think in architectural terms. Therefore, ecosystem designers need to break through the walls of the IT silo. That means it's time for a lot of organizations to move their desks around. In this new role the CIO should sit with the CEO, along with all the other "C-level" executives. The head of IT and technology for sales should sit with the head of sales. The people who set the objectives and requirements sit with the people who execute them, so that the ecosystem culture pervades the IT organization. The traditional IT support function staff will probably sit with the CFO.

Speaking "Business"

Because ecosystem design requires a fusion between business and IT, and because business processes are being radically transformed quickly, there is no time for a lag between a concept and its execution. The IT group must also become familiar with business language, and take on business performance indicators as their own. And because the value of smart services is largely predicated on proactive rather than reactive activities, internal IT departments need to become more service-focused and outward-facing, hiring consultants to train them if necessary.

Many IT staff will point to their not inconsiderable efforts over recent years to become business aligned in this manner. However, using the example of SOA, if looked at from the traditional perspective of the IT department the services will be defined and assembled to relate to the existing IT systems, procedures, and data models. It's a necessary approach, though wholly different from the business perspective that will want services defined around recognizable business tasks that can be reassembled or orchestrated to follow business change. Actually, both approaches are required in order to create the binding together of front office flexibility with back office stability.

The Ecosystem Designer

The skill set of the ecosystem designer, the person who holds an extended version of what has been the chief enterprise architect role, draws from both business and IT. If we were to write a job description of the archetypal ecosystem designer, it might sound something like this:

- The ecosystem designer must be able to convince partners that there is a market for the ecosystem if they collectively develop the skills.
- The ecosystem designer must give the target customers the confidence that there will be a party ultimately responsible for coordinating all the partners and technology and making the whole assemblage work. In our example, that's Energy Plus, which bears the most responsibility but also reaps the greatest reward. The designer's company must be able to provide a clear architectural implementation roadmap and manage integration.
- The ecosystem designer acts as guarantor of the project; he or she must find any missing pieces of technology, or missing partnerships, if the processes break or do not meet

expectations. He or she must become proficient in selecting and developing partners and managing those relationships.

- The ecosystem designer regularly and systematically reviews the ecosystem's functioning and makes recommendations for changes in design if expectations are not being met.

Question 3: What Obstacles Will Most IT Departments Face Adopting an Ecosystem Approach?

As we've seen, there are a number of objections in the Jabberwocky boardroom when Moneymaker announces her plan to transform Power Plus into Energy Plus. Almost immediately (leaving aside the protestations of business managers faced with changes in the responsibility structure) the folks down in the IT department join the chorus and state reasons why the plan won't work. They are being told that it's time to revolutionize their thinking about how IT is created, deployed, and managed. They calm down a bit when it's explained that they won't have to do it all themselves, but they remain somewhat resistant. This is not truculence. It's an understandable reaction given that they understand all too well the limitations and risks of change to the current systems and the amount of knowledge required to bring new technology into use safely.

If your company plans to implement smart services ecosystems, it's likely that you will come up against a similar scenario. We'll describe some of the types of IT issues that you'll likely encounter and offer suggestions about how to overcome them.

Three Categories of IT Obstructionism

Asking an IT department to move from a traditional model to an ecosystem model is asking your IT staffers to leave behind the comfort of having everything installed in their own data center, having everything under their control, and having a relatively stable set of partners that do a relatively defined set of things. Given that the level of experience they have in the IT systems that likely are heavily customized, their concern is well placed. The question is how to separate the new world from the existing IT in such a manner that safe corporate back office transactional IT services are maintained while building out to embrace the more open and shared work of the business ecosystem.

Of course, every company is structured slightly differently and will have different dynamics between its various executives. But here are three general types of resistance you will likely encounter as IT is presented with the smart services ecosystem concept, along with some handy suggestions for overcoming the resistance.

Fear Change but Want to Help

One category of IT staffers fears change but genuinely wants to help move forward. They demonstrate a lack of understanding of what's going to happen. They fear the unknown. They want to enable change. They understand it needs to happen, but the challenge is that they don't know how to accomplish it, because they can't visualize the roadmap. Their unfamiliarity with business objectives keeps them from doing so.

This group needs people—think of them as "coaches"—who can help them understand the vision and the roadmap. They need help to get them into a structured way of working toward the new goals—IT groups are incredibly structured, and that can be part of the problem, but also part of the solution. They need the business to leverage their need for structure and focus them on specific areas and specific tasks. They must be helped to understand that they are supplementing the ecosystem team and that they are making an important contribution to this new way of working. The coaches could be part of an internally assembled task force or outside consultants.

Naively Proactive

This naively proactive group believes that technological advancement is the key to business success, however, they are not particularly savvy in business. Sometimes they like to buy technology for its own sake.

This type of attitude is mostly found in organizations where the IT leadership controls the IT budget but the business approves the spending of that budget. This type of structure can lead to Technology being implemented with little relation to business objectives. This group sometimes makes locally optimized decisions without considering enterprise-wide consequences.

The first step to a solution is to take budget control away from this group and focus them toward the business values. This is usually the type of group that benefits most from reorganization around business verticals (the "move your desk" solution described in Question 2). The tension here is not fear of technology or fear of partnerships and sharing. The tension results from a lack of understanding between business and IT and the attitude that IT is an independent organization.

If reorganization along business lines is not practicable, the next step might be to place a layer of "service management" above your existing IT organization. This layer of personnel can direct the technology-focused people toward business objectives without making it seem as if the executives are watching over their shoulders. It's analogous to sending the brilliant but recalcitrant student to the "cool" ex-hippie guidance counselor rather than the stern headmaster.

NIMBYs

The third group, the "not in my backyards (NIMBYs)," or "obstructionists," is the most resistant to change. They've been running a world-class, locked-down, efficient IT enterprise for ages and they're doing fine on their own, thanks very much. Unfortunately, this must change. There are three possible ways of doing this.

1. Outsource the division completely. If your IT operation is focused on cost-cutting and static maintenance, there is no advantage to keeping them within the boundaries of your corporation when there are outsourcing companies that can do the same service more cost-effectively.

2. Replace the leader of the NIMBYs and reallocate the rest into new roles to break up the body of resistance.
3. Lastly, a softer option that will work for those who are merely concerned with their objectives and believe they are doing the right thing, change key performance indicators (KPIs) from IT-focused to business-focused measurements.

The clearest path to change is through economic incentives. NIMBYs tend to be able to obstruct change because they're in charge of IT-centric KPIs. They look at metrics such as cycle times, throughputs, and uptime. But you can change their KPIs to goals such as "percentage of deals closed" or, if the business is consumer-driven, "reducing the number of people who drop out of the sales cycle." A revenue target is another option. The senior IT people's KPIs should be focused on business successes and objectives. If IT's notion of success more closely matches the business' notion, you have a much happier family. This approach leaves the NIMBY IT staff with two choices: Continue to obstruct and fail against KPIs (and be very visible in that failure), or change behaviors to deliver the KPIs, receive bonuses, get pay raises, and keep their jobs.

Question 4: What Other Industries Have Adopted Smart Services through an Ecosystem Approach?

Smart services is an adaptation of a well-established industry business model for how services will be delivered in the future. The good news is that other industries, such as the automotive industry, have already been through this change. Around 15 years ago it was the norm to buy a car and once it was out of warranty you would take it to one dealer or another who would service it using socket sets, wrenches, and screwdrivers. Their value-add was their mechanics skills and their spares inventory, which they kept locally in their workshop.

Today this model is unthinkable: your car's complex electronics are remotely diagnosed by the manufacturer and the information passed to the dealer who uses it to fix the car and at the same time sell you other value-added services, such as financing for the next model. This has revolutionized the user experience and the dealer channel. Those who have embraced the change have grown and thrived and those who haven't—the back-street workshops—have either gone out of business or moved on to lower-value business. GM's OnStar model is another great example of a smart services platform resident in everyone of its core brand assets, consumer automobiles.

So this is a collaborative model, not a direct versus indirect model. It's a sort of "Your Company Inside" model to your partners, allowing them to transform their cost model by gradually moving out of low-margin business such as diagnostics and remediation and moving upstream to a new set of value-added services, which they wrap around the core value you provide them to deliver a new level of value to their customers.

It's not just relevant to car companies. A large number of companies providing products as diverse as airplanes, PCs, mainframes, cell phones, and home alarm systems are already implementing very similar business models. It's not about whether you are an IT company or not. That's completely irrelevant. It's about whether you believe that the partner ecosystem you have and the network you use to connect to them are capable of reinvention in this way. If you can think of a way in which they could be, you've started the process of reinventing your company and your partner ecosystem.

Question 5: How Does All of This Affect the Core IP Network?

Moneymaker's new vision for the role of IT in Energy Plus's business model has significant implications for how the IT department views its role. Rather than concentrating on managing in silos around the traditional IT system components, such as clients, applications, middleware, operating systems, servers, storage, and networks, she is asking for a new IT architecture. It is one of loosely coupled components that can be combined together on demand to produce managed services at any time, in any form, accessed by any device anywhere on the Internet. She wants to be able to create these managed services quicker than any competitor and to be assured they will behave in a predefined and predictable way. This last part will be essential for her to underpin her model with Service Level Agreements (SLAs) to her ecosystem partners and end customers.

Essentially Moneymaker is asking the IT department to build a new IT architecture similar in form to the ones that have been built by telecom service providers such as AT&T, Verizon, or British Telecom. In fact, she wants the Energy Plus IT department to think of its charter going forward as an internal service provider rather than an enterprise IT department.

The analogy is very relevant. Over the last 15 years, since the rise of the Internet, and in particular since the emergence of Voice over IP capabilities accompanied by massive fiber-based broadband capacity, the world's telecom companies have seen a huge disruption to their cost models as their core offering, voice services, has reduced in price to the point where it is for all intents and purposes free. In response, they dramatically reduced their costs by transitioning their IT architecture from multiple silos to a single end-to-end, IP-based, Next Generation Network or IP NGN. This IP NGN would virtualize all the hardware components that were connected to it; would host and deliver a new set of high-margin end-user services that ran on top of it; and would provide a layer of intelligence that controlled key aspects such as Quality of Service (QoS), billing, and application provisioning.

This model has been so successful that several major service providers now term themselves "Experience Providers," a term that captures their goal to provide end-user managed service experiences over their core network either from themselves or any of the hundreds of "over the top" players who don't own the core network, but use the deregulated telecom environment to offer additional services on top.

The key to this was a new role for the core IP network. No longer was it considered as a transport pipe whose primary function was to move packets from A to B as quickly as possible. Its new role was to provide a platform for the delivery of intelligent services such as security, authentication, encryption, presence, and QoS across not just data and voice but also video and mobility—the so called "quad play" strategy.

The same needs to be true for the IT team at Power Plus as they make their own transition to an internal service provider. They need to make their network an enabler of the new business processes now and in the future. However, to do this they need to have some sort of methodology for measuring what the current state of the network is, what the future state needs to look like and what steps are needed to get there.

One way of doing this is through applying Cisco's Service Assurance Roadmap process that the company developed after working with dozens of service providers and enterprises as they added rich services to their networks. The model clearly defines the stages of the roadmap that need to be followed and is used by many companies as a template for the transition.

The Service Assurance Roadmap Process

The chart in Figure Q10-1 shows the overall model. Using remote monitoring tools and on-site analysis the company categorizes the current state of a customer's network as one of three broad types:

- **The network and related processes focus on getting the Foundation right**. The network is seen as a collection of routers and switches and not holistically managed as an end-to-end system. Symptoms include reactive network operations management. The assets are too often unknown, and the IT staff spends too much time firefighting as the operations processes have not created consistent adherence to central policy guidelines for configurations, process, and governance.

- **The network and related processes focus on achieving Quality**. The installed base infrastructure has been brought under control and processes such as asset management and incidence management are working well. However, key process indicators such as end-to-end availability, QoS metrics, and closed loop change management for software updates still need to come under control. As a result new services can behave in an erratic fashion, service creation is slow, and too much money is spent on operating the network as opposed to innovating the business processes that are enabled by the network.
- **The network and related processes have reached a level of Operational Excellence**. A high performance quality has been established end-to-end and the network now consists of a number of standard service modules that can be combined together dynamically and on demand. This allows the company to now focus on services, which is where true value lies. New services can be created and deployed dynamically, each with a guaranteed SLA. The IT infrastructure is now a "real-time" infrastructure with applications responding in real time to events identified at the network level.

Service Assurance Roadmap

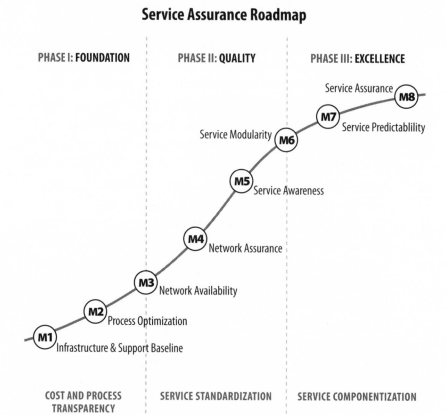

PHASE I: FOUNDATION   PHASE II: QUALITY   PHASE III: EXCELLENCE

Service Assurance **M8**

M7
Service Predictablility

Service Modularity **M6**

M5
Service Awareness

M4
Network Assurance

M3
Network Availability

M2
Process Optimization

M1
Infrastructure & Support Baseline

COST AND PROCESS   SERVICE STANDARDIZATION   SERVICE COMPONENTIZATION
TRANSPARENCY

Figure Q10-1. Network Operations Maturity Roadmap

Within these categories the company has defined eight maturity stages as follows.

- **M1—Infrastructure and Support Baseline.** The installed base is unknown. Companies should conduct an installed base discovery process and GAP analysis to determine the assets they have in order to create a solid plan for proactive asset management.
- **M2—Process Optimization**. The equipment is identified but the processes are often chaotic. Companies should

review their operational processes and governance and define the interlocks, with the intent to create a dashboard of Key Process Indicators (KPIs) to be used to track future adherence.

- **M3—Network Availability.** Processes are being adhered to on a well-known estate of equipment but end-to-end availability of the network still struggles to reach the target availability (99.9% uptime). Companies should focus on ITIL-based network optimization capabilities to improve incident management and resolution. The goal at this stage is to introduce the first SLA for network availability.

- **M4—Network Assurance.** The network performs well most of the time. More focus needs to be put on preproduction testing processes and software release management to improve moves, adds, changes, and deletions. The goal is a robust infrastructure that allows for prediction of network quality levels, such as performance, resilience, and scalability. The goal at this stage is to introduce SLAs for network quality.

- **M5—Service Awareness.** The network is constantly available but individual services cannot be guaranteed. Often, the exact service portfolio and reach is undocumented. Companies at this stage should focus on mapping existing and future services to the network, monitoring performance on a service level, and supporting service-centric processes, all backed up by a balanced scorecard.

- **M6—Service Modularity.** The mapped services and processes now need to be decomposed into single components that can be consistently reused and combined together in real time. An application services delivery architecture is created that needs to be implemented on top of a fully virtualized storage, CPU, and I/O IT infrastructure.

- **M7—Selective Predictability.** Controlling both network and service availability and quality, the challenge now is to be able to predict the impact of introducing new network or service components into the environment. All services must be predictable in terms of costs, quality, and time-to-market.

- **M8—Service Assurance.** The company is now ready to complete the transition to running IT as an internal Service Provider. End-to-end service management KPIs need to be implemented up to the business applications level such as SAP or Oracle. The result is that senior managers can launch new business initiatives involving new innovative services with SLA-based attributes at any time to any device in any format.

Throughout this roadmap, as optimizations are achieved, the company has an opportunity to reduce operating costs so that money is freed up to invest in new service creation. This is achieved through selective offload of processes that are not mission-critical to less expensive vendors who can deliver them through an SLA.

At this point the network is now a platform for the delivery of a rich array of services that enable the company's strategic business plan. Or put another way, the company is now officially using the Network of Everything to create new business value.

About the Authors

As vice president and business leader for Cisco Services, European Markets, Nick Earle is responsible for developing innovative services to help accelerate customer success and partner profitability, utilizing the network as the platform for business differentiation.

Nick Earle

With over 25 years of IT industry experience, Earle has held a number of senior management positions including CEO at StreamServe Inc. and President of EMEA Operations at Ariba. Previously, Earle spent 18 years at Hewlett Packard, where his various roles included Chief Marketing Officer for HP's $35 billion enterprise computing business. He also served as President of HP's Internet business, one of only two pan-HP business units. Earle is a recognized expert in emerging business models and the role e-business plays in delivering value and profit. He coauthored the book *From .com to .profit: Inventing Business Models that Deliver Value and Profit.* Earle was awarded an honorary doctorate in Computer Science by Liverpool University for his contributions to the IT industry.

Andy Mulholland

Andy Mulholland is a leading thinker and practitioner, helping clients recognize the impact of new technologies on their business models. Andy joined Capgemini in 1996 with 13 years of experience in senior IT roles. Mulholland's role of Global Chief Technology Officer includes advising the Capgemini Group management board on all aspects of technology-driven market changes. He has led Capgemini's advanced technology focus, and his blogging strategy and CTO blog has enabled Capgemini to build innovation through ecosystem collaboration.

In the last six years, Andy has also published seven white papers proposing technology architectural models, three of which have become the norm throughout the technology industry, and most recently led Capgemini's vision on business-driven technology clusters. Andy's first book, *Mashup Corporations The End of Business As Usual*, co-authored with Chris Thomas of Intel and Paul Kurchina of KurMeta, was published in October 2006.

Prior to joining Capgemini, Andy has been the founder, or co-founder, of four technology companies that have either been acquired by leading multinational technology companies or gone public on the small capital NASDAQ.